Mastering Swimming

Jim Montgomery
Mo Chambers

Human Kinetics

Linrary of Congress Cataloging-in-Publication Data

Montgomery, Jim, 1955-
  Mastering swimming / Jim Montgomery, Mo Chambers.
      p. cm. -- (The masters athlete series)
  Includes bibliographical references and index.
  ISBN-13: 978-0-7360-7453-7 (soft cover)
  ISBN-10: 0-7360-7453-8 (soft cover)
  1. Swimming. I. Chambers, Mo (Maureen), 1958- II. Title.
  GV837.M63 2009
  797.2'1--dc22

2008035439

ISBN-10: 0-7360-7453-8 (Print)   ISBN-10: 0-7360-8169-0 (Adobe PDF)
ISBN-13: 978-0-7360-7453-7 (Print)   ISBN-13: 978-0-7360-8169-6 (Adobe PDF)

The Web addresses cited in this text were current as of August 2008, unless otherwise noted.

Acquisitions Editor: Tom Heine; **Developmental Editor:** Anne Hall; **Assistant Editor:** Cory Weber; **Copyeditor:** Joy Wotherspoon; **Proofreader:** Anne Rogers; **Indexer:** Ann Truesdale; **Permission Manager:** Martha Gullo; **Graphic Designer:** Joe Buck; **Cover Designer:** Keith Blomberg; **Photographer (cover):** © EyeWire; **Photographer (interior):** James Wiseman, unless otherwise noted; **Photo Asset Manager:** Laura Fitch; **Visual Production Assistant:** Joyce Brumfield; **Photo Office Assistant:** Jason Allen; **Printer:** United Graphics

We thank the Southern Methodist University in Dallas for assistance in providing the location for the photo shoot for this book.

Human Kinetics books are available at special discounts for bulk purchase. Special editions or book excerpts can also be created to specification. For details, contact the Special Sales Manager at Human Kinetics.

Printed in the United States of America   10 9 8 7 6 5 4 3 2 1

Human Kinetics
Web site: www.HumanKinetics.com

United States: Human Kinetics
P.O. Box 5076
Champaign, IL 61825-5076
800-747-4457
e-mail: humank@hkusa.com

Canada: Human Kinetics
475 Devonshire Road Unit 100
Windsor, ON N8Y 2L5
800-465-7301 (in Canada only)
e-mail: info@hkcanada.com

Europe: Human Kinetics
107 Bradford Road
Stanningley
Leeds LS28 6AT, United Kingdom
+44 (0) 113 255 5665
e-mail: hk@hkeurope.com

Australia: Human Kinetics
57A Price Avenue
Lower Mitcham, South Australia 5062
08 8372 0999
e-mail: info@hkaustralia.com

New Zealand: Human Kinetics
Division of Sports Distributors NZ Ltd.
P.O. Box 300 226 Albany
North Shore City
Auckland
0064 9 448 1207
e-mail: info@humankinetics.co.nz

To the many masters swimmers who have the courage to show up at our workouts and bring the passion to give their best effort. You have been our inspiration.

Contents

Foreword   vii

Preface   ix

Acknowledgments   xiii

Part I   Taking the Plunge   1

Chapter 1   Start With a Vision, Train With a Plan 3

Chapter 2   Set the Stage for Success 11

Chapter 3   Develop Your Water Sense 19

Part II   Fine-Tuning Your Strokes   29

Chapter 4   Freestyle 31

Chapter 5   Backstroke .43

Chapter 6   Butterfly. 51

Chapter 7   Breaststroke 61

Chapter 8   Starts, Turns, and Finishes. 71

Part III Conditioning for Success   93

Chapter 9   Workout Essentials 95

Chapter 10 Pool Workouts 105

Chapter 11 Dry-Land Training. 125

Chapter 12 Open-Water Training 141

Chapter 13 Make Your Plan for Success 153

Part IV Competition   169

Chapter 14 Competing in Pool Events. 171

Chapter 15 Competing in Open Water 183

Appendix   201
Bibliography   203
Index   204
About the Authors   209

Foreword

The first time I met Jim Montgomery, one of my heroes in the sport of swimming, I broke a world record with him. How's that for an introduction? In 1978 I made my first national team for the World Championships, and one of the events I swam was the 400 freestyle relay. Jim was on that relay team with me. I had been swimming competitively for only about two years. Jim, of course, was coming off the 1976 Olympic team as one of their stars. We won the gold at the World Championships and smashed the world record.

I will never forget the encouragement Jim gave me as we prepared for that event. I admired his ability to keep his emotions on an even keel, just before competing on the world stage. He never got too high or too low. He was approaching the end of his competitive career, and before he retired I wanted to bottle the wealth of knowledge he had. I took advantage of his advice and will be forever grateful to him.

What a privilege it is for me to contribute to this book that Jim and Mo Chambers have so masterfully written. Although I don't know Mo as well as Jim, she is a talented masters coach in her own right—as well as a skilled wordsmith known throughout the swimming community. She was working as a software engineer for a large Silicon Valley firm when, at age 30, she decided to take a job teaching swimming to a group of eager adults. This "side job" soon became her all-consuming passion, and would eventually lead to her being named United States Masters Swimming coach of the year.

It's all in this book—the combined wisdom of two great masters coaches. In Mo's case it is apparent why, upon taking the helm of the Mountain View Masters Swim Club, it grew from an organization of 30 members to more than 350 swimmers. In Jim's case it's not surprising that he may now be better known as a masters swimming expert than as a great Olympian. He was perhaps the first Olympic swimmer upon leaving the elite ranks to generously pass on his trade secrets to ordinary masters swimmers; he went on to found what is now one of the largest masters teams in the country—Dallas Aquatic Masters—which maintains a strong emphasis on swimming for fitness for a lifetime.

In this book Mo and Jim show how to prepare for swimming success at any level, whether it's showing a lap swimmer how to execute her first flip turn or teaching a former high school star the strategies for his first open-water competition. The first chapter epitomizes Jim and Mo's shared training philosophy: Start with a vision, train with a plan. No matter what your eventual swimming goals are, the process Jim followed to win Olympic gold is now available to all of us. The book progresses to teach proper technique for all four strokes, the foundation for all swimming success. Also included are helpful tips on breath and balance, dry-land training, and planning workouts.

Jim won the same three events I won in 1984 (and he added a bronze in the 200). After I finished my last event, I reflected on the fact that it was such an honor to follow in the footsteps of some of the greatest freestylers of all time: Johnny Weissmuller, Don Schollander, and Jim Montgomery. It is rare to be able to take advantage of that greatness in order to reach your personal swimming goals. That is now possible with this wonderful book.

I can't wait to share this fantastic piece of work with all my fellow masters swimmers . . . and for that matter, all of my swimmer friends!

—Rowdy Gaines, three-time Olympic gold medalist

Preface

I t's 1969. The water in the Madison East High School pool is churning with the steady flow of the local swim team. In the center lanes, the veterans of the sport swim stroke for stroke with intensity and purpose. Coach Pat Barry pensively keeps his eyes on his charges. He scans across the lanes until his eyes stop at the far end of the pool: lane 6, home to the swimmers who lack the focus and the work ethic of team leaders. They are goofing around. There, in the center of the action, is Jim Montgomery.

Coach Barry asked Jim to get out of the pool. Holding up Jim's hand, he said, "Jim, you have more talent in this little pinkie than the rest of the swimmers in the whole pool have combined! You have so much potential—if you would just use it!" This defining moment sent Jim on a journey that to this day has affected his lifelong goals and career. This was when Jim realized that his potential was limitless.

With the help of first Coach Barry, then later college coach Doc Counsilman and club coach Jack Pettinger, Jim created a vision of becoming an Olympic gold medalist. Seven years later, in the 1976 Montreal Olympics, Jim became the first person to break the 50-second barrier in the 100-meter freestyle, winning the gold medal and anchoring two relays for two additional gold medals.

How did Jim go from goofing off in lane 6 to being the best swimmer in the world in just seven years? Jim was successful because he had incredible commitment to his vision and a training plan that worked for him. Now Jim Montgomery has come together with Mo Chambers with a vision to create a book specifically for adult swimmers who want to improve their strokes, add variety and purpose to their training, or learn more about this lifelong sport.

With a combined total of over 50 years of coaching adult swimmers, Jim and Mo have had the opportunity to meet, teach, and watch the improvement of thousands of adult swimmers who range in age from their teens to their nineties, and in skill from rookies to collegiate champions, triathletes, fitness swimmers, and competition-bound masters swimmers. Once immersed, all these athletes discovered that swimming is far more than doing lap after lap staring at a black line on the bottom of the pool. It is a medley of strokes to learn and perfect. It is an infinite number of training sets and drills designed to increase efficiency and improve fitness. It is a core-based, full-body exercise. The trip up and down the pool is a journey to a truly balanced and complete level of fitness.

Jim and Mo have written *Mastering Swimming* to guide your discovery of the fun and rewards that keep swimmers in the water throughout their adult lives. This book is for all adult swimmers, whether they swim on their own time in a private pool or public lap-swim program or they prefer the camaraderie of a structured adult setting like a masters program. Often misunderstood, masters programs are open to all adult swimmers regardless of their experience or goals. In fact, the vast majority of masters swimmers participate purely for fitness and stress relief; only a small percentage choose to compete. Regardless of your chosen venue, Jim and Mo want to improve your experience with this comprehensive guide to adult swimming.

Like in Jim's story, your journey will begin with setting goals. Your goals need not be Olympic sized—they can be as simple as learning a flip turn or increasing your stroke length. On the other hand, you may be dreaming bigger, thinking of competing in a pool meet or open-water event. Part I of this book, Taking the Plunge, guides you in goal setting and motivation. Your training plan must be flexible enough to accommodate the various responsibilities of the rest of your life. Do you train better on your own or in a group? How should you adjust your training for an injury or illness? Jim and Mo provide tips for staying on track throughout all the bumps in the road.

A successful swimming experience begins with an understanding of body balance, relaxed breathing, and efficient stroke technique. Part II of this book, Fine-Tuning Your Strokes, focuses on the mechanics of all four competitive strokes, beginning with the freestyle, and then moving on to backstroke, butterfly, and breaststroke. The discussion of each stroke examines three essential elements of swimming:

1. Maintaining a long body line that moves through the water with minimal resistance
2. Generating power from your core
3. Staying relaxed and in the flow of the stroke

The supporting photographs provide visual images that you can take from the book to the water. Peek inside the minds of champions when world-class swimmers, who continue to challenge the record books as masters, discuss their motivation and technique.

The final chapter of part II is dedicated to starting, turning, and finishing. Whether you choose to compete in a pool meet or simply want to improve your workouts, you must learn to negotiate the walls quickly, smoothly, and with minimal resistance. The simple, illustrated steps of the basic flip turn show you that turning is a lot less mysterious—and a lot more fun—than it looks.

Perhaps the most creative part of swimming is molding your workouts to achieve your goals. You may want to swim for improved fitness and stress relief or train for competition. Regardless of your goals, you'll be more successful and less prone to injury if you have a well-formulated plan that includes both in-water and dry-land training. Part III of this book, Conditioning for Success, guides you in creating a balanced training plan with a variety of workouts.

To improve your fitness, you must vary your heart rate and the use of different muscle groups by changing things up between workouts. Variations in the pool include swimming fast and swimming easy, building sets and descending sets, leg-specific sets, technique-focused sets, and starting and turning sets. After an introduction to the concepts of aerobic, anaerobic, and power swimming, this section provides workout samples and simple guidelines for designing your training weeks. If you're new to the swimming world, look for the sidebars that explain the pace clock and send-off intervals.

Consistent and well-designed dry-land workouts transform a good swimming program into a great swimming program. Your time in the gym and your time in the pool will work together to create a balanced and injury-proof training program. The exercises presented in this book focus on three critical areas for swimmers: increased flexibility, shoulder stabilization, and core strength and balance. Again, the illustrations and photographs provide visual images of excellent technique for these key exercises for swimmers.

Taking the plunge into lakes, rivers, and oceans certainly brings a whole new set of challenges, including the tides, the currents, the winds, the chop, and the absence of a black line on the bottom! The open-water swimming chapter begins with the basics of relaxation and navigation and progresses through more advanced racing strategies. Those new to the open water should note the tips for a great first experience. All swimmers, from triathletes and open-water competitors, will benefit from the sample workouts that take place both in the pool and in the surf.

Pool and open-water competitions are available to adult swimmers in all areas of the United States. These competitions are excellent opportunities to measure your progress and have fun while sharing your love of the water with other adult swimmers. Part IV, Competition, introduces you to these events, such as what to expect on race day and how to prepare yourself for competition.

It's time to dive in! Enjoy the ride as this book helps you create a vision, build better strokes, and design a training plan suited for your goals.

Acknowledgments

We could fill a second volume with the names and contributions of the friends and associates that provided support both directly and indirectly in bringing this book from concept to print. Our heartfelt thanks go to all the individuals and organizations that contributed their expertise and guidance.

Cecil Colwin, distinguished international coach and swimming historian, was the inspiration behind this book. His research and published works helped frame the stroke mechanics and training chapters.

Dave Tanner, PhD, and Joel Stager, PhD, both of the Counsilman Center for the Science of Swimming, provided invaluable information and feedback on anything to do with the science of swimming.

Innovative stroke technician Coach Bill Boomer generously shared his thoughts and ideas on relaxation, breathing, and body balance in the water.

Melon Dash, founder of Miracle Swimming Institute, provided helpful suggestions for chapter 3 and permission to use materials from her book *Conquer Your Fear of Water*.

Dr. Brent Rushall, author and publisher of *Swimming Science Research*, provided input on the fifth stroke and on starts and turns.

Coach Dick Bower pioneered the concept of cruise intervals, which are an integral part of our masters programs and discussed in chapter 10.

Nancy Ammann Pigeon, PT, STC, CSCS, served as our guiding light for the exercises and descriptions presented in chapter 11 on dry-land training. Ted Becker, PhD, provided valuable feedback, particularly in the area of injury prevention.

The coaching staff of Southern Methodist University swim team graciously allowed us use of their facilities to photograph the images in this book. We especially thank assistant women's coach Dominique Diezi for her help as a swim model and her suggestions on snorkel training.

Thank you to the champions who donated their time to model and also shared their thoughts on stroke technique and race tactics: Chris Derks (open water), David Guthrie and Katie McClelland (breaststroke), Martina Maracova (butterfly), Lia Oberstar (backstroke), and Richard Schroeder (racing). Thank you to Bart Fassino and Ed Wagner, who also demonstrated their expertise for the camera.

Michael Collins, head coach of MultiSports Orange County and the NOVA Aquatic Masters, shared his expertise in open-water swimming and racing.

Trip Hedrick, a phenomenal swim instructor and coach, shared his ideas and expertise on stroke mechanics and drills.

Steve Haufler, the very creative head coach of the Orinda Country Club swim program, was instrumental in providing information and feedback on starts, turns, and finishes.

The Hall family, of the Race Club, contributed in several areas. Our thanks go to Gary Hall Sr. for his help with Shoulder-Driven Freestyle and to Gary Hall Jr. for his insights into dry-land training.

Masters swimmers Meghan Gibbons, Dave Thompson, and Mike Weksler allowed us to share their stories and quotes. Tom Boyd and Mel Goldstein, of United States Masters Swimming, Inc., provided guidance on masters swimming organizations and clubs.

With special thanks from Jim to

Bobby Patten, head coach of Dallas Aquatic Masters—without his support in making Dallas Aquatic Masters one of the premier adult swim programs in the world, I would never have been able to experience and compile the information contained in this book.

James "Doc" Counsilman, my college coach at Indiana University, who taught me the science of swimming and coaching and inspired me to be a writer and coach.

Jack Pettinger, head coach of Badger Aquatics and my club swim coach, who took me from being a good swimmer to being a world and Olympic champion. I know of no swim coach more humble and dedicated to helping his swimmers succeed.

Stewart Ball, who helped me see my vision for writing this book and helped form the basis of chapter 1.

Art Luetke, traveling and swim buddy for life, who contributed to chapter 14.

With special thanks from Mo to

Art Stockin, who put Ulster County, New York, on the swimming map when he founded Stone Dock Swim Club in the early 1970s. Thank you, Coach, for showing me true passion and heart. I'll always be a "docker."

Kathryn Begley, my very proud mom, who continues to provide unending support for all of my endeavors.

My family and most enthusiastic fans, Dave, Trey, and Colton—I love you!

I

Taking the Plunge

Start With a Vision, Train With a Plan

I have been visualizing myself every night for the past four years standing on the podium having the gold placed around my neck.

—Megan Jendrick (née Quann), double gold medalist, 2000 Olympic Games

The big picture changed for Jim Montgomery while standing on the deck of his high school pool in Madison, Wisconsin. Jim, then a skinny 14-year-old boy without focus or drive, internalized the words of his coach, Pat Barry, who spoke to him about his untapped potential. These words opened up opportunities that Jim had never even considered, and a vision of what had seemed impossible suddenly began to seem possible. Olympic champions, as well as champions in every walk of life, have the ability to think outside of the box. Whether it's in the pool or out on dry land, every success story starts with a vision.

No vision or dream will come to fruition without a clear set of goals, the specific short-term and long-term milestones that map out your journey. In turn, you will never achieve your goals without a clearly charted plan to move you from one milestone to the next. In masters swimming, any practice session may have as many visions, goals, and training plans as there are swimmers in the pool. Although the swimmers are on individual journeys, their paths cross with others' when they swim as a team in a pool session. The most successful masters programs thrive on this diversity and welcome adult swimmers of all levels.

THE VISION

Every endeavor, whatever the level, begins with a vision. Consider the questions you ask yourself in the process of choosing a new job: Have you thought it through? Do the demands of the position fit into your life? Will you be able to make the commitment necessary in order to follow through? Before you dive into a swim program, ask yourself those questions to develop a vision of where you'd like to take your swimming.

Close your eyes for 60 seconds and let yourself dream about your goals. What is it that you want to gain from swimming? Is swimming just one facet of a bigger fitness program, or is it your main focus? Are you training for a specific pool competition, an open-water swim, or a triathlon? Are you swimming to reach a new level of fitness? Are you looking to improve your technique and learn new skills? Write down all your thoughts and ideas, even if they seem crazy and out of reach.

No matter how impossible your vision may seem, you can achieve it with the right amount of commitment to an appropriate training plan. Mo recalls the day that she first met Dave, a physically fit runner and bicyclist with a vision of completing an Ironman-length triathlon. Given his level of fitness and strong commitment to his goal, Mo's first impression was that the 2.6-mile (4 km) swim, 112-mile (180 km) bike ride, and 26.2-mile (42 km) run would be challenging for him, but possible. Dave then explained that he could not swim at all; in fact, on three different occasions in the navy, he had to be rescued while attempting a 75-meter swim test. Nevertheless, Mo was struck by Dave's absolute commitment to his vision and his ability to see it so clearly. Together, Mo and Dave worked on his swimming skills, set goals, and developed a training plan that would work with his busy life as a dentist and father.

In less than one year, Dave was standing confidently at the starting line of the New Zealand Ironman race. He surpassed his own expectations on the first leg of the race by swimming faster than expected. But while running up the ramp out of the water, Dave stepped on a piece of glass and lacerated the sole of his foot. As a doctor, he understood the severity of the wound and quickly hobbled into the medical tent. After receiving several stitches, Dave went back out on the course to live out his vision and completed the bike ride and the run. Not even a freshly stitched foot would prevent Dave from fulfilling his dream. He saw his vision clearly, he trained confidently with a smart plan, and he was 100 percent committed to it.

Goals

Goals are a series of milestones, or steps, that line the path toward the vision. Every great business plan includes yearly, quarterly, and monthly goals. The marathon runner slowly builds up to the 26.2-mile distance with runs of shorter distances. Likewise, the Olympic swimmer focuses on smaller, key swim meets in the years leading up to the big event. Short-term goals provide a means of measuring your progress and, if necessary, an opportunity to adjust your plan. As you achieve each milestone, you raise the bar of your expectations, build your confidence, and move closer to realizing your dream.

Jim reflects on the seven years of preparation for his Olympic bid: "I had a burning desire to avoid plateaus and improve my performance in every swim season. The amazing part was that getting better did not always translate into first place and faster times. Several times I had colossal failures, which gave me a better understanding of how I needed to train. I would make a change in my training and build back my confidence. My confidence turned into conviction, which then became certainty, knowing beyond a shadow of a doubt that I would succeed."

The dedication and work ethic of swimming champions are inspiring. What is it that sets these elite athletes apart? They have all of the elements essential for competing at the world level. They are young, extremely fit, and naturally gifted, but perhaps more important, they are incredibly competitive. They are singularly focused on their vision and they are highly motivated to succeed.

It is clearly not realistic for adults with families and careers to make this level of commitment to an athletic endeavor. Very few adults have an additional 6 to 8 hours each day to put aside for the in-water training, dry-land workouts, stretching, and bodywork that are required of world-class athletes. You can, however, assess your abilities in terms of age, fitness, available time, and motivation. Once you understand those factors, you can set realistic goals in line with your vision. Your goals should be challenging but within your capabilities.

Begin setting your goals by assessing your current skills. Are you new to swimming or a veteran of the water? All swimmers, regardless of experience, should have at least one goal specific to their stroke technique. If you are a novice swimmer, you should focus on gaining comfort in the water and developing a relaxed, streamlined, and efficient stroke, first in freestyle and then in the other strokes. More-experienced swimmers should concentrate on refining their strokes, gaining power, and learning competitive starts and turns.

As you read part II of this book, Fine-Tuning Your Strokes, you will encounter an incredible number of details about the four competitive swimming strokes, turns, and starts. Because it is not possible to think about all of them at once, focus on one or two concepts per workout. Think about your swimming strokes in terms of your priorities. What improvements in your stroke will move you toward your ultimate vision? Do you need to lengthen your stroke or perfect your flip turn? You can chart a clear path to your final goal with a calendar detailing your workouts with daily, weekly, and monthly goals. The process of learning and improving stroke mechanics requires time and concentration, but taken in small bits, one piece at a time, it can be accomplished.

As you set your goals, consider your life beyond your swimming: your family, your career, and your school, religious, or community obligations. How much time is available for training? Will you get enough sleep? You cannot meet your swimming goals without a comfortable balance between your life away from the pool and your fitness pursuits.

What Motivates You?

Motivation, or lack of it, is usually the tipping point in any fitness program. Coaches know that swimmers who regularly attend workouts are more likely to continue with the sport. Motivated swimmers find it easier to get to the pool and, as a result, are more likely to reach their goals. Therefore, take some time to think about what motivates you. What will keep you on the path toward your final goal?

As you read through the following list of motivators, you will likely find several that fit you. Many motivators are positive side effects of the sport that evolve into the main reasons that swimmers return to the pool year after year. Read through each one carefully, decide which ones apply to you, and take some notes. Understanding what motivates you helps you select appropriate goals.

1. *Fitness.* Swimming is a core-based, full-body exercise that can benefit every adult. It complements running and other weight-bearing sports because it puts less stress on the joints and tendons, therefore causing fewer injuries and allowing for more consistent training. Perhaps the main motivator for most masters swimmers is fitness. Swimmers often check their fitness progress by using specific, repeatable test sets. Samples of these types of swims appear in chapter 10, Pool Workouts. These test sets, or *benchmark* sets, lend themselves to setting goals.

2. *Science.* If you're intrigued by exercise science, the swimming pool provides you with an amazing laboratory. There are infinite measurable components, including your heart rate, the split times on the pace clock, your strokes per length, and your work-to-rest ratios. Swimmers motivated by the science of swimming are fascinated with fluid dynamics and the question of what makes champion swimmers fast.

3. *The water.* For many swimmers, water represents something natural, refreshing, and aesthetically pleasing. When they were children, their parents probably dragged them out of the swimming pool after hours of play and had to put time limits on their baths. Water simply is the place some people feel most at home. The buoyancy of water reduces body weight by 90 percent, making swimming attractive to people of all shapes and sizes. Water is indeed a great equalizer.

4. *Technique.* Swimmers never stop refining their strokes and learning to swim more efficiently. From the fundamentals to the finer points, such as generating more power and reducing drag, the mechanics of swimming provide endless opportunities for athletes to perfect their movements. Swimmers intrigued with improving their technique never miss an opportunity to join a swim clinic or watch another video of champion swimmers. They are always ready to embrace new and unusual stroke drills the coach tries out. They are students of the art of swimming.

5. *Overcoming fear.* A Gallup poll taken in 1998 showed that much of the U.S. population is not comfortable in water: 64 percent of people polled were uncomfortable in deep, open water, 46 percent experienced anxiety in deep water in pools, and 39 percent were afraid to put their heads underwater (Stillwell 2007). Many of these swimmers challenge their fears by either enrolling in adult swim lessons or joining a masters swim program. With commitment and good coaching, people can learn to swim with a relaxed stroke and proper breathing.

6. *Competition.* Masters swimmers who are motivated by competition will find plenty of opportunities. There are masters swim meets, open-water events, and triathlons. There are also *postal events*, in which you swim in the comfort of your own pool and send your results to an event coordinator who publishes a complete list of participants' results. Swimmers who thrive on competition are encouraged to consult a coach when planning their training programs to ensure that their efforts will properly target their events.

7. *Injury rehabilitation.* Many land-based athletes join masters swimming programs to maintain their fitness levels while rehabilitating their knees, ankles, or feet. These athletes may never leave masters swimming when they discover how perfectly swimming complements their weight-bearing exercises. Swimming is an excellent way for runners to build and maintain upper-body and core strength, which will make them more resistant to injury in all sports.

8. *Weight loss.* One hour of swimming can burn as many calories in an hour as high-impact aerobics, hiking, and ice skating. Because weight loss is about burning more calories than one eats, most masters swimmers who combine consistent workouts with sensible diets lose weight.

9. *Stress relief.* Many masters swimmers who are extremely motivated in their careers and family lives view their time in the pool as complete relaxation. Although some of them enjoy competition, the majority of them have no intention of ever competing. What they have in common with competitive swimmers is the ability to leave their worries behind when they jump into the pool.

10. *Self-esteem.* Building your level of fitness and achieving your swimming goals will feed your self-confidence and influence all aspects of your life, including your personal relationships and career. Jim attributes his success in building one of the largest adult swim programs in the country to the confidence he gained through swimming: "Through age and experience, I have grown less competitive in the water but more confident and committed to making a positive impact on people's lives."

11. *Friendship.* The team environment that characterizes structured swim workouts builds a unique bond among its members. Longtime swimmers often form their strongest friendships during their swimming experiences. The uniformity of the swimsuit and goggles wash away differences in occupation, social status, and financial standing. In the pool, a sense of belonging and the spirit of teamwork prevail.

In any given workout, the following kinds of people may be sharing a pool: a triathlete preparing for the next local multisport event, a runner who is staying active while recovering from knee surgery, and a CEO of a major corporation looking for one hour of relaxation in the day. The beauty of swimming in a structured workout group is that all of the swimmers' goals, ages, abilities, and levels of commitment blend together as a team when the workout commences. The swimmers get exactly what they want from the workout while enjoying the camaraderie of the group.

THE PLAN

Moving from a vision and goals to an attainable plan charted out by days, weeks, and months can seem like an overwhelming task. Many athletes abandon the vision and call it impossible during the planning stage. However, if you begin with a clear assessment of your initial skills and chart a steady progression toward your goal, your vision becomes attainable.

Each athlete's training plan consists of two parts: the technical aspect, which includes comfort level in the water and stroke mechanics, and the fitness and training aspect. For example, swimmers who would like to complete a 1-mile (1.6 km) open-water swim will plan to focus on building endurance and improving efficiency in the freestyle stroke. By building their skills slowly in each of these two aspects, swimmers can more easily write their plans and focus on their vision.

Although often overlooked, the technical aspects of a training plan are the most critical to the success of many swimmers. Part II of this book, Fine-Tuning Your Strokes, presents all four competitive strokes, beginning with the favored freestyle, or crawl, stroke. This basic conditioning stroke is preferred by triathletes and many fitness swimmers. Next is the backstroke, which nicely complements the freestyle with its similar rhythm. In addition, the backstroke works some opposing muscles to those used in the freestyle, creating a balance of strength in both strokes. Following the backstroke are the butterfly and breaststroke, which share many qualities and teaching progressions. The final chapter of part II focuses on negotiating the walls at starts, turns, and finishes—details that benefit every swimmer, whether competitive or noncompetitive.

Part III of this book, Conditioning for Success, focuses on physical training both in and out of the water. It outlines tools for developing your own personal training plan, including the kind and number of necessary workouts, allowing you to calculate the time commitment required to reach your goals. Will you want to complement your swim workouts with dry-land training or cross-train in another sport? How many times each week can you get to the pool? Ask yourself these questions to make a plan that complements your life.

The Three Cs

Three critical factors for a successful execution of your plan are commitment, confidence, and concentration. You must be able to commit to your plan. Be honest with yourself as you work through the details of your training plan. Think carefully through your current schedule to be certain that you can add this commitment to it. It is better to scale down your expectations and make a plan that truly will work in your life than create something untenable. Set yourself up for success.

Are you confident in the plan? As you begin this process, your vision might seem completely out of reach. However, a well-formulated plan will map out a series of achievable goals. These short-term milestones will serve not only to measure your progress, but also to build your confidence as you grow closer to your long-term goals. Believing in yourself is the first step to reaching your goals.

Concentration means staying focused on your goals and your vision. There are many tricks to maintaining focus, such as posting pictures or notes on your refrigerator, bathroom mirror, or desk. Tracking your workouts in a daily log is another excellent way to stay in tune with your plan and your progress.

There will be times in your life when the priorities of family, work, or other obligations will rise to the top, creating a blip on your path. You will need to be somewhat flexible with your plan. Give yourself permission to step back when you are unable to juggle your various commitments. Mo recalls the first six months after her twins were born when simply getting to the pool was her only goal. Despite the sleepless nights and seemingly endless days of diapers and bottles, Mo never let go of her vision of one day making her comeback.

With a clear vision and a commitment to achieving it, you can stay on track through the inevitable ups and downs of life. The key to maintaining your vision in those times is to be flexible and allow yourself to adjust your goals and your training plan.

Celebrate the Journey

Olympians will tell you that it is not the Olympic experience or a single event that has altered their lives and made them who they are. It was the entire journey: the years of workouts and competitions, the many achievements that sprinkled the path, the high moments, the disappointments, and the friends and coaches who surrounded them.

Take the time to reap the wonders of your journey. It's easy to get caught up in the details and obsessed with the struggle, while completely missing what is happening right next to you. Try to strike a balance between keeping your goals in sight, staying in the rhythm of day-to-day training, and taking in the scenery.

Cherish those few minutes with your teammates at the end of the workout. Allow yourself to be inspired by the people around you who are achieving their dreams within the ebb and flow of their lives. Look for the silver lining when things don't go the way you expected.

Jim's vision has evolved since 1976 in Montreal because the demands of his life have changed with a family and a business. "Like the competitive swimmer, I still have the desire to see how close I can come to those glory years. Like the fitness swimmer, I believe that the water gives me a healthy lifestyle and a satisfied spirit that transfer into all avenues of my life. Full of energy and passing through midlife, I keep coming up with new, satisfying goals on places to swim, groups to swim with, and creative ways to train. It's all worth striving for."

Set the Stage for Success

The silent solidarity of swimming the same set with others is an amazing motivator.

—Meghan Gibbons

Meghan Gibbons, a dedicated daily runner, began swimming after a hamstring injury led to complications in her back and a frustrating array of diagnoses. Somewhat uninspired with the transition from terra firma to water, Meghan tediously moved up and down the lanes until she saw a group of swimmers at the far end of the pool. "I noticed some people who seemed to be enjoying their swim. They swam in a group with a coach on the deck urging them on. But they weren't kids—they were in their twenties, forties, and up through their sixties. They joked in the lanes and chatted in the locker room." When she learned that they were masters swimmers, Meghan quickly dismissed the idea of joining in with the thought, *Oh, experts. No wonder. Forget it.* (Gibbons 2005). Now that she is also a masters swimmer, Meghan is quick to say that she, like many others, had misconceptions about the organization.

WHAT IS MASTERS SWIMMING?

United States Masters Swimming (USMS) is an organization with over 45,000 adult members that provides coached workouts, competitions, and clinics throughout the country, as well as a detailed Web site and a bimonthly publication, *USMS Swimmer*. Regardless of level of experience, any swimmer aged 18 years and older is welcome to join this growing fitness-minded group. An important aspect of the organization is providing a venue and support system for adults who choose to improve and maintain their fitness through swimming.

A masters swimming class is a structured swim practice or workout that is open to all levels of adult swimmers and has a professional coach or instructor. The coach's responsibility is to enforce the rules of practice etiquette, teach proper stroke mechanics, introduce appropriate training methods, and help establish personal and group goals for the participants. Masters swimming programs motivate their participants to exercise regularly in a safe and fun environment.

USMS was founded in 1970 by Arthur J. Ransom, a U.S. Navy doctor who was intrigued with the benefits of swimming for adults. He wanted to support his theory that swimming is the most healthful form of exercise in older age groups. When the first national masters swimming meet was held that year in Amarillo, Texas, Ransom and his associates were busy drawing blood and taking blood pressures to understand how the adult athletes tolerated the stress of the sport. The medical results of that first USMS meet were favorable, but the more important result of the event was the enthusiasm for swimming, competing, and socializing that the approximately 45 meet participants sparked. This love of the sport has helped the membership of USMS grow from 45 to 45,000 swimmers (Sowers 2006).

Courtesy of Robert Begley

Actor and Olympic gold medalist Larry "Buster" Crabbe (lane 4) was a competitor in some of the earliest masters swimming meets.

STRUCTURED WORKOUT PROGRAMS

Health clubs, YMCAs, universities, and public pools worldwide offer structured swimming workouts for adults that feature a coach on deck, a workout easily tailored to any ability level, and the camaraderie of others with a similar commitment to the water. These workouts are often called masters swimming and may or may not be affiliated with USMS.

Many people think that masters swimming programs are designed for experienced, competitive swimmers who live and breathe chlorine. On the contrary, many newcomers are amazed to learn that they do not have to know all of the strokes and how to do a flip turn before joining. Once they get their feet wet, new swimmers are pleasantly surprised to learn that many in the rookie lanes are also new to the world of swimming. Experienced swimmers do participate in masters workouts, but they swim in their own lanes, work at their own pace, and are the minority. In a recent USMS survey, less than 30 percent of masters swimmers considered themselves serious competitors (Boyd 2006).

FIND THE RIGHT COACH
AND PROGRAM

The United States has over 500 clubs registered with USMS in 53 regions. These clubs typically offer several workouts each week, and some have classes in multiple locations. Health clubs, YMCAs, and universities often offer masters swimming classes or structured workouts for adults. To find a local USMS chapter near you, visit their Web site at www.usms.org/lmsc.

How do you know which program is right for you? The feel of each program depends on the philosophy and the style of its coach. Finding a program that will work for your goals and schedule might take a little research, but the outcome will be worth the effort when you find the right match. Most clubs offer at least one trial swim to prospective members, which allow you to test the waters and ask a few questions. Don't be shy with your inquiries—masters coaches have been asked almost every question. The following top 10 questions from new swimmers address what you should consider when checking out a new club.

1. *What is the program philosophy?* Many clubs focus on fitness more than competition. Other clubs are highly competitive and train exclusively for meets and open-water events. The majority of clubs fall in the middle, with a mix of competitive swimmers, fitness swimmers, triathletes, and open-water enthusiasts.

2. *How much coaching in stroke technique will I receive from a coach?* New swimmers should differentiate between a structured workout program and a learn-to-swim program. Coaches on deck won't teach you to swim,

but they will bring your strokes to a higher level of efficiency by offering drills and tips as you train. The beauty of having coaches watch you swim through an entire workout is that they can monitor your stroke for change as you begin to tire. An attentive coach will remind swimmers to refocus on their technique during times of fatigue.

3. *Is there a coach on deck at all workouts?* The majority of masters swimming programs have coaches available who plan workouts and offer guidance throughout the sessions. Swimmers in less-populated areas of the country sometimes train without a coach, forming loosely organized groups. These swimmers may not reach their full potential because they are missing out on the benefits of stroke improvement and encouragement offered by a coach in daily workouts. Nevertheless, the camaraderie of a group provides motivation and the important social aspects of masters swimming.

4. *Can I learn or improve skills and strokes through private coaching, special clinics, or workshops?* Many coaches offer private instruction beyond structured workouts to help tune up your strokes so you can swim more efficiently and avoid injury. Clubs often host stroke clinics and offer underwater videotaping for members.

5. *How are workouts organized? Are like-level swimmers grouped together?* Coaches group swimmers of similar abilities together so they can tailor workouts for the needs and skills of swimmers in different lanes. This system allows lanes to flow more smoothly. Swimmers are also more motivated and inspired by each other when they are working within a compatible group.

6. *What if I can't swim butterfly?* This is one of the most common questions for prospective swimmers, along with "What if I can't do a flip turn?" and "What if I never swam on a team?" The majority of new masters swimmers don't have competitive swimming experience and typically can swim only freestyle. Most masters swimming programs offer primarily freestyle conditioning workouts that do not require flip turns. Furthermore, coaches can modify the nonfreestyle sets so new swimmers can participate using strokes they know. Over time, newcomers learn the other three competitive strokes, the proper turns, the order of the individual medley, and more.

7. *What is the workout schedule? How long are the workouts?* You should find a practice schedule that complements your work and family schedules. Even the best masters program will not help you if you can't attend the workouts.

8. *Are the facilities suitable to your needs?* Take a good look at the pool, the size and the number of lanes, and the water clarity. You should also tour the locker room facilities. Consider your personal needs with these questions: Are you planning to swim on your way to work? Will

you need to shower and prepare for a day in the professional world after you swim?

9. *How much will it cost?* As you consider the cost of the program, you'll need to know how many times per week you plan to swim. Many variables affect your perceived value of the club, including the coach and the facility. In some cases, your program membership fee includes discounts at local businesses and access to additional facilities, such as weight rooms or other pools.

10. *Is there a social aspect to the club?* Many swimmers are social animals. Friendships formed in the swimming lanes can last a lifetime. For many, the social side of masters swimming is the most important feature.

SWIMMING SOLO

If the masters workouts in your area don't suit your schedule or your style, you could choose to sign up for a local lap swim or train in your own pool. This is a great choice for those who need a flexible workout schedule. However, it is more difficult to stay motivated without the encouragement of a coach and other swimmers. Many resources, including a growing number of Web sites dedicated to helping swimmers who train independently, address issues such as stroke technique and planning workouts. This book provides basic information for a safe and successful independent swimming program.

Athletes who swim on their own must understand the importance of varying their workouts for maximum fitness benefits. Solo swimmers should seek out a swimming clinic or private lessons with a professional coach. Experienced coaches can offer advice on safe and efficient swimming, your training plan, and workout structure.

RULES OF THE POOL

For some, the first visit to a masters workout can be intimidating. The lanes are churning with swimmers who all seem to know what they're doing and where they are supposed to be. The coach is talking in what seems to be a foreign language while the swimmers come and go to the rhythm of the poolside pace clock. Once you've learned some workout and lane etiquette, you too will be navigating the waters like a veteran. This list of workout and lap swim guidelines should get you started, but you should be aware that individual lap swimming programs and workout groups may have their own variations.

- *Allow time to warm up.* You will benefit most from the planned workout if you allow enough time to complete the warm-up before the main sets start. Naturally, if you're swimming without a group, your workout starts when you get there. Even if you're short on time, you should complete a proper warm-up. Coaches understand that it is not always possible to be on time. If you arrive late, be sure to check in with the coach for lane placement and to find out what the group is doing. Once you are in the water, swim with an easy effort behind the other swimmers in the lane until your muscles are warm.

- *Pick up your equipment.* Before arriving at your lane, bring over a kickboard, pull buoy, and any other toys you think you'll need. If you keep all your equipment within arm's reach, you'll be ready for whatever the coach prescribes. At the end of your workout, be sure to return your training equipment to the proper place.

- *Pick the right lane.* When you are new to a workout, check in with the coach to see which lane is a good fit for you. Swimmers often refer to lanes in a workout by their *lane base* or *cruise interval*, which is a simple way to describe the speed of the swimmers in the lane. Chapter 10 discusses the pace clock, interval training, and finding your lane base.

  Lap swimming sessions often have lanes labeled as slow, medium, and fast. These are, of course, relative terms and you will want to observe the speed and ability of the swimmers in the lanes to determine which lane fits you best. When in doubt, ask a lifeguard for guidance.

- *Listen and ask.* Listen closely when the coach discusses the various sets within the workout. Not all coaches provide a written or posted set of instructions, so it is important to listen carefully. If you're new to the workout group, you may not understand all the instructions. Take a few extra minutes to absorb the instructions while the rest of the swimmers in the lane begin the set. You will reap more from your training when you understand and swim the sets as prescribed, rather than simply following along.

- *Swim in a circle.* Most participants in workout groups and lap swimming programs practice *circle swimming.* This means that swimmers stay on the right side of the lane and swim in a counterclockwise direction. If the pool is sparsely populated, swimmers may choose to split the lane, with one swimmer on the right side and another on the left. This situation is more common in lap swimming. If you would like to join a lane where two swimmers are already splitting the lane, make sure that both swimmers know you're entering the water, and ask to change the lane to circle swimming.

- *Who's going first?* Many swimmers find it easier to swim behind someone so they can draft, or take advantage of the reduced resistance provided by the slipstream of the preceding swimmer rather than to lead a lane. This is why swimmers sometimes migrate to the back of the lane at the start of a practice or set. Talk with others to find out the strokes and pace each swimmer prefers. Don't be left staring at each other when it's time to swim.

- *Watch your swing.* Because of the nature of the arm's recovery in the butterfly and freestyle strokes, swimmers' hands will sometimes collide. As you swim butterfly, be aware of swimmers near you, take an extra kick when your arms are extended, and avoid swinging wide when passing others. Take extra caution in all strokes when you use hand paddles.

- *Leave the wall safely.* It is standard for swimmers to leave the wall in 5- to 10-second intervals, which keeps swimmers of equal ability a safe distance apart. If a lane becomes crowded, swimmers should reconsider their order or lengthen the send-off interval between athletes.

- *Negotiate the walls safely.* The majority of collisions occur at the ends of the pool. With a few basic turning guidelines, swimmers can avoid most collisions.

    As you approach the area 5 yards (5 m) from the wall and prepare to turn, safely move into the left side of the lane. Make this shift after the swimmer ahead of you has completed the turn and left the wall. After making your turn, you will be positioned to swim on the correct side of the lane for your returning length.

    For maximum safety during circle swimming, all swimmers in the lane must be aware of the position of others. If swimmers follow each other too closely, the ends of the pool will become a traffic hazard. Good lane teamwork and the advice of the coach help prevent accidents.

- *Rest away from others.* Sometimes you'll want to sit out one or two lengths to rest, adjust your goggles, or talk with the coach. The ideal place to stop is at the end of the pool in the corner of the lane where the swimmers are not turning. This spot is in the right-hand corner of the lane as you approach the wall. Remember that incoming swimmers will cross over and make their turns on the other side of the lane. When you're ready to rejoin the group, leave the wall safely away from other swimmers.

- *The passing zone.* When you find yourself ready to pass swimmers in front of you, lightly touch their feet once or twice as you approach. At the next wall, they will pull over into the right-hand corner of the lane, giving you room to cross over and turn in the left-hand corner. After you've made your turn, they will follow at a safe distance.

MAKE A SMART START

There is a wide variation in the background of swimmers entering masters programs. Swimmers from 18 to 88 may be embarking on a swimming fitness program for the first time in their lives or returning to their competitive swimming roots after a short hiatus or perhaps years out of the water. Regardless of their swimming history, newcomers should take time to build up their distance safely and should consult with a coach about their strokes.

New swimmers often get caught up in the excitement of masters swimming and try to dive into every workout offered in a week. This level of enthusiasm is admirable, but the approach often leads to injury or burnout. You should consider several factors when planning the start of your swimming program. Do you have any swimming experience? How long ago did you last train? How old are you? Do you participate in other sports? Swimmers new to organized workouts should start with 3 to 4 swim sessions 20 to 30 minutes long each week.

They can gradually build the length of their workouts to one hour or longer over several weeks. Swimmers with a history of participating in organized workouts can begin with sessions 40 to 60 minutes long.

In the early weeks of training, all swimmers should focus on swimming correctly and gradually building an aerobic base. They should also have a coach or swimming instructor watch to see if their strokes are safe and efficient. The ideal time to make changes that will prevent injury and improve efficiency is early in the swimming program.

It's time to settle back and enjoy the ride! Taking the time to make the right decisions about where, when, and with whom you will swim ensures a fun and successful experience.

The learning never ends in this sport. Your experience will broaden if you are open to new ideas about stroke technique, training, and possibly pool and open-water competitions.

3

Develop Your Water Sense

The water is your friend. You don't have to fight with water; just share the same spirit as the water, and it will help you move.
—Aleksandr Popov, four-time gold medalist, 1992 and 1996 Olympic Games

How do world-class swimmers move so incredibly fast while making it look so effortless? They are extraordinarily fit and have good stroke technique, but there is more. Experienced swimmers are at home in their bodies, which allows them to relax completely in the water. They breathe naturally and maintain a balanced body position that allows them to cut through the water with minimal effort. This is called superior water sense. This chapter describes four building blocks for developing your sense of the water: relaxation, breathing, balance, and streamlining.

The four basic elements of water sense are all interrelated. When you are relaxed in the water, you are able to establish a natural breathing pattern within your stroke. If you are breathing comfortably, you can focus more on creating a balanced body position. Finally, with relaxed breathing and great balance, you'll be in position to streamline your body, seeking the path of least resistance as you move through the water. Conversely, better balance and a streamlined body position make breathing easier, which allows you to relax more in the water. Swimmers who have developed good water sense are better prepared to improve their stroke mechanics.

RELAXATION

Do you feel safe, confident, and at ease in any depth of water, whether you are in a pool, a lake, or an ocean? When you feel in control, you can relax in the water, whether you're in shallow water or deep, at the surface or underneath it, or in the middle of a crowded practice or alone in open-water. You can breathe comfortably as your muscles contract and release with each stroke cycle. You won't need to think about when you will take your next breath; you'll just breathe because you'll feel secure.

Many swimmers who are not comfortable in the water believe that learning the freestyle will help them feel confident and safe. However, the opposite is true. Swimmers breathe comfortably and swim efficiently only *after* they feel safe in any depth of water.

When you release the tension in your body, you can relax and allow the water to embrace you. The water lifts you higher and your strokes will feel more fluid. Being present in your body, having control over your movements, and feeling held by the water are fun. You will learn quickly how to swim effectively and confidently in any body of water.

Coach Bill Boomer has worked with swimmers of all skill levels. In the late 1980s and early 1990s, Bill revolutionized the way swimming coaches teach strokes with his theories on body position and balance in the water. Most recently, he has focused on teaching his swimmers to feel more relaxed in the water. He suggests that every swimmer, from rookie to veteran, should begin training sessions with a relaxation sequence to ready the mind and body for swimming.

At the heart of Coach Boomer's relaxation strategy is the aquatic signature, which is an opportunity to explore your relationship with yourself and your relationship with the water. In essence, you have to learn to trust the water enough to completely give yourself to it and let it manage you. An aquatic relationship is built upon emotional trust and physical awareness that is not dominated by survival reactions. "Only when you establish an emotionally satisfying coexistence with the water's remarkably consistent intentions can you truly understand how to move from point A to point B efficiently," says Coach Boomer.

Start in a vertical position in deep water and place your face in the water. Let your body float freely and surrender to the water. Keep your lungs full of air and let your body rotate from a vertical position to its natural place in the water. No two swimmers will have the same position, which is why your natural resting place is called your signature. Some swimmers will actually be in a vertical position when completely relaxed! Most people, however, will float to a position somewhere between 90 degrees (vertical) and 0 degrees (horizontal). By repeating this one-breath experience, lasting 12 to 14 seconds, you can gradually learn to give yourself freely to the water for longer periods.

Traditional relaxation exercises performed out of water often focus on deep breathing. Deep breathing includes a prolonged exhalation that expels carbon dioxide from the body. Many swimmers who are uncomfortable in the water hyperventilate because they do not exhale fully or are holding their breath. By performing bobs with an exhale focus, swimmers can learn to relax as they regulate their air exchanges. To do a bob, begin in water 6 to 8 feet (2-3 m) deep. From a vertical position, with water over your shoulders and your arms at your side, exhale sufficiently enough to allow your body to fall feet first to the bottom of the pool. Pause for a moment at the bottom, then push off with your feet and travel up to the surface while completing your exhale. Inhale at the surface, then submerge again, exhaling as you go down. Swimmers who are relaxed in the water will see a decrease in their heart rate after several bobs.

If you find you are not comfortable in the water and cannot fully exhale while doing bobs, try wall hangs in place of bobs. Place two hands on the wall, put your chin under the water, expel the air from your lungs, and allow your body to drop while holding the wall. Repeat this process until you feel comfortable with the exhalation. In time, you will feel ready to do bobs without the wall.

After doing several aquatic signatures and a bob sequence, swim four lengths of the pool, staying present in your body and breathing naturally with an exhale focus. If you count your strokes, you will likely find that you take fewer strokes to cross the length of the pool than you did before the exercises. You will feel relaxed and ready to pursue your aquatic goals.

BREATHING

When you can breathe as easily in the water as on land, you can cover long distances faster and with less effort. When you're relaxed, you can control breathing rhythm throughout the changing phases of the stroke and can easily swim at higher speeds and stay relaxed.

Novice swimmers are not the only ones who find it challenging to get good air exchanges. While training for Olympic competition, swimmers spend hours focusing on breathing strategies that will maximize their performance. In competition, they no longer think about when or how to breathe; their training has made breathing a natural part of their rhythm. Therefore, masters swimmers should certainly consider spending some of their training time working on breathing. A swimmer who learns to breathe naturally will achieve a longer, more relaxed stroke. Use these tips to master the art of inhaling and exhaling comfortably while you swim.

Tips for Better Breathing

1. *Relax.* Relaxation of the muscles in the face, jaw, mouth, and neck is perhaps the most critical skill for proper swimming breathing. Imagine how your facial muscles feel when you run or ride a bicycle. Your breathing should feel the same during swimming as during other aerobic activities. Swimmers who tense their faces in the water are most likely holding their breath underwater, which forces them to both exhale and inhale when they are above water. This inefficient air exchange creates anxiety and inevitably leads to exhaustion.

2. *Exhale.* As your face enters the water, your mouth should be slightly open with a trickle of air going out between your lips. Some swimmers exhale through the mouth and nose, while others exhale gently through

the mouth only. Many swimmers find a nose plug allows them to breathe more comfortably. Select the method that is most comfortable for you.

It is important to blow your air out slowly. Exhaling too quickly will cause you to gasp in your next inhalation, which may make you hyperventilate. By exhaling slowly, you can develop an awareness of any facial tension, especially around your mouth, lips, and teeth. As your face begins to leave the water, increase your rate of exhalation, and expel the remaining air with a forceful puff. Many swimmers use both their nose and mouth for this crescendo in exhalation as they turn their heads to breathe.

3. *Inhale.* Inhaling is a natural reflex—it is quick but not forced. If you exhale adequately, air will flow in on its own. Again, most swimmers breathe in through their mouths.

4. *Make your exhalation long.* Your exhalation should be twice as long as your inhalation. A longer exhalation leads to a more relaxed exchange of air.

5. *Don't panic if you breathe in water.* If you gulp in water, shape your tongue as if you're pronouncing the letter *K*. This tongue position keeps the water from going down your throat. Even the greatest swimmers breathe in water from time to time.

When should you breathe? During freestyle, breaststroke, and butterfly strokes, swimmers complete their exhalation at the end of the underwater pull phase, just before their faces leave the water. In the freestyle, increase your rate of exhalation toward the end of the underwater phase of the stroke as your body slides forward and rotates to the breathing side and your face leaves the water. In the breaststroke, complete the majority of your exhalation as your arms sweep in, the hips snap forward, and your head and shoulders rise up out of the water. In the butterfly, expel your air as your body is passing over your arms, your chest is rising, and your face is clearing the water. Although breathing takes place out of the water in the backstroke, it is important to establish a smooth, rhythmic transition between inhalation and exhalation, similar to the other strokes. The key is finding a consistent place in each stroke cycle when your face clears the water and timing your exhalation to allow a quality inhalation at this point.

BALANCE

Good balance in swimming means moving horizontally along the surface of the water. Experienced swimmers make this look easy as they cut through the water with their legs streamlined behind them. Their long body lines are positioned to swim extended distances with less effort, less resistance, and greater ease of breath. Balancing and streamlining are interrelated concepts that use the body's core muscles. Learn to create horizontal swimming balance from your aquatic signature by manipulating your body's length through its internal core connections and applying downward pressure with the upper chest. As you swim, begin to think from the center, or core, of your body. Imagine yourself more as a racing boat and less like a life raft.

Swimmers who do not exhibit good balance will assume a more vertical position in the water, dropping their hips and legs below the water line as they move. To keep their legs from sinking, they kick harder and lift their heads above the water line to breathe. They lose length at the front end of their strokes and tire quickly. The following progression of balance drills will help you rotate your lower body to a horizontal position in the water without kicking. If you are swimming on the surface in a well-balanced position, the energy you exert to kick will propel you forward.

Begin this balance drill by floating in deep water. Imagine your body as a teeter-totter floating horizontally in the water. Think of your lungs, the center of flotation in your body, as the fulcrum in the middle of the teeter-totter. Your head and neck are at the front end of the teeter-totter, and the lower part of your spine, your hips, and your legs are at the back end. How do you maintain your balance? First, keep your head and neck in alignment with your spine. If you pick your head up to breathe, your lower body will drop below the surface of the water. Next, keep your eyes positioned on the bottom of the pool, and gently press your face, chin, and chest toward the bottom of the pool. Your lower body will rotate toward the surface. You will probably not reach a horizontal position with this drill, but you will begin to come closer.

Try the balance drill again. When you have reached a position as close to horizontal as possible, slowly extend your arms over your head. Your ears should be between your biceps. In this position your lower body rotates up even higher because your lungs are now more centered in the teeter-totter and your extended arms help redistribute your body's weight. Maintain this position while you swim, particularly during the long-axis strokes of freestyle and backstroke. The extension of one or both arms contributes to better balance and a longer body line while swimming. Think of yourself as a boat moving through the water: the longer the boat, the faster it will move through the water. Shape your body into a long, streamlined boat with good head-neck-spine alignment and core muscles engaged.

Although several factors can upset balance and body position, the most common is breathing. Some swimmers may initially assume a balanced body position in the freestyle, but then upset the body line by lifting their heads out of the water each time they take a breath. They must then reposition themselves after every breathing stroke, which makes progress slow and tiring. Swimmers who learn to synchronize their breathing with the rotation of their hips and shoulders in the freestyle are able to inhale easily while maintaining good head-neck-spine alignment, making it unnecessary to lift their heads. Imagine keeping one goggle under the water and one goggle above the water when you breathe. As you move through the water, you create a bow wave, similar to the wave created by the bow of a ship, next to your face. By breathing behind this bow wave, it is easier to inhale quickly while keeping good body alignment.

Your balance will improve as you work through this next section on streamlining. Excellent streamlining is one of the hallmarks of world-class swimmers. They have perfected the art of cutting through the water with perfect rhythm, continually shaping their body throughout each stroke cycle to minimize resistance.

STREAMLINING

Streamlining means decreasing resistance. The process of streamlining your swimming doesn't necessarily require great effort, but rather recognition, concentration, and commitment. You must practice and perfect your motor skills, and become aware of the water and the resistance created by your body. Streamlining also means aligning your body and limbs to reduce the resistance of oncoming water throughout the stroke cycle. Timing the changes in your alignment sequences is crucial. Skilled swimmers spend most of the freestyle stroke cycle tipping their bodies equally to one side or the other rather than holding a flat, central posture that produces increased resistance. They focus on eliminating any inefficient vertical and lateral body movements.

Create as little resistance as possible by keeping your strokes long and your body balanced by maintaining proper head and body alignment throughout the stroke cycle. A longer body will travel through the water faster. The following set of streamlining drills, or flow shapers, will teach you how to recognize pressure against your body during every phase of the freestyle stroke cycle. Flow shapers are exercises that teach swimmers to create and detect specific flows in the water. They produce positive results because they synchronize the hand and arm for an accurate stroke pattern.

Reducing Resistance

Before you learn to reduce resistance, you must know what resistance is. If you understand the three types of resistance, you can better decide which type of stroke correction to make first. The three types of resistance in swimming are frictional, form, and wave resistance.

The water creates frictional resistance when it comes in contact with the swimmer's skin, suit, cap, goggles, and body hair. To help reduce the effects of frictional resistance, swimsuits are designed to fit tightly and hold minimal amounts of water. For decades, competitive swimmers have shaved body hair and worn silicone or latex swim caps and streamlined goggles to reduce frictional resistance. When swimmers double their speed, frictional resistance also doubles.

The shape a body makes in the water creates form resistance. It's no surprise that a long, streamlined, arrowlike body shape is better for a swimmer to maintain than a bargelike shape. When evaluating a swimmer's body shape in the water, you must think dimensionally, or about what is happening above, below, and to both sides of the body. When swimmers double their speed, form resistance increases four times.

Streamlining Drills

Begin by learning how to properly streamline your body out of the water. While standing on a pool deck or in shallow water, extend your arms over your head and place one hand on top of the other. Wrap the thumb of your top hand around the pinkie side of your bottom hand. Reach your fingertips to the sky and press the insides of your arms against your face just in front of your ears. Squeeze your body toward its centerline. If possible, have a partner help you make alignment adjustments. By raising your shoulders toward your ears, you can streamline yourself even more.

Ship drill While in the water, push off from the wall in streamlined position with your body outstretched and your arms extended. Your shape will resemble the bow of a ship (see figure 3.1). Hold the streamlined position, tightening the muscles from your core through your trunk and out to your fingertips. How far can you glide after your push? Do you glide farther underwater or on the surface?

Figure 3.1 Streamlining the body.

Practice making your body shape like a destroyer, ocean liner, or barge. These variations of the ship drill show the transition from the streamlined flow of the destroyer to the more turbulent, cumbersome flow of the barge. Move your head away from the long axis of the body to detect the sensation of the oncoming water's pressure.

Kick with head leading Maintain a neutrally aligned spine position on the water's surface, hold your arms to your side, and add an easy, relaxed flutter kick. Rotate your whole body, maintaining alignment of the head, neck, and spine to take a breath.

Kick with one arm leading Extend your right arm forward, hold your left arm to the side, hold your body in streamlined balanced position, and begin to flutter kick lightly. Think: no noise and no white water. Focus on proper body position and strive for a feeling of going downhill. Take one arm stroke as you roll your left side down and allow your right side to rotate toward the surface to breathe and then repeat the exercise with the left arm extended, rotating to the right side to breathe (see figure 3.2).

(continued)

Streamlining Drills *(continued)*

Figure 3.2 Kick with one arm leading.

Kick with an underwater recovery Extend your right arm forward, hold your left arm at your side, and kick lightly 6 to 10 times. Pull your right arm through to your side as you roll your left side down and recover your left arm forward underwater. Breathe to your right in the natural flow of the stroke.

Focus on relaxing the muscles in your neck, jaw, and face in this breathing sequence. During the drill, keep your body line long and breathe with your head in line with your spine. This practice maintains your balance during the transition between sides. Again, imagine yourself as a long boat.

Clock drill Lie on your side, extend one arm in the water in streamlined position, and extend the other arm out of the water, holding your fingers toward the sky at the 12 o'clock position. Hold this position for 1 to 2 seconds, then bend the elbow of the arm above water and reach it forward to entry position. Pull your underwater arm through, switch to the other side, and continue the drill. Maintain the body alignment you have built throughout the streamlining sequence. Most masters swimmers would find this drill challenging. Swimmers with limited ankle flexibility can use fins for this and other drills, being careful not to overkick or gain dependency on them for body positioning.

The motion of a person swimming through the pool generates wave resistance. This type of resistance is evident when swimmers' vertical or lateral movements create waves, which dissipate energy in great amounts. When swimmers double their speed, wave resistance increases eight times.

In the freestyle, the forward extension of the arm and shoulder places the body in streamlined alignment. Recovery of the shoulder and arm is important for reducing form and wave resistance. Based on the previously mentioned speed-to-resistance ratios, swimmers should focus first on reducing wave resistance in the water, then reducing form resistance. Form resistance can be reduced with improved flexibility.

Several factors affect swimmers' ability to maintain ideal form and body alignment. Many adult swimmers are limited by poor flexibility or injury. Stay focused on creating a streamlined position that works best for you.

The concepts of relaxing, breathing, balancing, and streamlining are great basics to revisit during the warm-up and the cool-down sections of your swim workouts. Swimmers at all levels should spend time focusing on these building blocks to better develop their water sense. Great water sense builds more fluid strokes and enhances your partnership with the water.

Fine-Tuning Your Strokes

4

Freestyle

I could make good time because I was so long and skinny, shooting through the water like a stick.

—Johnny Weissmuller, five-time gold medalist,
1924 and 1928 Olympic Games

Johnny Weissmuller, better known as the movie actor who played Tarzan, gave this amazingly accurate explanation for his swimming successes, including five gold medals and 52 national championship titles. Although there is a little more to the story of his success, Johnny was correct when he described his form as long, lean, and streamlined.

In a freestyle competition, swimmers can choose any stroke style, including front crawl, backstroke, breaststroke, butterfly, sidestroke, or even dog paddle. As long as swimmers do not touch the bottom of the pool, pull on the lane line, or interfere with others, anything goes. The vast majority of swimmers choose the front crawl for freestyle swimming because it is the fastest stroke. This book refers to the front crawl stroke as the freestyle stroke.

Several factors contribute to great freestyle technique. The first facet to consider is breathing and how it fits into the rhythm of the stroke. You should next approach the stroke from three dimensions: width, length, and depth. When considering width and length, think about reducing your lateral movements and streamlining your body as you move through the stroke cycle, making yourself like the shooting stick that Johnny Weissmuller described. The depth element of the stroke is about making a great catch, or holding more water as you move into the propulsive phase of the stroke. Finally, consider kicking technique, which can vary greatly among swimmers.

BREATHING

Controlled breathing is perhaps the main factor for efficient freestyle swimming. Breath control involves timing air exchanges with the rhythm of the stroke and ventilating the lungs. Swimmers who lengthen their exhalation to blend smoothly with the flow of the stroke can better master the fundamentals of balance, relaxation, arm timing, streamlining, stroke length, and the effective application of power. Swimmers with good breath control take deep breaths quickly and easily, followed by long exhalations. This process provides swimmers with enough time within each stroke cycle, or each series of cycles, to keep their bodies long, loose, and rhythmic.

New swimmers are encouraged to establish a comfortable breathing pattern, either to one side every arm cycle or alternating. Experienced swimmers typically prefer the former, as it provides the most oxygen, thus allowing for greater effort and faster speeds. By mixing a breathing pattern of every four, five, or six strokes into their training, swimmers are able to concentrate more on their stroke mechanics. Conditioning the mind for breathing repetition is crucial to mastering an efficient and relaxed breathing pattern.

The freestyle breathing sequence begins with a quick inhalation. If you have properly expelled your breath during the exhalation phase of the previous stroke cycle, this act of inhaling will be a reflex; in fact, you may not even be aware that you have taken in a breath. As your face returns to the center position, refocus your eyes on the bottom of the pool. Pull your breathing-side arm out of the water and slide it forward to reenter the water. As your hand enters the water and your arm extends forward, exhale gently and steadily. Continue exhaling throughout the next stroke cycle, allowing yourself time to complete the body roll to the opposite side as you complete the cycle with the other arm.

Some swimmers hold their breath for a moment before exhaling. Regardless of when you exhale, you must make the process longer than your inhalation, and build it to a crescendo just before your face exits the water for the

next inhalation. This means that when your entry arm is almost fully extended and your mouth is just about to clear the water, you should expel the remainder of your air with a puff (see figure 4.1). Many swimmers use both their mouths and noses for this final puff, which not only clears the lungs for more air, but also moves water away from the face, so they can inhale without taking in water. If your head and body are

Figure 4.1 The remainder of the air is expelled with a puff.

properly streamlined, your head will create a natural bow wave (a wave that is curved like a ship's bow), allowing you to inhale with your mouth slightly below the water line (see figure 4.2, *a-c*).

Your exhalation should always be at least twice as long as your inhalation. Advanced swimmers increase their outward-to-inward breath ratio even more than 2:1. Prolonging your exhalations and allowing the air to flow out easily gives you more time within each stroke cycle to streamline, balance your body, and maintain your stroke length and rhythm. Once you master this process, you will glide through the water smoothly and effortlessly. Experiment with mouth-only and mouth-and-nose breathing to find out which technique is more comfortable for you.

Maintain body balance throughout the stroke cycle by keeping your head, neck, and spine in alignment as you breathe. Novice swimmers often lift their heads out of alignment, which causes their hips and legs to drop and reduces the extension of their arms in the front of the stroke. As a result, they lose their long *body line*, or the streamlined shape of an extended and aligned body, which is critical for a long exhalation and a more relaxed stroke. If swimmers are having problems getting their faces out of the water to breathe, they should exaggerate their rotations toward the breathing side (their belly buttons should face the wall of the pool) to make sure their

Figure 4.2 Complete freestyle breathing.

mouths clear the water's surface. This is especially helpful for swimmers who have limited flexibility in their shoulder girdles and necks or have shoulder impingement, a condition in which the scapula puts pressure on the rotator cuff when the arm is extended. As their skills progress and they become more flexible, they will be able to reduce their rotation and resume a more streamlined position.

WIDTH AND LENGTH

Examining the width and the length of a swimmer's freestyle means looking at the whole stroke with emphasis on the arm recovery, head position, and core rotation. World-class swimmers spend hours perfecting their strokes to minimize lateral movements and maximize forward momentum. Chapter 3,

Develop Your Water Sense, asserts that reducing resistance is the fastest way to improve swimming speed and efficiency. Johnny Weissmuller likened himself to a shooting stick. Jim Montgomery imagines his body carving through the water like a knife. Coaches will sometimes tell their masters swimmers to imagine they are swimming through a narrow hallway.

In the freestyle stroke, reducing lateral movements and increasing stroke length begins with maintaining alignment of the head and spine. If a swimmer's head moves out of this line, either vertically or horizontally, the body will compensate by sliding out of position in the opposite direction. To reduce head movement, imagine that you are being pulled down the pool by a rope attached to the top of your head. Practice swimming slowly without breathing for several strokes to perfect the head-on-the-spine position.

Efficient freestyle begins with maintaining forward momentum throughout the stroke cycle. This is particularly important as the arms recover over the water. Arm recovery begins as your body rotates to the side and you lift your shoulder girdle, elbow, and hand out of the water. Think of this process as taking your hand out of your side pocket. In Texas, Jim says, "Take a gun out of its holster." Visualize your arms as relaxed hinges or as pendulums swinging forward as they recover from your elbows down to your fingertips.

Swimmers with reduced flexibility sometimes recover their arms in a wide swing just over the water's surface. This less-efficient style has the same result as when swimmers take their heads out of alignment: Their bodies compensate by snaking from side to side. They can correct this mistake by increasing the rotation of their shoulders and bringing their hands straight forward, close to their bodies.

Relaxation is crucial for arm recovery in the freestyle. Experienced swimmers who churn out lap after lap make it look so easy because they truly are relaxing their arm muscles throughout their recovery. They appear to simply toss their elbows forward with the lower part of their arms swinging loosely underneath. Two great stroke drills that help swimmers maintain a relaxed, high-elbow recovery are the fingertip drag and the zipper, which are explained in the freestyle stroke drills section on page 39.

A freestyle arm recovery that is technically correct sets you up for a great hand entry into the water at the front of your stroke. As you swing your lower arm forward in the recovery, visualize placing your hand, thumb, or middle finger into an imaginary hole in front of your shoulder. Your forearm and elbow continue through this hole, creating a clean entry with a minimum amount of bubbles (see figure 4.2). Imagine that the water's surface is a thin sheet of ice and you have created a small

Figure 4.2 Fingertips, hand, and forearm positioned to slice cleanly into the water.

hole, through which you poke your fingers, hand, forearm, and then elbow. You can actually listen to your hand enter the water while you are swimming. Does it slice in quietly or does it ker-plunk? If the entry seems noisy or creates many bubbles, you may be reaching too far over the water. This causes your elbow to drop down and enter the water at the same time as your hand, trapping air bubbles. Simply adjust your entry point for a cleaner feel.

After the entry, reach forward with your fingertips to maximize the length of your underwater stroke. The front end of the freestyle stroke is called the *front quadrant*; focus on it to maintain great length in your stroke. Imagine yourself with one arm fully extended under the water, your head aligned with rest of your body, your opposite arm in a recovery position with your shoulder blade, shoulder, and bent elbow high out of the water. You are the blade of a knife cutting through the water. Your shoulders and hips should roll about the same amount on each side, regardless of whether or not you are on a breathing stroke. The ship drill, described in the streamline section of chapter 3 on page 25, is a great way to begin working on streamlining and lengthening your stroke. You might also try the long-armed dog drill on page 39.

In the Mind of a Champion

What do swimming champions think about? Jim shares what goes on in his mind while he swims the freestyle stroke.

"When swimming freestyle, I think of several key words to help me concentrate on my stroke mechanics. For the arm recovery, I use the term *draw*. It reminds me that when I begin my arm recovery, I want to lift my elbow, arm, and shoulder out of the water like I take my hand out of my side pocket, or in Texas, where I live, like I draw a gun out of its holster. The next term is *reach*. This is where my hand, then my arm, enters the imaginary hole in front of my shoulder and reaches forward into a streamlined body position. The next term is *dig*. This is the catch phase of the pull, when I press my fingertips down while popping my elbow up. And finally, I *extend*. This reminds me to accelerate and finish my pull past the hips to full arm extension.

"It's important to note the sequence of these mental images. My arm recovery comes first. I want to feel that everything is moving forward, not sideways. Streamlining comes next, where my head and the front of my body feel the least resistance to the oncoming flow of water. With the resistance minimized, my focus turns to propulsion. Are my arms anchored with the palms of my hands facing straight back through my entire pull?

"As soon as I jump in the water, I begin to concentrate on my stroke deficiencies. Am I carrying my head too high, dropping my right elbow midway through the pull, or not finishing through with my left arm? All these things can occur in my freestyle stroke when fatigue sets in.

"I have to remember that there is no perfect stroke. Striving for near-perfect technique is a good goal, but many great swimmers have won with unconventional freestyle techniques. As one of my swimming coaches said, 'What is good for you is good only for you.'"

DEPTH: THE CATCH AND THE POWER PHASE

The power in swimming comes from the core group of muscles, which this book defines as the area from the neck to the knees, including all of the upper-back and shoulder muscles, the abdominal muscles, and the trunk and upper-leg muscles. The best way to access this power is with a great setup at the beginning of the freestyle underwater pull, or what is commonly called the *catch*. This term, which first became popular with the development of the crawl or freestyle stroke in the 19th century, refers to the point in the stroke when a swimmer's hand connects with the water and starts to pull.

The catch itself is not the main propulsive part of the stroke, but when properly executed, it sets your stroke up to be more effective through the propulsive power phase that follows. The freestyle catch occurs in the first 9 to 12 inches (23-30 cm) of the stroke, where you begin your pull by pressing the fingertips down while keeping your elbow up. Imagine yourself reaching over a waterfall and anchoring your palm and forearm on the rocks so that you can pull your body over. The late Doc Counsilman, former head coach of Indiana University and coach to 48 Olympians, including Jim Montgomery, was well known for his analogy of pulling over a barrel. Great freestyle swimmers anchor their hands in the water and use their core muscles to rotate their bodies past their hands. To properly achieve this catch position, internally, or medially, rotate your shoulder and open your armpit. Imagine driving your elbow toward the pool wall in front of you.

Consider the effect of body rotation on the depth of your hand catch. The forward reach and downward press of your arm at the entry and catch causes your body to rotate to the side. Keep your hand planed directly back (toward the wall behind you), with your fingertips toward the bottom of the pool, until your arm has reached midstroke. This is a key point for maintaining a powerful application of propulsive force. Finding the right amount of body rotation will automatically help you find the ideal depth in the pull. Once you set the high-elbow position in the underwater pull, maintain it throughout the stroke cycle. By keeping your hand and elbow anchored in the water at the catch spot, you will be able to recruit core muscles to rotate your body past that spot on the longitudinal axis. At midstroke, the bend of the elbow is approximately 90 degrees and then opens up again as your hand finishes the stroke. Your hand moves slowest at the catch phase of the stroke, but gradually picks up momentum until it is moving fast under your hips at the end of the stroke. Keep your wrist flexed to hold your hand perpendicular to the water's surface at the finish of the pull. The acceleration of the hand through the underwater pull synchronized with the rotation of the body's core creates the power phase of the freestyle stroke.

With a well-executed hand entry and extension followed by an effective catch and follow-through, your hand will actually come out of the water in front of the point where it entered! The hands of world-class swimmers exit the water several feet (about 1 m) in front of their entry points. These swimmers have an incredible amount of shoulder and back flexibility, allowing them to position their hands, forearms, and elbows in the catch position much earlier in the stroke. This creates a longer and more propulsive power phase. The following series of photos depicts the freestyle stroke from catch to power phase (figure 4.3, *a-d*).

Figure 4.3 Moving from catch to power phase.

Many adult novice and intermediate swimmers lack the body rotation, strength, and flexibility to hold their shoulders and elbows above their pulling hands throughout the freestyle pull. A well-designed dry-land program that includes stretching and strengthening helps swimmers learn and perfect the underwater stroke. Use the following teaching progression of both on-deck and in-water skills to learn the mechanics of the catch position and the correct muscle recruitment for transitioning into an efficient underwater pull.

1. Begin by standing on the pool deck in a streamlined position. Have a partner hold a hand against yours, applying slight pressure against your palm as you proceed to simulate the freestyle pull pattern. Start by

pressing your fingers and elevating your elbow. Feel the different use of muscles during a high-elbow, a straight-arm, and a dropped-elbow pull. When you do a high-elbow pull, you should feel your core muscles come into play, including the upper-back, chest, and shoulder muscles.

2. Use stretch cords to manipulate your hand and forearm into the desired movement of the stroke cycle. Start with your arms fully extended at shoulder-width and your wrists slightly flexed. Pop up your elbows and move your arms back in a curved path, first diagonally outward and then inward. Once your hands have moved across and under your body, extend your elbows and straighten your arms. Notice that your hands travel farther than the elbow.

3. Another great teaching tool is the in-water press-up. Position yourself at the deep end of the pool, facing the wall. Place your palms flat on the deck or gutter of the pool. Start with your head and body submerged, and then press up, using the buoyancy of the water to lift your body out. Maintain a high-elbow position and lift your body as high as you can.

4. Sensitizing your hands and forearms can dramatically enhance your feel for the water. This allows you to make subtle adjustments in the pitch of your hand so you can hold the water more effectively, whether anchoring in the catch position or finishing the propulsive power phase. You will learn to recognize water pressure against your hand and forearm during every phase of the stroke. Here are three simple ways to sensitize your hands: press the fingertips of one hand hard against the fingertips of the other, press your fingertips against the pool deck while resting, or rub your hands together or on the pool deck.

5. Swimming with hand paddles generates more water pressure against the palms of your hands, which activates the muscle groups that propel your elbows up. Novice masters swimmers should use smaller paddles, preferably with holes in them. Try eliminating the wrist strap of the paddle and use a single strap or tubing around your middle finger. Focus on keeping water pressure on the paddle. If you drop your elbow, the paddle tends to slide off your hand.

6. Whether you are from the American South or not, the A-OK and the Hook 'em Horns drills can effectively teach you to recognize flow and to angle your hands efficiently for good stroke patterns. To begin, swim freestyle with your fingers in the A-OK position, pressing together the tips of your thumb and forefinger to form a tunnel to channel the water flow as your hand changes direction in the stroke. If you drop your elbow during the pull, the water will not flow through the tunnel. To form the Hook 'em Horns hand position, hold your middle and ring fingers against your palm at the base of your thumb and point your forefinger and pinky finger up to signify horns. Begin the freestyle with this hand position, pointing the horn fingers toward the bottom of the pool during the pull.

KICKING

Although the legs do not provide as much propulsion as the pull of the arms in the freestyle stroke, they do play an important roll in streamlining the body as it rotates from side to side on the long axis. As your arm finishes a stroke, the leg on that side of your body naturally counterbalances the movement by kicking downward to keep your hips high. At the same time, your other leg moves up as your opposite arm prepares to enter the water. This basic rhythm of your arms and legs occurs naturally, without conscious effort, during each arm cycle.

There is more than one type of kicking pattern in freestyle swimming. Two-beat, four-beat, and six-beat kicks are all common patterns for the balancing, rudderlike, or stabilizing action in the freestyle stroke. A two-beat swimmer kicks twice (once per leg) for each complete arm cycle. A four-beat swimmer kicks four times per cycle and a six-beat swimmer kicks six times per cycle. The kicking pattern you choose depends on the strength of your kick and the distance you are swimming. Freestyle sprinters often choose a six-beat kick, but swimmers going longer distances, particularly open-water swimmers and triathletes, may kick less.

The flutter kick is an undulating action that starts in the hip joints, passes through the legs, and ends with a whiplash movement of the ankles and feet. As you kick, imagine that your legs, from hips to toes, are two long rubber fins. Keep your knees and ankles loose and relaxed to allow the motion from your hips to flow down your legs. The most efficient and natural freestyle kickers are those with finlike flexibility in their ankles, knees, and hips. Masters swimmers use all kinds of freestyle kicks, and some are more efficient than others. New swimmers are inclined to initiate the kick from their knees, which increases resistance and compromises their body position. Visualize your legs, from hips to toes, as long fins or made out of rubber to learn the feel of the kick.

If done improperly or overemphasized, freestyle kicking adds significant drag to whole-stroke swimming and quickly drains swimmers' energy. Swimmers should do all they can to maximize benefit while minimizing the effort they put into their kicking by incorporating flexibility conditioning into their workouts.

With so much to think about, how can swimmers expect to perfect their strokes? Refining the details of your swimming strokes is much like working on your golf swing. Many things happen within a fraction of a second. While swimming, focus on only one or two things at one time. In a typical workout, coaches often incorporate stroke drills early in the session to isolate one or two specific aspects of the stroke. As the workout progresses, they transition into full-stroke swimming for the main set, paying attention to technique with increased aerobic effort. Coaches may include stroke drills into low-heart-rate swimming at the conclusion of the session to allow swimmers to refocus on the details of their stroke when their muscles are fatigued. With practice, swimmers' muscle memory improves and the new skill or stroke change becomes a natural part of their stroke.

Freestyle Stroke Drills

All masters swimmers should have a toolbox of stroke drills for focusing on technique and specific aspects of the stroke. The following exercises help swimmers work on all phases of the freestyle stroke, including body position, length, breathing, the catch, the propulsive pull phase, and arm recovery. Swimmers who lack a strong freestyle kick should use fins for these drills. A kickboard is often used to help learn the single-arm and catch-up drills by holding onto the end of the kickboard with your fingertips, arms kept straight.

Single-arm freestyle Push off in a streamlined position with both arms extended over your head, then swim freestyle moving only one arm, leaving the other arm extended. Focus on the feeling of pressing your fingertips down and your elbow up in the first 9 to 12 inches (23-30 cm) of the pull. Maintain a streamlined position throughout the pull, rotating your body as it passes over your underwater hand and elbow in the catch position. Ride out each stroke and recover over the water, relaxing your arm and leading with your elbow. Swim one length of the pool using your right arm and then swim another length using your left arm. Breathe every third or fourth stroke to better observe your underwater stroking arm.

Catch-up stroke This drill is similar to the single-arm freestyle, but it alternates stroking between the right and left arms. Be sure to return the stroking arm to the streamlined position before beginning to stroke with the opposite arm. For both drills, keep your arms extended slightly under the water's surface to prevent your elbow from dropping below your wrist and hand. If you are having trouble keeping the opposite arm extended throughout the pull, it is usually because you are lifting your head out of the water to breathe, causing a break in your body's alignment.

Fists To complete this drill favored by many masters swimmers, simply swim freestyle holding your hands clenched into fists. Start each stroke with your arm fully extended and the thumb side of your fist angled down. Focus on your hand and forearm rotation throughout the first half of the stroke. You want to feel as though you are pulling the water back with both your hands and forearms. Imagine that your forearms are as big as Popeye's!

The following three stroke drills help develop a relaxed, high-elbow recovery and length in your freestyle stroke.

Fingertip drag Swim freestyle, keeping your fingertips in the water on the recovery. Imagine that you are leading the recovery with your elbow, maintaining a high elbow position and rotating your shoulder internally. This is a favorite warm-up and cool-down drill for many swimmers.

Zipper The zipper drill is much like the fingertip drag, but you maintain contact between your thumb and your body throughout the recovery. When your thumb reaches your armpit, reach forward and put it in the water. This excellent drill encourages the forward momentum that characterizes an efficient arm recovery.

Long-armed dog Swim freestyle making your arm recovery completely underwater. You are essentially combining a long-armed dog paddle with the head position and side breathing of the freestyle. Reach long on each side and make a good catch, then rotate your body past your arm as you focus on lengthening your stroke.

Different Strokes

Take a look at any pool of swimmers and you will quickly see that no two freestyle strokes are built the same. Each swimmer seems to move through the water with a different tempo, some rotating more or less and others kicking harder or softer. At the world-class level, the individuality in styles continues, particularly when you look closely at the distance swimmers and the sprinters. Recently, a portion of sprint freestyle specialists are moving toward a straight-arm freestyle stroke, resembling more of a windmill, than that of the more accepted front-quadrant-dominant stroke. The success of straight-arm freestylers, such as American Gary Hall Jr. and Australian Eamon Sullivan, calls us to take a closer look at this nonconventional style.

Sometimes referred to as a rotary or windmill stroke, this straight-arm technique has been appropriately dubbed the *shoulder-driven* freestyle by Coach Mike Bottom, to differentiate it from the traditional freestyle stroke. Coach Bottom, one of the most prominent sprint coaches in the world and coach of four-time Olympian Gary Hall Jr., trains his elite sprint specialists to be versed in both stroke styles, thus stocking their stroke toolbox with everything they need to maximize their opportunities in both training and racing. The energy demands of the shoulder-driven stroke make it suitable for only the shortest freestyle events—the 50 meter and some, but not all, of the 100 meter. In contrast, the traditional stroke is more suitable for events of 200 meters and up.

As you read about the shoulder-driven stroke, you will quickly realize how dramatically different this technique is from the traditional emphasis on the long body line and extended front quadrant of the traditional stroke. The objective of the shoulder-driven stroke is to take all the dips out of the speed curve and keep the body moving. To this end, one hand is always *on the water*, or positioned with water pressure on the palm in a propulsive movement. The following key features of the shoulder-driven stroke are what make this continuous motion possible.

- *A quick catch.* This means that as the hand enters, it immediately executes the catch beginning with the fingertips and followed by the palm and arm. The moment just after the catch is executed is considered the *power position* in the shoulder-driven stroke.
- *Early release.* As the entering hand is catching the water, the other hand is releasing the water at the finish of the underwater phase and transitioning into the recovery. The hand releases the water earlier than the traditional freestyle so as to carry the momentum of the powerful underwater pull into the recovery.
- *Fast recovery.* Perhaps the most noticeable feature of the shoulder-driven stroke is the fast and powerful arm recovery. Unlike the traditional relaxed high-elbow freestyle recovery, the arms are *whipped* over the water, rushing up to the front to quickly assume the power position, preventing even the slightest dip in the speed curve.
- *Flatten the hips and kick, kick, kick.* The legs drive a hard and fast kick, again propelling the charge forward. As a result, the hips remain relatively flat compared to the traditional stroke.

We all get a little tired just *reading* what it takes to swim the shoulder-driven freestyle. Why would a masters swimmer begin to tackle this nontraditional style? Remember that the shoulder-driven style is something you pull out of your stroke toolbox for quick, short bursts of speed. This is not the style of stroke you use through your workouts, but only on specific, targeted short-distance sets. We suggest that any masters swimmer who prefers sprint events consider adding this style to their repertoire. Those swimmers with flexibility through their shoulders, legs, and ankles will have the most success, as they will be able to take advantage of the full range of shoulder rotation as well as the strong driving kick.

(continued)

Different Strokes *(continued)*

You can get a taste of the shoulder-driven stroke by speeding up your arm recovery by swimming freestyle with the butterfly kick. Maintain a rhythm of one kick per single arm stroke. Increase the tempo of your kick and speed up your arm recovery to keep the pace. Imagine that your shoulders are connected to your spine as you fling your arm over the water much like a discus thrower. Remember not to worry about how pretty your stroke looks; it's all about speed. If you choose to wear fins on this drill, be sure to pick short ones. As with all training and racing with shoulder-driven freestyle swimming and drills, keep the distances short and allow yourself enough rest to maintain your technique.

Because the shoulder-driven freestyle is purely about speed and not about maintaining speed over long distances, it has been likened to the Indy driver with the pedal on the floor. The gas tank empties sooner, but you get there much faster. Try it for yourself and enjoy the ride!

Backstroke

I moved across the water like a rowing shell slipping across the Thames.

—John Nabor, gold medalist, 100-meter backstroke, 1976 Olympic Games

The backstroke is so similar to the basic crawl stroke that it is sometimes called an upside-down freestyle. These two strokes are often grouped together as the long-axis strokes because swimmers rotate primarily along the vertical (head to toes) axis of the body. As a matter of fact, many of the world's great freestyle swimmers were backstroke specialists earlier in their careers.

The teaching progression for backstroke begins with body position: how to use balance, core strength, and kick to position yourself like John Nabor's rowing shell. Once you're comfortable with the isolated kicking drills, move on to arm movement, both underwater pull and overwater recovery. Lastly, the discussion of stroke tempo, rhythm, and the importance of relaxation bring the whole stroke together.

Backstroke is an excellent complement to freestyle and should be a part of every swimmer's workout. It opens up the chest muscles, works opposing muscle groups, and conditions the legs. Many swimmers who invest the time to learn and perfect their backstroke are paid back with both a better backstroke and a faster freestyle!

BODY POSITION AND KICKING

When swimmers' bodies are properly aligned for backstroke, their lungs are positioned at the surface of the water with their body underneath. This differs from the freestyle, where the swimmers' backs are on the surface of the water and their lungs are pushing up from underneath. Lacking this push from the lungs' buoyancy, backstroke swimmers sit slightly lower in the water and depend more on the strength of their kick to achieve the balanced, horizontal body position from chapter 3, Developing Your Water Sense. A good relationship between body position and kicking technique is essential for a successful and efficient backstroke.

Begin by resting on your back in the water with your arms at your sides. Kick lightly and maintain a relaxed and steady head position with your ears underwater. As in the freestyle, your head, neck, and spine should be aligned and your core muscles should be engaged. Gently press the base of your neck lower in the water to keep your hips on the surface of the water. Resist the temptation to tuck your chin and lift your head to look around, which will cause your hips to drop. Ideally, your head will not move in any direction. Imagine that you are swimming with a cup of water on your forehead; try not to spill a drop!

Begin the kick by dropping your leg below the horizontal line of your body at the hip. Bend your knee at the lowest point of the kick, or just as you begin to move your leg up (see figure 5.1*a*). Finish the kick by whipping or snapping your foot as it reaches the surface of the water (see figure 5.1*b*). Imagine you are trying to flick water off your toes. When kicking properly, the bubbles you create on the water's surface make it look like it is about to boil.

Great backstrokers have very powerful kicks and maintain a steady six-beat rhythm throughout their strokes. Many coaches of backstroke technique believe that a great kick leads to a great body position, which leads to a great catch, which leads to more power. Practice making your kick small and constant, and focus on relaxing your jaw and neck muscles. Avoid the temptation to lift your knees in a bicycling motion, which compromises your body position and causes additional resistance. Swimmers can improve their technique by increasing flexibility in their hip flexors, knees, and ankles and working with fins.

Figure 5.1 Backstroke kicking mechanics.

The following body position and kicking drills give you a great foundation for building an efficient backstroke.

1. *Kick with your arms at your sides.* Focus on excellent body alignment and a steady kick. Visualize yourself as a rowing shell. Keep your spine in a neutral position by engaging your abdominal muscles.

2. *Kick with one arm extended.* Once you are comfortable kicking with your arms at your side, try extending one arm over your head while keeping the other relaxed at your side. Hold your extended arm straight with your palm facing the side of the pool. Your body will rotate toward the extended arm, dropping that shoulder deeper and raising the opposite shoulder out of the water, while keeping your head in a neutral position. To minimize resistance and streamline your body, hold your extended arm tight against your head, just behind your ear.

3. *Streamline your kick.* Swimmers with good shoulder flexibility should kick holding both arms overhead in a streamlined position. Hold your arms tight against your head, extend your elbows, and stack your hands, locking the thumb of your bottom hand around the pinky of your top hand. Activate your abdominal muscles to avoid arching your back. Keep your kick small, fast, and streamlined with the long axis of your body. Make yourself into a torpedo.

Because a strong core and an efficient kick are so essential to this stroke, great backstroke swimmers practice these drills frequently. All swimmers, regardless of stroke preference, are encouraged to practice these exercises to isolate their core muscles and strengthen their legs. Masters swimmers with reduced ankle flexibility may prefer to use fins with these exercises, which will help them develop the mechanics of the kick.

ARMS

As in the freestyle, in the backstroke your body rotates on its long, vertical axis with each stroke, using power from your core and relieving stress from your shoulders. An efficient backstroke requires an effective catch at the top of the underwater pull phase and accelerated hand motion through the end of the stroke during an extended power phase.

Begin the arm pull by placing your hand in the water with your palm facing out and your pinky finger entering first. Your hand should be directly in line with your shoulder. The point of entry depends on shoulder flexibility and varies with each swimmer. Imagine you are lying on the face of a clock with your head positioned under the number 12. As you swim, your arms should enter the water near 11 o'clock and 1 o'clock.

Continue to lead with the little finger driving the arm and shoulder underwater with your palm out and your arm straight until your fingertips are 8 to 12 inches (20-30 cm) deep. Your body should be rotated approximately 45 degrees at this point, which is the deepest point of your catch and your opposite shoulder is raised out of the water. Children learning this entry to the catch motion like to think of it as a *karate chop*.

Begin the catch by rotating your arm and bending your elbow to point toward the bottom of the pool. Open your armpit and point your fingers toward the side of the pool. In a great backstroke catch, the entire underside of your arm holds the water. Continue the stroke, maintaining pressure on the water with your hand, forearm, and upper arm and pushing the

Figure 5.2 Backstroke catch.

water toward your feet. Increase the bend in your elbow during the underwater phase, allowing your hand to sweep closer to your body as it accelerates through the end of the stroke (see figure 5.2). Your hand should finish under your hip, which will rise up as the opposite arm begins its entry and catch.

The recovery, or above-water, phase of the backstroke pull begins as soon as your hand finishes the underwater pull. Your shoulder and hip will be high in the water and perfectly positioned to lead the recovery. Keep your arm straight

In the Mind of a Champion

Lia Oberstar-Brown, a two-time American record holder, four-time NCAA champion, and former member of the U.S. national team now trains under the guidance of Coach Jim at the Dallas Aquatic Masters. Her record-setting trend continues in her career as a masters swimmer, where she is a two-time world record holder, two-time national record holder, and 10-time national champion. Lia shares these thoughts about her backstroke: "When swimming backstroke, there are three major thoughts running continuously through my head.

"The first thought is about my kick. I want to feel that a majority of my forward motion comes from an effective and strong kick. I am constantly trying to keep the rhythm of my kick at least twice as fast as or faster than the rhythm of my arms. Although I was taught to kick three times per arm pull, I make myself kick harder. I want to double that rate, even triple it, if I can. My speed increases during a backstroke swim when my kick increases.

"The second thought is a good push-through at the bottom, or end, of my stroke. There is only one small phase of each backstroke pull that actually moves me forward in the water. Everything else is either out of the water (recovery) or setting up for the power phase (catch). Each time that I push my arms through, I envision throwing water toward my feet. When I'm really tired, I imagine arm-wrestling someone. This has the effect of keeping consistent and equal power moving forward from both arms. When finishing my stroke, I want to bounce my hands out of the water.

"Finally, there is tempo. Because my legs play such an important part in maintaining forward motion, my upper body can't have slowdowns in the arm-stroke rate. I don't want any points of hesitation or outright stopping with my arm strokes; I think of backstroke as one continuous stroke until the turn."

as you lift your hand, thumb-side first, up out of the water as if you were reaching out to shake somebody's hand (see figure 5.3*b*). Continue to keep your arm straight as it recovers directly over the line of your body with the palm facing in (see figure 5.3*a*). As your hand approaches the entry point (at 11 or 1 o'clock), your shoulders and hips should rotate naturally, allowing you to place your pinky finger in the water first (see figure 5.3*c*).

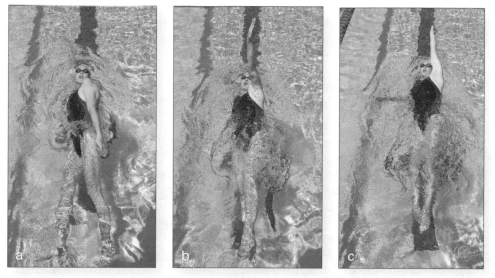

Figure 5.3 Backstroke arm recovery sequence.

Learning the backstroke pull can be tricky for beginners because the recovering arm is straight while the underwater arm is bent. Many new backstroke swimmers want to either pull underwater with a straight arm or recover with a bent arm. Three drills that isolate segments of the backstroke pull and facilitate the development of correct mechanics are the Single-Arm Backstroke, the Six-Count Drill, and the Double-Arm Backstroke.

STROKE TEMPO

For a great backstroke, you must rhythmically combine body position, kicking, and arm movement and maintain your momentum. World-class backstrokers have a high stroke rate (arm turnover), a fast kick, and a powerful pull that starts with an early underwater catch. Their success is partially due to their flexible shoulders, legs, and ankles. However, their true mastery of backstroke lies in their ability to execute the fundamental elements of the stroke with a relaxed tempo that is driven from their core.

Unlike the freestyle, there is no catch-up effect in the backstroke. Your arms and hands never stop moving. Imagine that your two arms are now one arm; keep them flowing together through your core as you swim. Many beginners fail to maintain their momentum in the backstroke because they stop their hands

Backstroke Drills

Swimmers use these drills to isolate specific aspects of the stroke before integrating them into full-stroke swimming. Use the first three drills to focus on all phases of the stroke, including hip and shoulder rotation and the recovery and underwater phases of the arm stroke. Use the last two drills to work on the timing and rhythm of the stroke.

Single-arm backstroke Relax one arm at your side and swim backstroke with the other arm. Stay focused on rotating to both sides: the shoulder of the stroking arm should be underwater at the catch and above water as you start your recovery. Keep your kick steady and maintain body alignment from the top of your head through your core. Alternate lengths of this drill concentrating on various aspects of the stroke: first the entry, then the catch, the finish, and the recovery. Switch arms and repeat.

Six-count drill Extend one arm above your head with the palm facing the side of the pool. Hold your extended arm underwater and your other arm above water in the finishing position (at your side with your shoulder up). Your body will be rotated to about 45 degrees. Kick in this position for six counts, then rotate to the opposite side and reverse your arms. In other words, complete half of a full stroke cycle. Kick for another six counts and switch. As you kick on your side, stay focused on maintaining a long body line with your head, neck, and spine in alignment. As you switch from one side to the other, keep your head still and your kick steady. Swimmers with more flexibility may do this drill holding the palm of their extended hand facing the pool bottom.

Double-arm backstroke In this drill, you will swim backstroke with both arms at the same time. You will not be able to execute a deep catch in this drill because you won't be rotating side to side. Use this drill early in the teaching progression when you're learning to coordinate holding your bent elbow underwater while your straight arm recovers

Rhythm drill Building on the single-arm backstroke drill described previously, swim two strokes using your right arm, then two strokes using your left arm. As before, keep the arm that is not stroking at your side. In this drill, you essentially complete a full stroke cycle as you transition from side to side. Focus on setting the tempo of the stroke with your hips, keeping your head steady and your kick constant.

A good variation of this drill is to swim three single-arm strokes with the right arm, then three strokes alternating arms, then three single-arm strokes with the left arm. Continue in this pattern for a full length of the pool.

Long-axis combo This drill, sometimes called the Russian Roll-Over, is a combination of the two long-axis strokes: freestyle and backstroke. Swim two strokes freestyle, and then roll onto your back for two strokes of backstroke. Focus on the catch in your freestyle and the follow-through in your backstroke.

Vary this drill by increasing the number of strokes for backstroke and freestyle to three or four. As you do the drill, feel the similarities in rhythm between these two strokes. Focus on working from your hips to rotate on the long, vertical axis of your body.

as they finish each stroke. These swimmers are encouraged to finish and go, immediately initiating the arm recovery with a thumbs-up hand exit at the end of each stroke.

Proper breathing, often overlooked when learning backstroke, is a critical part of stroke tempo. Although your nose and mouth are out of the water, you should establish a relaxed and regular pattern of inhalation and exhalation within the rhythm of the stroke. Backstroke swimmers typically inhale and exhale through their mouths, breathing in as one arm recovers and breathing out as the other arm recovers. This breathing pattern coordinates the inhalation and exhalation with the rhythm of the stroke in a manner similar to freestyle. One option for swimmers working to become more comfortable with their breathing is to practice swimming the backstroke inhaling through their mouths and exhaling slowly through their noses. The focus is on relaxing the jaw, face, and neck muscles and breathing comfortably. Exhaling through the nose is recommended as a practice exercise only; swimmers primarily breathe through their mouths when training and competing in the backstroke.

Good backstroke rhythm comes with practice and relaxation. The long-axis combo drill and the rhythm drill can help swimmers with tempo.

BACKSTROKE STYLE

Backstroke styles vary considerably among swimmers, and depend on the strength and flexibility of their shoulders, legs, and ankles. Swimmers with greater shoulder flexibility can angle their palms toward the bottom of the pool as they begin the catch, which sets up the stroke more efficiently. Swimmers with highly flexible shoulders will be able to achieve an effective catch with less rotation. Flexible feet and ankles are crucial for strong kicking motions.

Swimmers with less flexibility can improve their stroke efficiency by rotating their shoulders slightly more than normal and starting the catch by holding their palms perpendicular to the pool bottom. A well-designed dry-land program with massage, stretching, and core-strength exercises will increase strength and flexibility, making it easier to swim a more efficient backstroke.

No two backstrokes look the same. Swimmers at the world level exhibit an amazing variety of underwater strokes, tempos, and uses of their core muscles. With time, practice, and the guidance of a coach, you will find the stroke style that works best with your strengths.

Although many new swimmers resist learning or training in any stroke but the freestyle, they are encouraged to add the backstroke to their repertoire. The benefits of mastering the backstroke and mixing it into training are many, including better muscle balance, improved feel and sense of the water, and the opportunity to add variety in the pool. For example, the kicks for the backstroke and freestyle work opposing muscles, which makes the two strokes complementary and mutually beneficial. The two strokes share a similar rhythm with the common element of shoulder and hip rotation through the long axis of the body. Every freestyle swimmer can improve by adding a little backstroke.

Where Am I Going?

Perhaps the most frustrating challenge that new backstrokers encounter is learning how to navigate. It is truly difficult to relax when you are swimming blindly down the pool, not really knowing who or what you may run into next. How do experienced backstrokers swim in a straight line? How do they know where the wall is? Remember these navigation pointers for safer backstroke swimming.

- *Keep your head on straight.* The key element to swimming in a straight line is to keep your head still and in line with your core. Often, swimmers lift their heads or look from side to side to see where they are going. This practice will surely take them off course. Like in the freestyle, your head must remain steady and still on the water's surface. Again, imagine being pulled down the pool by a rope attached to your head.

- *Hands enter the water at 11 and 1 o'clock.* Another contributing factor to weaving backstroke is improper hand placement at the entry. Entering the hand at 12 o'clock, instead of 11 or 1 o'clock, changes swimmers' direction, particularly if their shoulder flexibility is limited. Keep your elbow straight and your palm facing out as your hand enters the water.

- *Position your palm for success.* After your hand enters the water, it should slice down 8 to 12 inches (20-30 cm) before beginning the catch. In the catch, rotate your palm and forearm to an angle of attack that will move the water toward your feet. However, if you begin to push the water before you are properly positioned (for example, if you push while your palm is facing the side of the pool), then you will certainly weave off course. Try to minimize the water pressure on your palm and forearm until you have initiated the catch and you are positioned for the follow-through and finishing phases of the stroke.

- *Recover over the line of your body.* A great recovery, with a straight elbow held directly over the line of your body, will set you up for an efficient entry and catch. At the top of your recovery, look over your shoulder and down the line of your arm as if you were aiming a gun at the sky. Maintain the momentum of the recovery as you drop your arm into the water at the 11 or 1 o'clock position and continue your hand's slice into the catch position.

- *Watch for the flags.* At the end of every lap pool, there should be overhead flags placed 5 yards (5 m) from the end of the pool. These flags are appropriately called *backstroke flags* and they warn you that you are approaching the wall. Count how many strokes it takes you to swim from the flags to the wall. Once you are comfortable with your stroke count, simply begin counting as you travel under the flags on each lap and you will never be surprised by the wall again.

Butterfly

I knew I was doing well. I knew if I just stayed with my rhythm that it would carry me through.

—Misty Hyman, gold medalist, 2000 Olympic Games

Rhythm, flow, and relaxation are just a few elements of a great butterfly stroke. At the 2000 Olympics in Athens, Misty Hyman did not think about pushing harder or muscling up as she was being chased by the gold-medal favorite during the 200-meter butterfly. She held onto her lead in one of the biggest upsets in Olympic swimming history by focusing on her stroke rhythm. Great rhythm in butterfly allows swimmers to move through the water with minimal resistance, to apply their power at critical parts of the stroke, and, perhaps most important, to relax through other phases of the stroke.

This chapter discusses the following elements of the butterfly: positioning the body, kicking, breathing, and using the core, or center, of the body for stability and power. The butterfly kick, often called the dolphin kick, is both fun to do and is a great core-strengthening skill. Once swimmers are comfortable with core rhythm and kicking, they should focus on arm movement, tempo, and timing the full stroke.

If you are new to the butterfly or if you have limited flexibility, you may want to consider using a pair of fins while learning this skill. Swim fins will help you feel the flow of the kick through your legs, ankles, and feet. Shorter fins are a good choice because they better maintain the speed of the kick, and thus the stroke tempo, or timing. Resist the temptation to motor down the pool while wearing fins; keep the energy coming from your core and let it flow from your hips through your legs and the fins. Fins are not designed to make you swim faster, but rather to help you feel the stroke rhythm better.

When executed with an easy rhythm and tempo, the butterfly can be a lot of fun. Too often, swimmers try to swim butterfly with their shoulders and arms, which is definitely not fun and leads to injury. Stay focused on the key concepts of core rhythm and forward momentum and you will learn to swim a great butterfly.

BODY POSITION AND KICK

Over the past decade, the butterfly stroke has evolved to a more efficient, flatter stroke than the up-and-down stroke of the 1970s. Contemporary world-class butterfly swimmers maintain a gentle undulation, or pulsing, while focusing on forward momentum. This gentle undulation, produced by the body's core muscles, is at the heart of a relaxed and efficient butterfly stroke. For this reason, this chapter's skills progression begins by discussing pulsing motion and then moves on to kicking and breathing. The range of butterfly kicking drills, all designed to improve the efficiency and power of critical components of the stroke, will help you build strength and confidence.

Pulsing Relax your arms at your sides, position yourself horizontally in the water, and place your head in alignment with your neck and spine. Keep your eyes focused on the bottom of the pool and imagine your neck as long and straight. Begin to undulate your chest under and over the water line. Lead with the top of your head, and think about lifting your lungs and flowing the motion forward. If you're doing the movement properly, you will feel your abdominal muscles working. Focus on engaging the upper abdominal muscles as you press the chest under the surface. Keep the energy flowing from your center, resist the temptation to kick, and do not rush.

Kicking When done correctly, the butterfly kick fits into the undulating rhythm quite naturally. Keep your arms at your sides, imagine that your legs are an extension of your chest and hips, and let the energy flow through your thighs, knees, shins, ankles, and toes in a whiplike fashion. Think of your legs as unfurling or unrolling with this release of energy. As your chest goes down, your feet finish their final snap, and your hips sit high on the water surface (see figure 6.1*a*). As your chest rises up, both of your legs lift up together and your knees are straight (see figure 6.1*b*). Work your leg muscles through both the up and the down movements. Perhaps the most common mistake that beginning

Figure 6.1 Butterfly kicking rhythm: *(a)* chest low and hips high while feet finish snap and *(b)* chest high while legs lift with knees straight.

butterfly swimmers make is initiating the kick from the knee. Remember to keep your legs straight and connected to your core and to move them using the power of your abdominal and hip muscles. Ideally, your knees will be relaxed enough to allow the pulsing motion of your core to move down your legs. Keep the height of the undulations to a minimum and concentrate on forward momentum.

Breathing Breathing in butterfly, as in all strokes, must be synchronized with the rhythm of the stroke. Inhale when your chest is at the highest point of undulation and keep your eyes focused down on the water. As you inhale, visualize having a long neck without wrinkles. Keep your neck long and straight and lead with the top of your head. Exhale slowly as you press your chest and lungs below the surface of the water again. Accelerate the flow of air and blow the remainder out with a final puff, then inhale as your chest rises back to the top. Relax your face and jaw muscles, focus on breathing in and out, and maintain a steady, pulsing rhythm.

Begin practicing kicking by holding your arms at your sides and taking a breath on every fourth upbeat of your legs. Next, kick with your arms extended in front of you. Again, breathe every fourth kick. Minimize any disruption to the flow of the undulations by inhaling quickly and exhaling slowly as you press your chest under the water.

All swimmers will improve core strength through butterfly kick drills, whether they practice on their backs, underwater, horizontally, or vertically, which is described later in this chapter. The dolphin kick was recently introduced into the underwater pullout of breaststroke as well as freestyle and backstroke starts and turns, so it can now be legitimately used in every stroke for masters competitions.

ARMS

Keeping the motion of the arms in rhythm with the movement of the core is critical to keeping the butterfly stroke relaxed and sustainable. The section reviews the mechanics of the butterfly's arm motion by examining a complete stroke cycle, which begins and ends just after your hands enter the water at the top of the stroke. This progression allows you to focus on one stroke cycle at a time, and then gradually build into swimming the complete stroke.

At the beginning of the stroke cycle, your hands and arms enter the water, your chest presses down, your hips are at the surface of the water, and your legs are finishing the snap of the kick. Your hands will spread naturally, moving your arms into a Y position just beyond your shoulders (see figure 6.2*a*). This phase of the stroke feels as though you are grabbing up high on the sides of an open doorway and leaning through it with your chest. Although you do not actually stop moving, you may feel like you are pausing at this phase as you ride out the momentum of the previous stroke cycle and set up for the next. Beginning butterfly swimmers often err by rushing through or completely omitting this critical extension of the body, press of the chest, and momentary pause. This mistake makes it difficult to achieve a rhythmic and flowing stroke.

As in every stroke, a proper catch will set swimmers up for a more powerful and efficient butterfly. Similar to the freestyle catch, butterfly swimmers maintain a high-elbow position as they press their fingertips, hands, and forearms down and slightly out to effectively grab the water for the underwater pull. The hand position at the widest point in the catch phase is often called the *corner*. During the underwater phase of the stroke, swimmers pull their arms back from the corner and under the body, maintaining the high-elbow position (see figure 6.2*b*). From there, they push their arms back and out to the finish of the stroke. At the transition between the pull and push, swimmers hold their hands about a hand's width apart, just in front of their bellies (see figure 6.2*c*).

During the underwater phase of the stroke, the chest moves from the lowest point of undulation to the highest point, which is just above the water's surface. Your hands must increase to their peak speed through the powerful press to the stroke finish. This acceleration of your hands and forearms from the slower catch to the faster finish provides maximum power and lift as you transition into the recovery. In a breathing stroke cycle, take a quick breath while your chest moves up and over the water and your hands accelerate through the push phase of the stroke.

The recovery of the arms in the butterfly is wide: the arms are straight, relaxed, and in line with the shoulder blades, the pinky fingers are up, and the backs of the hands are leading forward. The arms should be just above the surface of the water during the recovery. Resist the temptation to bend your elbows, as you would in the freestyle, by imagining you are making a snow angel: Hold

Figure 6.2 Butterfly stroke mechanics: *(a)* arms in Y position, *(b)* sweeping in from the corners, and *(c)* pushing through to the finish.

your elbows straight while your fingertips draw large semicircles on either side of you. Relaxation is essential during this phase of the stroke in order to ride the surge of power to the front of the stroke. Imagine that you are tossing your arms to the front as your chest moves forward over the water (see figure 6.3). Your arms, chest, and head should reach the front of the stroke and the water's surface at the same time.

A critical element to maintaining the rhythm in the butterfly stroke is to quickly and cleanly connect the underwater phase with the low, above-water recovery. New butterfly swimmers sometimes get their hands stuck at the back of the stroke, which makes it difficult to initiate the recovery. To avoid this, finish the stroke just before the elbows straighten out completely. Your elbows should lead as your arms exit the water, followed by the forearms and hands. The back of the hand should always face forward (see figure 6.4).

Figure 6.3   Front view of arm recovery.

Figure 6.4   Butterfly stroke finish with transition into recovery.

BUILD THE STROKE

The butterfly stroke can be mastered with the right combination of skills, time, and practice. The following progression is used for both novice and advanced butterfly swimmers and is good for both teaching and refining the stroke.

1. *Pulse and kick, extending your arms in front.* Focus on working from your core and keeping your head in alignment with your neck and spine. Breathe on every fourth kick.

2. *Pulse and kick, sculling your hands in and out.* As your chest moves down and your hips rise up, spread your arms to scull, or sweep, your hands out to the catch position. Sweep the hands back in as you move your chest up and your hips down. Keep your head in alignment as you focus on the catch, on your hips, and on the finish of each kick. If you are doing this drill properly, you will feel like a band director holding your elbows high and sweeping your hands in and out. Using a snorkel may help you focus on body position and head alignment.

3. *Four kicks, one stroke cycle.* This step is similar to the first one, but differs on the third kick. At this point, when your chest is pressed under the water, initiate your catch and then follow through with a full stroke cycle. Accelerate your hands through the underwater phase and into the recovery without stopping. Make your fourth kick as your hands push back and leave the water.

   Concentrate on the placement of the two kicks in each cycle, the first as your hands enter the water and the second as your hands exit. Coaches say, "Kick your hands *into* the water and kick your hands *out* of the water."

4. *Two kicks, one stroke cycle.* Once you're comfortable with step 3, reduce the number of kicks at the front of your stroke, but maintain a visible pause at the start of each cycle when your arms are extended just prior to the catch. Hold your chin on the surface of the water when you grab your breath and keep your eyes on the water to maintain the alignment of your head and body. Resist the temptation to drop your head or tuck your chin.

Once you've mastered these four steps, you are ready to transition to full-stroke butterfly. Maintain stroke rhythm by emphasizing a long ride on the forward momentum of each stroke. Resist the temptation to rush into the catch of the next stroke. As you begin to integrate butterfly into your workouts, begin with two to four full butterfly strokes from the wall, then swim easy freestyle for the remainder of the length. Select a breathing pattern that is comfortable for you and fits with the flow of your stroke. With consistent practice, you will eventually be able to swim butterfly for the full length of the pool.

Butterfly Drills

All butterfly swimmers, regardless of their experience, can use the preceding skills progression and the following drills to review fundamentals such as body position, stroke timing, rhythm, flow, and kicking.

One arm only Hold one arm at your side and swim butterfly using the other arm, breathing to the side of the stroking arm. This is a good drill for reinforcing the rhythm of the stroke and the timing of the two kicks.

As you recover your arm, roll slightly to the side and imagine making the largest arc possible with your arm. This helps you keep your arm straight during the recovery. This excellent drill is also good for connecting the underwater phase of the stroke to the recovery. Accelerate your motion through the finishing press and into the recovery without slowing down.

Single, double, single This favorite drill to help with rhythm and timing begins with a streamlined kick from the wall. Keeping your right arm extended in front, swim one stroke cycle using only your left arm, then swim another cycle stroking with your right arm and the left arm extended, and finally, swim a stroke cycle using both arms. You can either repeat this pattern or alter it to make a sequence of two right-arm cycles, two left-arm cycles, two full-stroke cycles. You can increase this sequence to sets of threes or higher as you progress.

Underwater dolphin kick You may practice this kicking drill with your hands at your sides or with your arms overhead in a streamlined position. Focus on working your abdominal and lower-back muscles to move the flow of energy through your hips and legs as you snap your feet at the end of the stroke. Successful underwater dolphin kickers move the chest and arms up and down very little.

Dolphin kick on your back Lie on your back, hold your hands at your side, and keep your head out of the water during this excellent abdominal strengthening drill. Focus on kicking up and snapping your feet just under the surface of the water. Try to create a small splash. Use your hands to scull slightly at your sides.

Vertical dolphin kick Perform this drill in the deep end of the pool, maintaining an upright position with your arms crossed over your chest (see figure 6.5). Use fins if your kick is not strong enough to keep your head above the water. Focus on working through both directions of the kick and generating energy and power from your core muscles. Sprint in place for 10 to 15 seconds and then rest, working up to sprints 30 seconds long. When you are ready for a greater challenge, hold your arms above your head in streamlined position as you kick.

Figure 6.5 Vertical dolphin kick

GET IN THE RHYTHM

Great butterfly rhythm includes lengthening the body at the front of the stroke, maintaining forward momentum, and reducing the amplitude of stroke. Imagine yourself as a surfboard skimming over the waves. World-class butterfly swimmers execute this stroke with minimal undulation. One of the defining characteristics of Olympic champion Michael Phelps' butterfly is the way he keeps his stroke flat while breathing in each stroke cycle. He has been likened to a stone skipping across the water.

As in the other strokes, head position significantly affects the efficiency and rhythm of the butterfly. Many butterfly swimmers err by lifting their heads and looking forward to breathe, or dropping their chins down after they breathe. Both of these misalignment problems cause swimmers to bob up and down instead of lunging forward. It is critical to keep your head in alignment with your neck and spine. Elongate your neck as your chest rises to breathe. As you breathe, keep the back of your neck high and free of wrinkles, and fix your eyes on the water. When you aren't breathing, keep your neck long and resist the temptation to tuck your chin or drop your head. The top of your head leads the forward momentum throughout the stroke cycle.

Learning to swim the butterfly will take some time, but stick with it! Because relaxation, stroke rhythm, and timing are essential to this stroke, butterfly drills can be integrated into workouts for swimmers at every level. As they learn the basics, novice swimmers often use kicking and drill swimming as an alternative to swimming butterfly. Butterfly is an excellent conditioning stroke, and mastering it will give you a better command of all strokes, since you will have learned how to use your core to manage stroke rhythm and tempo.

In the Mind of a Champion

Martina Moravcova, a sprint butterfly and freestyle specialist, shows no signs of losing her winning rhythm. Martina's 67 medals, including 2 Olympic, 22 world, and 43 European, combined with her impressive resume of records, including 3 world, 16 European, and 203 Slovakian, make her one of the most decorated female swimmers of all time. Like many elite swimmers, Martina feels her stroke mechanics are primarily guided by instinct. Here, she shares her thoughts about dry-land training, the butterfly kick, and race management.

"When swimming butterfly, it is important to involve my core muscles and maintain my lower-back flexibility. For dry-land training, I typically do Pilates exercises to balance strength and flexibility through my abdominals, back, and hip muscles.

"I feel as though the kick makes the difference between a great flier and mediocre one. My first kick, when my arms enter the water, is what I call my *balancing kick*. I stress the upbeat of the legs, which helps me maintain a flat body position. The second kick, when my arms leave the water, is my *power kick*, where I stress the downbeat of the legs, boosting the forward momentum in my stroke. There is a fine line between the amount my body needs to undulate up and down and generating the necessary balance and power in my stroke with my kick. I want to stay as low in the water as possible, not wasting any energy moving up and down.

"Off the start and turns, I take 8 to 10 underwater kicks, depending on how deep I dive in or how tired my legs are. As I kick, I focus on a tight streamline, interlocking my head between my arms so my whole torso moves smoothly along with my kick. I kick slightly tilted on my left side because I've found that I am faster and stronger on that side, and it also relieves the lower-back tightness that I occasionally have.

"When I race, I have a tendency to overwork the first 25 meters of a 100-meter butterfly event. To avoid this, I focus on making sure my stroke stays long, maintaining the same stroke rate, and managing the energy I put into my kick. In the final 15 meters of the race, I focus on entering my arms shoulder-width apart in order to catch the water effectively, even if my shoulders and back are tightening up. In addition, I increase my tempo, thus maintaining my stroke rate into a strong finish."

Breaststroke

Think of your breaststroke as a jewel: You never hammer it; you only polish it.

—Kurt Grote, gold medalist, 1996 Olympic Games

Over the past 20 years, the breaststroke has undergone a metamorphosis unlike any other stroke. In the late 1980s and early 1990s, Coach Josef Nagy of Hungary pioneered the *wave style* of breaststroke, in which the swimmers' shoulders rise up and over the water, creating the appearance of a wave. Under the tutelage of Nagy and the University of Michigan's Jon Urbanchek, Mike Barrowman rose to the top with this then-controversial style of the stroke. Although the execution of the wave stroke varies according to an individual's build, flexibility, and strength, this style of the breaststroke has replaced the conventional breaststroke in most levels of competition. Many masters swimmers prefer the conventional, flatter breaststroke that they honed in their youth, but the majority of adult swimmers choose the wave style for its proven success in making swimmers faster and more efficient. This chapter discusses the wave style of breaststroke.

As with butterfly, the heart of the breaststroke is the undulating rhythm of the body's core. These two strokes are often referred to as the short-axis strokes, because swimmers rotate through the hips on the short axis of the body. Because of their similarities, this chapter follows a teaching progression similar to the butterfly, beginning with the kick, then moving on to the arms, and finishing with the integration of all the components for the full stroke.

KICK

The kick in the breaststroke is more crucial for stroke power and efficiency than any other stroke's kick. The most successful breaststrokers have a unique degree of flexibility that allows their legs and feet to hold, or grab, more water while kicking. This is why many coaches say, "Breaststrokers are born, not made." Regardless of level of innate flexibility, all swimmers can learn the breaststroke kick and integrate it into a wave style that works for them. Adult swimmers with a history of knee injuries might consider substituting a butterfly kick in training if they experience any pain with the breaststroke kick.

The three phases to the breaststroke kick are called the *recovery*, the *catch*, and the *propulsive phase*. Although these terms are traditionally used to describe the arm movements of a stroke, they serve quite well to discuss this unique kick.

In the recovery, draw your heels up toward your buttocks (see figure 7.1*a*). During this first phase of the kick, pay particular attention to minimizing resistance by hiding your legs behind your hips and torso. You can keep your body streamlined by minimizing the angle you create between your torso and upper leg, and keeping your knees and ankles together with your feet pointed back. New breaststroke swimmers often draw their knees up under their bodies to start this kick, which creates a significant amount of resistance and breaks the line of the body. Practicing breaststroke with a kickboard can reinforce this habit and make it difficult to correct. For this reason, once you understand the basic mechanics of the breaststroke kick, practice it without a board.

At the top of the recovery, set your feet up to catch, or connect, with the water. Turn your toes outward so the sole and the arch of your foot can grab the water, flex your toes toward your knees (ankle dorsiflexion), and position your heels just under the water's surface (see figure 7.1*b*). Keep your knees close together during the catch, but move your feet apart and outside the line of your body to hold more water. Feel the water pressure on the insides of your legs, ankles, and feet. It is important to position your legs for the most effective hold on the water, regardless of the width of the kick.

The final phase of the kick is the propulsive phase, when your feet grab the water and your legs straighten out. Keep your heels just under the water line and push your feet straight back in an elliptical pattern around your knees. Use the insteps of your feet to sweep the water back and use your inner leg muscles to accelerate the motion. Close your feet at the end of the kick by clapping your arches together and pointing your toes (see figure 7.1*c*). If you have made a good connection between your feet and the water, you will look and feel as though you have launched forward.

The breaststroke kick can be a bit tricky for many swimmers. If you are learning it for the first time, practice first on dry land. The following progression of skills takes you through the fundamentals of the breaststroke kick. First, learn the mechanics of the kick, and then integrate the kick into your stroke in the water.

1. *Kick on the pool deck.* Lie face down on the pool deck or across a starting block and work with a partner to feel the three phases of the kick: draw your heels up, set your feet out for the catch, then fire your feet back through the propulsive, or thrust, phase to the finish. Extend your legs out to your toes at the beginning and end of each kick.

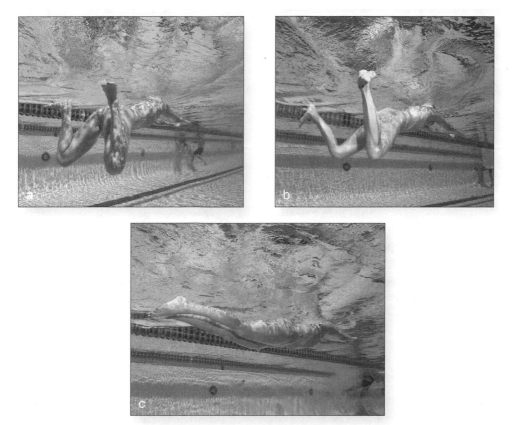

Figure 7.1   Kick cycle: *(a)* recovery, *(b)* catch, and *(c)* propulsive phase.

2. *Kick while holding onto the pool wall.* Hold onto the pool wall for support and stretch your body out horizontally on the water's surface. Draw your heels up toward your buttocks, set your feet out to catch the water, and then freeze. Make sure that your toes are pointing out to the sides, and then push your legs back from the knees with a whiplike motion, squeezing your legs together as they extend at the end.

3. *Kick with your hands at your sides.* Lie on the surface of the water with your head, neck, and spine in alignment and your eyes focused on the bottom of the pool. As you draw your heels up in the recovery, imagine your hips sliding forward as your upper back, neck, and head rise above the water's surface. At the catch point of the kick (your toes are pointing outward and are poised to push back), your upper body will be at its maximum height. Keep your neck long, lead with your head, and focus your eyes on the water. Inhale quickly, use your abdominal muscles to press your chest under the surface, and fire your kick through the propulsive phase to the finish. Ride out the kick as you return to your starting position, flat on the water's surface.

The breaststroke kick has an uneven flow because the underwater recovery of the legs and feet is followed by the force of the propulsive phase. You must *ride out*, or glide through, the propulsive phase of the kick before drawing your heels up for another kick cycle. As you learn the breaststroke, count how many kicks you take to complete one pool length. Challenge yourself to reduce the count by decreasing your resistance as you recover your heels, accelerating through the propulsive phase, and riding out each kick.

Resist the temptation to bob your head throughout the cycle of the kick and the resulting body undulation. Keep your head and neck in alignment with your spine and work the up and down undulation with your core abdominal muscles. Ideally, the three phases of the kick will meld with your body's undulation into one movement that flows from the lift of your heels to your toes snapping together at the finish.

Breaststroke specialists spend a significant amount of time refining their kick technique and building strength, power, and endurance through a variety of kicking drills. The ideal way to stay sharp and maintain the critical timing and rhythm of the stroke is to mix kicking drills with stroke drills and full-stroke swimming. For that reason, the drill section of this chapter includes several kicking drills.

ARMS

The three phases of the breaststroke arm movement are the sweep-out, the sweep-in, and the recovery. Begin each stroke cycle on the surface of the water in a streamlined position, with your head, neck, and spine aligned and your eyes focused on the bottom of the pool. In the sweep-out phase, angle your hands slightly so that your pinky fingers are just under the water line and your thumbs are pointing downward. Sweep or gently press your hands to a spot just beyond your shoulders (see figure 7.2*a*). The sweep-out is more of a slow and deliberate stretch than a propulsive movement. The hands glide just under the water surface to what are called the *corners* of the pull. Visualize these as the first two corners of a triangle.

At the corners, reposition your hands so that your thumbs are angled slightly up and your pinkies are angled slightly down. Next, pull your hands down (see figure 7.2*b*) and sweep them in toward each other. Think about bringing your index fingers together to form the third point in the triangle (see figure 7.2*c*). Because the sweep-in is the power phase of the pull, it is essential that the speed of the hands *accelerates* from the corners through the recovery, thus providing lift to the body and forward momentum to the stroke.

Breathing fits smoothly into the flow of the wave breaststroke. As your hands accelerate through the sweep-in from the corners, your shoulders naturally rise up, making this propulsive phase of the arm movement the ideal time to take a breath (see figure 7.2*c*). If you allow your body to lift your head within the flow of the stroke, you don't need to bend your neck to breathe, which disrupts body alignment. To maintain proper body alignment and forward momentum, shrug your shoulders and keep your eyes on the water in front of you (see figure 7.2*d*).

For the recovery phase, shoot your hands forward in a straight line out from your chest, which brings you back to a streamlined position (see figure 7.2*e*).

Perhaps the most common error masters swimmers make while learning the wave breaststroke is lifting their heads to breathe during the sweep-out phase. To reinforce correct technique, practice the arm pull using a pull buoy. Freeze your hands at the corners as you finish the sweep-out, then check your head position, reposition your hands, sweep in, and recover. Gradually transition from this skill to a more flowing movement of streamline, sweep out, sweep in and breathe, and recover back to the streamlined position. Emphasize the explosive nature of the sweep-in and the recovery and the extension of your body from your fingertips to your toes at the end of each stroke cycle.

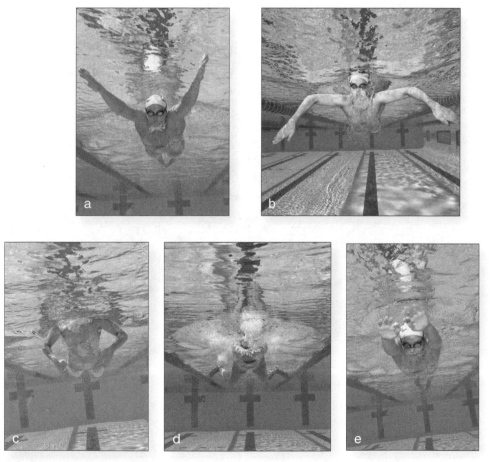

Figure 7.2 Stroke cycle: *(a)* sweep-out to the corners, *(b)* pull down and sweep-in, *(c)* head rising up during sweep-in phase, *(d)* maintaining proper body alignment, and *(e)* recovery to streamlined position.

PULL, LUNGE, KICK

With a basic knowledge of the kick and the arm motion, swimmers are ready to integrate the two into the wave breaststroke. Like the butterfly, the timing of the arms and legs with the undulation of the body is critical to swimming breaststroke efficiently. Novice breaststrokers find stroke timing less complicated when they keep the following two key points in mind:

1. Each stroke cycle begins and ends in a streamlined position on the water's surface with head, neck, and spine in alignment and eyes focused on the bottom of the pool.
2. Each stroke cycle begins with the sweep-out phase of the pull, while the legs remain streamlined on the water surface until the hands transition for the sweep-in.

Begin with just one stroke cycle, moving through it slowly until you become comfortable with the timing, then gradually add more cycles, remembering to extend your body from fingertips to toes at the end of each stroke.

Begin in a streamlined position on the surface of the water, and sweep your hands out to the corners of the triangle. While you're learning, freeze at this point to check that you have not lifted your head or started to kick your feet.

At the corners, transition your hands into the sweep-in phase, arch your back and let your upper body rise above the water as you slide your hips forward. This allows your heels to recover behind your hips and your feet to position themselves to catch the water (toes pointed outward). Continue accelerating your hands through the sweep-in into the recovery phase, then shoot your hands forward and return your body to a streamlined position as your feet fire through the propulsive phase of the kick. Think "kick your hands forward" through this explosive phase of the stroke, commonly referred to as the *lunge*. As you lunge forward over the surface of the water, lead with your fingertips, and follow with the crown of your head, keeping your head, neck, and upper back moving as one unit. This explosive phase of the stroke is often likened to the uncoiling of a cobra (see figure 7.3).

Figure 7.3 Keep your head, neck, and upper back moving as one unit during the explosive lunge phase.

The heart of the timing sequence for each cycle of the breaststroke can be summarized as *pull, lunge, kick.* Initiate the cycle with your sweep-out, recover your feet during the powerful sweep-in (pull), lunge forward, streamline, and fire the kick. Four important tips for successful wave breaststroke include:

1. *Accelerate from the corners through the lunge.* Think "fast hands." You should transition from the sweep-in into a streamlined recovery and lunge with a fast and powerful acceleration. The explosive nature of this movement allows your body to lunge forward at the highest point of the stroke. Any hesitation between the sweep-in and recovery will cause your body to drop down, increase resistance, and lose its forward momentum.

2. *Streamline between strokes.* After completing the lunge and the kick, keep your body in a tight streamline to minimize resistance while maximizing the forward momentum of the stroke. The timing between the kick and the lunge varies for each swimmer and depends on the length of the race. Distance breaststroke swimmers fire their kick later in the stroke than sprint breaststrokers.

3. *Maintain forward momentum.* Focus on maintaining a flat, even line throughout the entire stroke cycle. This is particularly important at the point in the stroke when you are positioned over the water. Your shoulders should be shrugged as you inhale and move your hands through the inward sweep into what is sometimes called the *prayer position.* Maintain a strong line between your back, neck, and head as you move forward.

4. *Ride on the surface.* Don't go too deep as you lunge forward. This causes more resistance and slows your momentum. Lunge forward as though you are diving just under the top sheet of your bed.

Breaststroke swimmers routinely incorporate a variety of pulling, kicking, and stroking drills into their sets to stay focused on the individual components of the stroke. They do less whole-stroke swimming than specialists of the other strokes to keep their stroke timing crisp. The wave breaststroke, like butterfly, is not a stroke that can be swum both leisurely and correctly; your heart rate will always be up if you are swimming with proper form. For this reason, you shouldn't swim whole-stroke breaststroke for extended distances. The following breaststroke drills provide conditioning and help you develop and maintain great stroke rhythm.

When you watch breaststroke swimmers both at the world-class level and in your next masters swimming workout, you will notice a wide spectrum of styles. More than any other, this stroke varies between swimmers, depending on their size, strength, and flexibility. All swimmers are encouraged to learn and practice the wave breaststroke drills. Over time, they will develop the wave breaststroke best suited to them.

Breaststroke Drills

Two-count glide This drill for new breaststrokers focuses on streamlining and riding out the forward momentum of the pull, lunge, kick sequence. After the lunge, streamline for a full two counts, thinking, "One one-thousand, two one-thousand."

One pull, two kicks This drill is a breaststroke cycle with two kicks (pull, lunge, kick, kick). Stay streamlined for two full kicks before sweeping out to begin a new stroke. This is a great timing drill that integrates nicely into conditioning sets.

Two down, one up In this conditioning drill, complete one full cycle of breaststroke, and then stay underwater for more streamlined breaststroke kicks. You can change this to three kicks down, one kick up, or any other combination.

Breaststroke arms with dolphin kick Swimming breaststroke with a dolphin kick helps you feel the flow of the stroke and is a nice alternative to full-stroke breaststroke for swimmers with a history of knee problems. Although this stroke modification is great for workouts, it is not legal in competitions.

Breaststroke arms with flutter kick Use this drill to practice the fast hands required in wave breaststroke. Make fast transitions between the sweep-out, the sweep-in, and the lunge. Maintain forward momentum by keeping your hands and elbows in front of your nose throughout the pull. Think, "Out, in, punch!"

Head-up breaststroke Imagine a wall extending from your chin to the bottom of the pool. As you perform this drill, keep your hands and arms in front of the wall. This drill is ideal for novice breaststroke swimmers who pull too far under their bodies. In breaststroke, your hands and arms should stay in front of your face.

Kicking Drills

Kick on your back Begin on your back, hold your hands and arms at your sides, lead with your head, and do the breaststroke kick. Focus on keeping your hips on the surface throughout the cycle of the kick. As you recover your heels toward your buttocks, be careful not to lift your knees out of the water. Explode through the propulsive phase of the kick with a powerful finish and ride out each kick. Although you won't cover much distance kicking on your back, you will learn a lot about minimizing resistance.

Kick with a pull buoy Kicking with a pull buoy between your legs forces you to keep your knees closer together than your heels and feet, thus generating more power.

Superman kick Kick with your arms extended in front of you like Superman. Accentuate the undulation of your body by kicking downward, which pops the hips up.

Egg beater This vertical kick drill favored by water polo players allows you to feel the water pressure on the inside of your lower legs. Begin vertically in deep water, and go through the motions of the breaststroke kick, alternating one leg at a time. Challenge yourself to keep your hands above the water or streamlined over your head.

Kick underwater, lead with your head Do the breaststroke kick underwater, keeping your hands and arms relaxed at your sides. Maintain body posture, keeping your head, neck, and spine aligned and your eyes focused on the bottom of the pool. Focus on minimizing resistance as you sneak your heels up to begin each kick and streamlining your whole body as you ride out each kick.

Kick underwater in streamlined position Begin underwater again, but hold your hands and arms in a streamlined position. Like in the underwater kick leading with the head, the focus in this conditioning drill is on cutting through the water with the minimum of resistance.

Kick and pulse, leading with your head This kicking drill allows you to feel the integration of the kick into the stroke rhythm. Leading with the head and relaxing your arms at your sides, do the breaststroke kick on the surface of the water. Focus on recovering your heels behind your hips as your head and chest rise up. Inhale quickly, press your chest down, and fire the propulsive phase of the kick.

Kick progression 25s This progression of four lengths of a 25-yard (25 m) pool is a fun way to work your legs as you integrate the kick into the stroke. In the first 25, streamline kick for 3 kicks, and then swim one full stroke cycle. In the second 25, streamline kick for 2 kicks, then swim one full stroke cycle; on the third, kick once, then swim a full stroke cycle; on the fourth, swim full-stroke breaststroke. Rest at least 10-20 seconds after each length.

In the Mind of a Champion

David Guthrie, 1984 Canadian national champion, continues to stay on the cutting edge of breaststroke technique. His resume as an adult competitor includes 22 masters world records, 31 masters national titles, and 15 years as an All-American champion. Clearly a student of the mechanics of this detailed stroke, David shares his insight on maximizing his power.

"My starting position for each stroke cycle is exactly like the glide position on a push-off: tight streamline, firm core, head lower than the hips. I concentrate on maintaining this 'downhill' position and pressing down with my chest as I initiate the press-out with my arms. There's a real temptation to lift my head at the beginning of the pull, but it's the last thing I want to do. Instead, I concentrate on keeping my neck fixed through the entire stroke, never allowing my head to tilt back or duck forward on a hinge. My head and neck essentially become an extension of my torso—the key to leverage.

"On the in-sweep of my pull, I concentrate on sliding my hips forward, literally bringing my hips to my hands, instead of pulling my elbows back. I like to create a mental image of my hips sliding forward on rails on the water surface. Drawing my hips forward automatically pushes my upper body up out of the water. It's a misconception that the upward movement of the torso comes from lifting with the head and shoulders; it comes from the combination of the hips sliding forward and the powerful sweep-in of the hands.

"As my hips slide forward, I focus on keeping my legs near the surface in the slipstream, extended but relaxed, until the last possible moment before it's time to initiate the kick. It's easy to get into the habit of lazily drawing the heels up and pausing before driving the feet backward, which is the least hydrodynamic position possible! Instead, I maximize my kick by delaying the recovery of my heels until my hands are ready to shoot forward. Then I make sure that I wait until I am streamlined before firing the legs back and applying power. Otherwise, it's wasted effort."

8

Starts, Turns, and Finishes

Stick the wall! ... I do not breathe the last four or five strokes so I can keep my rhythm and zero in on the wall like radar.
—Rowdy Gaines, triple gold medalist, 1984 Olympic Games

In a 25-yard (or 25 m) pool, approximately one-third of a competitive swimmer's time is spent moving from the flags to the wall and back to the flags. Therefore, swimmers who make the effort to polish their starts, turns, and finishes are in an advantageous position. Even masters swimmers who don't participate in organized competitions can gain speed and improve the quality of their workout with more efficient turns.

Unlike running, cycling, and speed skating, where athletes strive to reach their maximum speed in the first moments of the race, swimmers reach their top speed within hundredths of a second as they dive from the starting block through the air. One of the main objectives of the start is to transition the speed of the dive into the water and carry the momentum into swimming speed. Elements that affect the quality of a swimming start include body position in the air, entry into the water, quality of underwater streamline, and timing of the initial kicks and first strokes. Similarly, when pushing off the wall after a turn, an explosive drive from the legs and a tight, torpedolike streamlined body position moves swimmers through the water faster than they can swim on the surface. For a seamless transition between pushing off the wall and moving down the length of the pool, swimmers must maintain the momentum of the push-off and underwater streamline through the breakout strokes and into the rhythm of the stroke.

THE STARTING PROTOCOL

This chapter begins with a review of the protocol that meet officials follow to start a swimming race. Because every race starts the same way, swimmers quickly come to know what to expect when they step onto the starting blocks, freeing their mind to focus on their race strategy. This simple starting procedure varies very little, whether the meet is for age group swimmers, masters swimmers, or Olympic contenders.

1. The deck referee blows a series of short whistles that signal swimmers to ready themselves to swim. If they have not already done so, swimmers remove their T-shirts and sweats, make final adjustments to their swim caps and goggles, and give their attention to the referee. At this time, the referee may announce the event and the heat.

2. Next, a long whistle signals the swimmers to step onto the starting block, or platform, and place one foot or both feet at the front of the block. Swimmers who opt not to use the starting block should position themselves adjacent to the block with one foot or both feet at the edge of the pool. Those who elect to start in the water should wait for the referee's approval, and then enter the pool feet first, place one hand on the edge of the pool, and wait for the race to begin. In a backstroke race, all swimmers enter the water when the long whistle sounds. A second long whistle blast will signal the backstroke swimmers to position themselves at the block for the start.

3. At this point, the referee hands over control to the meet starter. The starter checks that the swimmers and timers are ready, then proceeds with the race by commanding, "Take your mark." Swimmers then move into the starting position and await the starter's next command, which indicates the start of the race. This final command may be a simple whistle, the sound of a gun, or an electronic beep, which is the most common signal.

Safety First!

Safety is of the utmost importance when practicing starts.

- Swimmers should learn to dive in a pool specifically designed for this activity at a depth that is approved for competitive springboard diving.
- Swimmers should dive in an area of the deep end with a minimum of 15 meters of unobstructed water for the dive and glide.
- Swimmers should dive away from the sidewalls and any ledge or slope that leads to the shallow area of the pool.
- Starting blocks should be secured and covered with a nonskid surface.
- Diving practice should be directly supervised by a coach or lifeguard.
- All pools should post the following warning: "Diving into shallow water is dangerous and may result in permanent spinal cord injury or possible death."

With experience, swimmers quickly fall into the rhythm of starting procedures at meets. The consistency in the whistles and commands lets swimmers focus more on what they will do after they leave the block than on the logistics of the start procedures.

THE FORWARD START

Freestyle, breaststroke, and butterfly events all start from the blocks with what is called a *forward start*. Because the majority of swimmers who come into masters swim programs have little or no competitive swimming experience, coaches allocate time to teach the forward start in the weeks leading up to a competition. The following teaching progression has helped many swimmers learn and improve their off-the-block starts. Take your time to move through these steps, letting yourself grow comfortable with each one before moving to the next. You should always practice your starts in water that is 6 feet (2 m) deep or greater.

1. *Streamline.* First, review the streamlined body position that is essential for diving from the starting blocks and into the water. Begin by establishing a straight body line on the pool deck. Place one hand over the other with two squeezes: Squeeze the thumb of your top hand around your bottom hand and squeeze your ears between your biceps. Align your spine by moving your chin away from your chest, contracting your abdomen and buttocks, and placing your feet together. To further perfect your streamline, lie down on the deck with your toes pointed.

2. *Dive from the pool deck.* Practice diving from the pool's edge, maintaining a streamlined body position throughout the entire dive. Imagine your whole body entering the water through a single hole created by your fingertips. Visualize diving through a hula hoop resting on the water's surface without touching the sides. Move the imaginary hula hoop farther away from you as your confidence grows. Resist the temptation to look up as you enter the water, which increases your frontal resistance and hinders your momentum. If your goggles leak or slip off, tighten them. Focus your attention on keeping your hands together, streamlining your body, and aligning your head and neck with your spine.

3. *Standing broad jump.* Position yourself on the starting blocks with your feet almost shoulder-width apart and your toes just over the front edge. Jump from the blocks into the water feet first. Maximize your distance by using your hip and leg muscles to explode off of the blocks. Swing your arms to increase your momentum.

4. *Swinging dive.* Position yourself at the front of the starting block as you did in example 3 and imagine a hula hoop on the water's surface in front of you. Swing your arms up, forward, and around to create

momentum, and dive from the block, piercing the center of the hoop with your fingertips. Keep your body tight and streamlined as it follows your fingertips through the center of the imaginary hoop.

5. *Transition from swinging dive to breakout.* Build on the swinging dive by maintaining your underwater streamlined position until the *breakout*, which is the transition from the underwater phase of a start or turn to full-stroke swimming. When done well, this transition will carry the momentum of the start or turn seamlessly into the rhythm of the stroke. Later sections of this chapter outline specific details on breakout execution.

6. *Take your mark.* This step makes swimmers more comfortable with the starting protocol and the process of positioning themselves on the starting block as they wait for the starter's commands.

The forward start favored by most masters swimmers is the *track start*, which features a staggered foot position similar to the traditional start in a track meet. Many adult swimmers like this start because it is fast and suitable for those who have limited flexibility and those who like more stability. Swimmers who begin with the *grab start*, another common option, position both feet at the front of the block, wait for the starter's commands, then grab the block either inside or outside of their feet (see figure 8.1a). Although the track start is recommended for new swimmers, experienced swimmers who prefer the traditional grab start often choose not to switch to the newer start.

As the referee sounds the long whistle, step onto the starting block and position yourself at the front edge with your feet almost shoulder-width apart, your toes over the edge, and your eyes focused down the pool. When you hear the command "Take your mark," move one foot back on the block, bend down, and grab the underside of the block with both hands. Keep your elbows slightly bent and your arms tensed as you pull back from the block for balance. Bend your back leg to at least 90 degrees, lifting the heel slightly, and bend your front leg slightly. Draw your weight forward with your shoulders and arms so that your center of gravity is held over the ball of your front foot. Keep your head down, but don't rest your chest on your legs.

Naturally, swimmers may vary this track start position to accommodate reduced flexibility or personal preference. Swimmers with limited flexibility in their back and hamstring muscles may be better able to grab the block if they position their back feet farther back on the block and lower their hips. Others prefer not to grab the blocks at all, keeping their hands free for a traditional relay-style start. Furthermore, many swimmers prefer to keep their weight in a neutral position or to lean back slightly, keeping their weight over the back foot.

As you learn the forward start, take the time to get comfortable with bringing one foot back, coming down, and then holding your start position for at least two seconds. Experiment with your foot and hand position until you find one that fits you well.

7. *Go!* When the starting beep sounds, pull your body forward slightly using the underside of the block, which will shift your center of gravity over the water. As you feel yourself falling forward, push with your legs as your body unfolds over the water and assumes the streamlined position. Imagine your whole body shooting through a narrow tunnel of air into a hole in the center of your imaginary hula hoop (see figure 8.1, *b* and *c*).

It is crucial that you become comfortable with your starting mechanics by practicing the entire sequence from the starting commands to the breakout. Begin your practice slowly by reviewing the steps in the progression. As you become more comfortable, add power to your leg drive, or push from the blocks, and visualize exploding as you unfold from the starting position.

Figure 8.1 Off the blocks: *(a)* grab position, *(b)* push off, and *(c)* entry.

Forward Starting Drills

For variety and an opportunity to improve your freestyle, breaststroke, and butterfly starts, try these fun drills.

Clapping drill Stand on the pool deck with your hands at your sides, and ask a coach or swimming buddy to clap their hands. When you hear the sound of the clap, immediately place your hands and arms in streamlined position. When practiced consistently, this drill can improve your reaction time.

One-leg drill This starting drill, recommended for swimmers who have good stability and are comfortable with the track start, is performed from the starting blocks and is designed to improve leg power. Assume your starting position on the block and raise your back foot off of the block. When you hear the starting command, perform your start using your front leg only.

Diving over a pole Ask a coach or swim buddy to hold a maintenance or shepherd's hook safety pole in front of the starting block for you to dive over when performing your start. The farther away the pole is from the block, the more leg power you will need to clear it. Similarly, adjusting the pole higher or lower forces you to change your body position to clear the bar. The goal of the pole adjustments is to achieve a clean entry into the water with minimal frontal resistance.

THE BACKSTROKE START

The hallmarks of a great backstroke start are very similar to the forward start: an explosive leg drive, a streamlined body position, movement focused through a single hole in the water, streamlined underwater kicking, and breakout strokes. Swimmers who take the time to perfect their backstroke starts will have a significant advantage over swimmers who take the in-water start for granted by simply pushing off the wall when the starting beep sounds. The following backstroke start skills progression is recommended for both new and experienced backstroke competitors. You should get comfortable with skills 1 through 5 by holding onto the edge of the pool or gutter before moving to skills 6 and 7, which use the starting block handles. As in the forward start, these skills must be performed in water more than 6 feet (2 m) deep.

1. *Ready position.* Begin in the pool, hold onto the pool edge or gutter with both hands, and position your feet against the wall shoulder-width apart, just under the water's surface. Although most swimmers prefer to stagger their feet, you should choose the position that is most comfortable for you. Your head and neck should be aligned with your spine and your knees should be bent to a 90 degree angle, as if you were sitting down.

2. *L-seats.* Assume the ready position, then drive with your legs and keep your arms at your sides as you shoot up and over the water. As you move through the air, form an *L* shape with your body, then land, buttocks first,

Figure 8.2 L-seats: *(a)* launch and *(b)* seat.

in the pool. Focus on the leg thrust that gets you up, out, and over the water (see figure 8.2, *a* and *b*).

3. *L-seats with leg kick.* Repeat skill 2, adding an upward kick with both feet as you enter the water.

4. *Streamline the entry.* Repeat the previous drill adding the motion of the arms to create a more streamlined entry and to transition into the underwater phase of the start. As you drive with your legs and lift your hips up, out, and over the water, throw your arms back to the sides, or over your head, into the streamlined position. Your hands now enter the water first, creating a single hole. Maintain your streamlined position as your whole body follows your fingertips through the hole. If you land on your back or drag your body through the water, focus on driving your legs, arching your back, and thrusting your legs up before entry.

Once you're underwater, maintain your streamline. As you feel yourself losing momentum, begin to underwater dolphin kick or flutter kick to the surface for your breakout. The high-amplitude underwater dolphin kick is sometimes called a *double-leg kick* to distinguish it from the dolphin kick used in the butterfly stroke. Remember to blow water out of your nose, to keep your nose clear of water while underwater on your back.

5. *Take your mark.* Once you're comfortable with the backstroke start from the side of the pool, move to the starting block to fine-tune your start. Begin in the pool with your hands positioned on the handle of the starting block and your feet positioned shoulder-width apart on the pool wall. United States Swimming (USS) and USMS rules require your feet to be completely submerged. While you wait for the starter's commands, stay relaxed and focused.

When you hear the command "Take your mark," pull your head closer to the block and bring your knees into the 90-degree position. Your buttocks should be held away from the wall (see figure 8.3).

Figure 8.3 Backstroke start: take your mark.

6. *Go!* At the starting signal, drive with your legs as you lift your hips and body up, out, and over the water and throw your arms back into a streamline. Ideally, your body will be arched over the water and poised for a clean entry through a single hole in the water created by your fingertips (see figure 8.4, *a-c*). Here is a practice drill for getting your hips up during the start: Place a soft kickboard or a pool noodle behind you and practice your start, trying to get your buttocks over the board.

Figure 8.4 Backstroke start: *(a)* drive the legs, *(b)* hips up and arms back, and *(c)* streamlined entry.

You will only learn what works best for you in the backstroke start by practicing and experimenting with foot and hand positioning. Some swimmers have more success using the pool edge or gutter than the starting block. Although learning to arch the body over the water is a great challenge, most swimmers master it after investing some time in the progression of skills.

THE RELAY START

Perhaps the most exciting portion of a swim meet for competitors and spectators alike is the relay. The critical timing of relay exchanges can make a close race even more exciting as swimmers aim to minimize their exchange time. Each of the two swimmers in the exchange have different, yet equally important responsibilities for a quick and legal relay start. Swimmers leaving the block must time their movements to leave the block the very moment the incoming swimmer touches, and incoming swimmers must maintain their stroke tempo and rhythm until the finish.

The first swimmer in a relay performs a forward start for a freestyle relay and an in-water backstroke start for a medley relay. The second, third, and fourth relay swimmers do a relay start, which is faster than a forward start because of the momentum gained from the swing of the arms and the fact that the outgoing swimmer can begin the movements of their start before the incoming swimmer touches the wall. Like other starts, great relay starts come with practice.

Rhythm and timing go hand in hand in successful relay exchanges. Because the outgoing swimmers have synchronized their movements on the block to the stroke tempo and speed of the incoming swimmers, any deceleration in the incoming swimmers' stroke as they approach the wall can cause an early, or *false* start, resulting in a disqualification. As you perform the following set of relay starting skills, allow yourself to fall into the rhythm of the movements. You will make a more timely exchange and gain more momentum and power leaving the block.

1. *Get into the rhythm.* Begin by standing straight up on the pool deck, away from the pool, with one foot forward and one foot back. Bring your back foot forward while swinging your arms forward, up, and around, and use the momentum from your arms to jump straight up. The jump uses both feet and feels like a standing broad jump. If you bend your knees and lower your body as you swing your hands, you will find that you can jump higher, which will translate into more power off the block. For maximum height, do not bend your knees past 90 degrees and hold your feet a little less than shoulder-width apart for the takeoff. Repeat the sequence—step, swing, squat, jump—on the deck until you are comfortable with the timing and rhythm.

2. *Off the blocks.* Stand at the front of the block, holding the toes of one foot just over the edge and your other foot back. The diving sequence is the same as the one you practiced on deck, but you will now use the

momentum of your arm swing to move your center of gravity forward over the water. As you leave the block, maintain the momentum of your arm swing, throwing them forward until your fingers are pointing at your entry spot in the water.

3. *Streamline your entry.* For a clean entry with minimum frontal resistance, streamline your body as it follows your fingertips through the hole you created in the water. As you practice the dive, experiment with the timing and depth of the bend in your knees to maximize your power. Keep your shoulders low and your momentum moving forward, resisting the temptation to stand up.

4. *Time the start.* Once you are comfortable with the rhythm of the start, begin synchronizing your movements with the strokes of incoming swimmers. As swimmers approach, keep your arms stretched out in front of you and follow them in with your fingertips, allowing your body to drop lower as they move closer.

   Freestyle and backstroke swimmers should begin their step and swing sequence just as the incoming swimmers begin their final stroke to the wall. However, the nature of butterfly and breaststroke make it more difficult to time the finish, so swimmers are more prone to mistime their relay starts. If you don't have the opportunity to study the rhythm of the incoming swimmer's stroke before the race, a conservative relay exchange is recommended.

Relays truly are team events in which every swimmer contributes to the success of the relay exchanges. The most successful relay teams have practiced the timing of their starts and their members are confident in the stroke rhythm of the swimmers they will follow. Masters swimmers who cannot afford this extended practice time should choose more conservative relay exchanges.

TURNS

Like the start, the success of a turn depends on how well the swimmer maintains momentum both in to and out of the wall. The previous section on starts discusses how to carry the momentum of the dive into the water. This section on turns focuses on maintaining stroke speed and rhythm going to and from the wall. To achieve this seamless transition from swimming to turning and back to swimming, you must think of the turn as more than just what happens at the wall. The turn can be quantified by four phases that play a critical role in maintaining momentum:

1. The approach
2. The turn itself
3. The push-off from the wall and streamline
4. The breakout

As you learn to do turns, focus first on the technical aspects of each of the phases and then on your turning speed. By mastering the mechanics of the turn at slower speeds, the individual phases of the turn will blend together smoothly.

Freestyle Flip Turns

Learning a freestyle flip turn should be a priority for all masters swimmers because it raises the quality of their workouts by improving momentum to and from the walls. The freestyle flip turn also stresses the shoulders less than the *open turn*, also called a *nonflip, touch-and-go turn*, in which swimmers grab the wall. With consistent practice, swimmers master the flip and soon improve their speed and flow in workouts. The following progression begins with the very basics and advances to a complete turn. As in the forward and backstroke start progressions, swimmers should become comfortable with each skill before moving to the next.

1. *Bubbles.* You must expel air out through your nostrils while doing a flip turn or water will go up your nose. Begin this skill set by getting comfortable with blowing bubbles out of your nose while underwater.

2. *Somersault.* This step makes you comfortable with the flipping part of the turn. Remember to blow bubbles from your nose as your body flips around. Begin by lying on the surface of the water, face down, with your arms at your sides and your palms facing the bottom of the pool. Tuck yourself into a ball by moving your nose toward your knees and your heels toward your buttocks, and then sweep your arms over your head in a large and powerful circle, as if you were pushing a tall stovepipe hat off your head. Keep your elbows in front of your face where you can see them. You will flip completely over and find yourself lying on your back with your fingertips pointed the same direction that you started (see figure 8.5, *a-d*).

   If you have trouble completing your flips, you are probably rolling to the side during your somersault, preventing your hips from going straight over your shoulders. Focus on aligning your head, neck, and spine. You might also try holding a pull buoy or kickboard in each hand on the surface of the water as you flip to give your body the sensation of coming over the top.

3. *Approach to midpool.* This skill adds the approach strokes to the flip, but does not yet approach the wall. Swim four to five strokes into a head-lead position with your arms at your sides and your palms facing down, press your chest slightly under the water, then do the flip from the previous exercise. Many swimmers err in this step by rushing into the flip before both hands are back at their sides. You must be in a *submerged* position at the start of the flip, holding your arms at your side, your palms down, and your chest pressed down slightly.

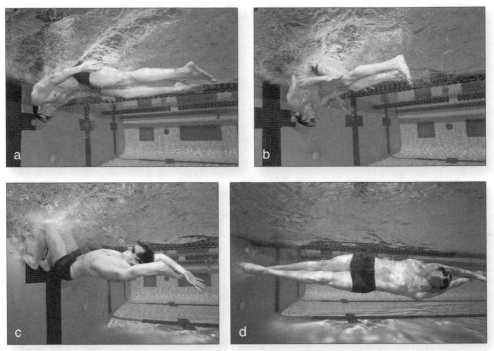

Figure 8.5 Somersault flip turn: *(a)* approaching the wall, *(b)* flip, *(c)* streamline, and *(d)* break out.

4. *Approach to midpool and streamline.* This skill, which is also performed away from the wall, adds the streamline to the end of the flip. Swim 4 to 5 strokes into the head-lead position with your arms at your sides and your palms facing down, submerge, and then flip, moving your arms into a streamline (their position after they knock off your imaginary stovepipe hat). You should finish the movement lying on your back with your arms in a tight streamline. Repeat the previous exercise several times, perfecting your streamlined finish by aligning your head, neck, and spine and engaging your core muscles.

5. *Add the wall.* The goal of this step is to learn to judge when to initiate your flip. When you come through the flip and position your arms into the streamline, both your feet should be firmly planted on the wall and your knees should be bent to 90 degrees and poised for an effective push-off.

   Start at a point past the backstroke flags and begin swimming toward the wall, using the underwater markings on the wall to judge your distance. Move into head-lead position on your final stroke, submerge, flip into your streamline, and plant your feet on the wall.

   Learning to judge the distance and timing of the flip requires trial and error and consistent practice. Swimmers make all kinds of mistakes during the learning process, including coming up in the next lane, missing the wall completely, and hitting their buttocks on the wall. With practice, all swimmers can successfully master the flip turn.

6. *Approach, flip, and streamline.* Once you are comfortable with judging the distance and can successfully plant your feet, begin adding the push-off. Approach the wall, submerge your chest, flip into your streamline, and then drive with your legs as you rotate your body to the side. The moment between the foot plant and the push-off is critical for gaining or losing momentum. Swimmers who are slow to streamline after the flip lose momentum; their bodies drop lower in the water and their resulting push-off is weak and often too deep. Imagine that the pool wall is a hot stove and make your foot touch a quick touch and go, transitioning quickly from the flip to the streamline to the push-off (refer back to figure 8.5, *a-d*).

7. *Approach, flip, streamline, and break out.* This final step completes the freestyle turn with a rotation to the abdomen. Approach the wall, submerge into the flip, transition to the streamline, push-off, rotate to your side, and finally, rotate onto your front.

   As you rotate, you might choose to add either deep dolphin or freestyle kicks to maintain the momentum you gained from your push-off. The type and amount of kicks depend on your strengths and your chosen distance. Sprinters with a strong dolphin kick will maximize their underwater time with several dolphin kicks. However, distance swimmers with weak kicks will fare better by swimming on the surface.

   As you feel your body nearing the surface of the water, focus on keeping your stroke long and maintaining a strong body line as you take the first two strokes without breathing and then settle into your stroke rhythm.

The beauty of learning a flip turn is the multitude of opportunities to practice. Every time you approach a wall, you can choose a flip turn over an open turn. You may want to start by flipping only at one end of the pool in your workouts, and then gradually build up to flipping for all your turns. It is fine to incorporate this new skill slowly. Focus on the various phases of the turn separately and slowly link them together into a faster and more elegant turn. Here are more tips and ideas for rotating at the walls:

- Don't slow down as you approach the wall, but either maintain or increase your swimming speed. Swimmers who decelerate as they approach the wall lose momentum and turn more slowly.

- As you approach the wall, keep your head down and resist taking a final breath or lifting your head. Focus your eyes on the underwater target of the wall.

- Don't let your body roll to either side as you approach the wall. Press your chest down slightly to lift your hips and spring your heels toward the wall. Think, "rush your hips to the wall" to engage your abdominal muscles as your hips move over your body toward the wall.

- Before your feet hit the wall, sweep your hands toward your head, keep your elbows close together, and move your hands into streamlined position. With your upper body streamlined early in the turn, you are positioned to push off the wall the moment your feet make contact.

- Don't bring your hands and arms down or sweep them outside of the line of your body. This delays your turn at the wall because you will have to realign yourself to streamline before pushing off.

- Start kicking as soon as you have rotated onto your front and have moved 5 to 6 feet (about 2 m) from the wall. Maintain momentum by kicking throughout the breakout stroke and into your swimming.

- If your push-off is too deep and you feel more like a submarine than a swimmer, you are most likely starting your flip turn too close to the wall. Try initiating the turn a little farther away and check that your knees are bent to 90 degrees when your feet plant on the wall.

Backstroke Flip Turns

Once you have mastered the freestyle flip turn, you can transition easily into the backstroke turn, which differs only in the approach and breakout phases. The following skills progression focuses mainly on these two phases and the process of carrying the stroke rhythm through the flip and the streamline.

1. *Begin the approach midpool.* This drill starts in the middle of the pool. Don't worry about the wall at this point. Start swimming backstroke with your left arm up and your right arm at your side, and count your *hand hits*, or hand entries, as you go. On your fifth stroke, move your right arm across the body over your left shoulder and roll onto your front, pulling through into the head-lead position of the freestyle flip turn. Practice the approach several times with both the right arm and the left arm to become comfortable crossing over and rolling to either side.

2. *Know your finishing stroke count.* If you have not already done so, count your strokes from the backstroke flags to the wall. Begin swimming several strokes outside of the flags to reach your normal stroke tempo when you pass under the flags and begin counting.

3. *Transition from the approach to the flip.* Position yourself outside the flags again and begin swimming toward the wall, counting your strokes as you pass under the flags. Begin to cross over two strokes before you reach the wall. For example, if your stroke count from the previous exercise was five strokes, you should begin your crossover and roll stroke after three strokes. Once you are on your front and pulling through with the arm that crossed over, begin your flip and plant your feet on the wall. Check your position as you plant your feet on the wall. Like in the freestyle flip turn, look for the 90 degree knee bend and the streamlined upper body.

The Fifth Stroke

Over the past decade, the underwater element of competitive swimming has evolved to become a critical part of competing at the world-class level—so much that coaches have come to refer to the streamlined dolphinlike underwater swimming used to maximize distance after starts and turns as the *fifth stroke*. With proper training, swimmers are faster and more efficient with this underwater technique than with surface swimming and the flutter kick (Clothier 2004). It is now a fundamental skill taught to swimmers of all ages. Masters swimmers are quickly jumping into the action as well, enjoying the benefits of a stronger core, improved body position, and faster swimming.

Before implementing this skill into your training, it is important to understand how the mechanics of the underwater dolphin action differs from the butterfly kick. The dolphin action of the legs used in the underwater phase of dives and push-offs differs in both the magnitude and the *tempo*, or rate, of the kick commonly used in the butterfly stroke. To differentiate between the two kicks, coaches often refer to this deeper, underwater dolphin kick as a *double-leg kick*. Because swimmers are underwater when performing the double-leg kick, they are able to achieve a higher upbeat of the legs, thus creating a more powerful backward thrust on the downbeat than when kicking on the surface. In backstroke, this is reversed— the swimmer's downbeat is increased, resulting in a more powerful upbeat. Furthermore, because the double-leg kick is performed independent of any arm motion, the swimmer is able to increase the tempo of the kick for improved speed. Because of the difference in both magnitude and tempo, swimmers must specifically develop and train the unique aspects of the underwater double-leg kick.

The following sample training exercises strengthen the double-leg kick in the underwater push-off of all four strokes. Although we consider this essential training for competitive swimmers, *all* swimmers can reap the core strengthening benefits of this skill. Feel free to slip on your fins as you are learning and improving the technique.

Freestyle. If you are not already doing so, try taking two underwater double-leg kicks after pushing off the wall before switching to a conventional flutter kick. If you are already double-leg kicking, then try adding two additional kicks. Again, follow with a powerful breakout stroke and then easy freestyle to finish.

Backstroke. Push off the wall and kick your normal number of underwater kicks plus two more, then break out into two fast strokes and finish the remainder of the 25 yards or meters with easy backstroke.

Butterfly. Push off the wall and kick your normal number of underwater kicks *plus* two more, then break out into two full strokes on the surface and finish the remainder of the 25 yards or meters with easy freestyle.

Breaststroke. Push off the wall and take two complete underwater pulls instead of the normal one. Focus on getting a good double-leg whiplike kick at the finish of each pull.

As you perform the double-leg kick, focus on these keys to success:

- Maintain a tight streamline from fingertips to toes as you focus on minimizing the undulation of the upper body.
- Kick with a tempo much higher than in normal butterfly kicking.

(continued)

The Fifth Stroke *(continued)*

- Exaggerate the lower-leg upbeat in freestyle, butterfly, and breaststroke and the lower-leg downbeat in backstroke to achieve a more powerful backward thrust.
- Focus on "stabbing" the legs backward instead of up and down while the body maintains a streamlined wavelike motion.

With practice, most masters swimmers are able to integrate the double-leg kick into their training and thereby gain more distance off every wall, which translates to faster times. Swimmers with limited flexibility may discover that it is faster for them to minimize their double-leg kicks, get to the surface quicker, and swim. All swimmers should mix the underwater dolphin kick into their training at whatever level works for them. The benefits of building core and leg strength as well as the variety it brings to training make the fifth stroke essential for all swimmers.

Practice stroking into the wall and making the flip while crossing over to both the left and right sides.

4. *Transition from the streamline to the breakout.* Before you combine the streamline with the flip, practice the push-off, streamline, and breakout strokes alone. Push off from the center of the wall, extending your arms and legs in a tight streamlined position. Remember to exhale through your nose. You may choose either a traditional backstroke kick or a dolphin kick to maintain the momentum of your push-off. Begin your first breakout stroke when your head is about 1 foot (.3 m) below the surface, and follow with the second stroke just as your head is about to break the surface. As you reach the surface of the water, focus on keeping your kick steady, maintaining a long body line, and settling into your stroke rhythm.

    When you swim in competition, your head must break the surface within 15 meters of the wall, which is typically marked on the lane lines. Experiment with your push-off, streamline, and breakout to determine your ideal amount of kicking. Strong dolphin kickers do three or more underwater dolphin kicks before their two breakout strokes. Swimmers with weaker kicks might transition into backstroke kick more quickly.

5. *Approach, flip, streamline, and break out.* This step completes the backstroke turn by adding the breakout. As in the freestyle flip turn, focus on maintaining your momentum into the flip and exploding off the wall through the underwater phase and breakout until you are swimming again. Resist the temptation to drop your chin or lift your head to look around as you approach and leave the wall. Breaking your head alignment slows momentum, disrupts the consistency of your stroke count during the approach, and increases resistance as you leave the wall.

Open Turns for the Short-Axis Strokes

Unlike turns for freestyle and backstroke, in which swimmers can touch the wall with any part of their bodies, when making breaststroke and butterfly turns, swimmers are required to touch the walls with both hands simultaneously. For this reason, traditional flip turns, in which the feet touch the wall first, are not effective. Instead, swimmers choose an open, or nonflip, turn for these short-axis strokes. However, like both the backstroke and freestyle turns, swimmers with successful open turns maintain their stroke rhythm and momentum as they reach the wall and throughout the turn, streamline, and breakout.

In the following skill progression for short-axis turns, the first steps cover the *ready* position, or a swimmer's position on the wall when preparing to push off. Swimmers are encouraged to leave the wall for every repetition in a workout from this position, since it transitions smoothly into a streamlined push-off and reinforces the mechanics of good short-axis turns.

1. *Assume the ready position.* Extend your wall-side arm and hold the pool's edge or gutter, and extend your other arm underwater toward the opposite end of the pool with your palm facing up. Plant the balls of your feet on the wall of the pool, and keep your knees flexed but relaxed. Position your chin over your wall-side shoulder and look down your arm at the wall. Visualize all the body parts between your two hands connected in a single line: the hand on the wall, elbow, chin, shoulder, the elbow in the water, and the other hand (see figure 8.6*a*).

2. *Push off and streamline.* From the ready position, move the hand that is on the wall toward your ear, as if you were answering a phone. Think, "call the police." As your body drops underwater, slide that hand past your ear, over your head, and toward your outstretched hand to form a streamlined position (see figure 8.6*b*).

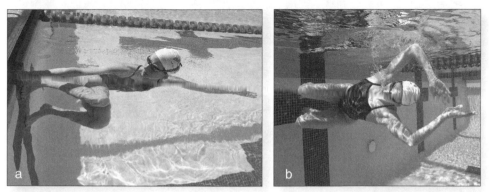

Figure 8.6 Short-axis turns: *(a)* ready position and *(b)* push off and streamline.

Drive with your legs and push off the wall. Practice transitioning from the ready position to the streamline and push-off until you are comfortable. Challenge yourself to see how much distance you can gain as you move from the wall.

3. *Approach.* Swim toward the wall, maintaining your stroke rhythm and speed. As you get close, keep your head in line with your spine as you extend your arms and reach for the wall (see figure 8.7a). Ideally, your body should be stretched out on the water's surface completing a kick as your hands touch the wall. With practice, you should be able to judge your distance several strokes away from the wall and adjust your stroke length to achieve this optimum body position as you approach every wall, including the one at the finish.

4. *Approach to the ready position.* Swim to the wall, touch it with your arms extended, and begin your turn by drawing one arm back, leading with the elbow as if you were about to poke somebody behind you. Think, "elbow the robber" (see figure 8.7b). At the same time, bring your knees up toward your chest and position your feet on the wall, pointing either to the side or diagonally up.

Maintain your momentum and speed by making your body small as you spin and keeping your center of gravity low. Think, "call the

Figure 8.7 Short-axis turns: *(a)* approach, *(b)* "elbow the robber," *(c)* "call the police," and *(d)* extend arm while moving into ready position.

police" (see figure 8.7*c*), and move into the ready position by turning your palm up and fully extending your arm toward the opposite end of the pool (see figure 8.7*d*). Practice this approach and turn several times, freezing when you reach the ready position.

5. *Approach to turn to push off.* As you perform the complete two-hand touch turn sequence, remember these cues to connect the pieces of the turn together. Swim to the wall and touch it with two hands, pull your knees up and your elbow back ("elbow the robber"), move your wall-side hand up ("call the police"), streamline, and push off.

6. *Butterfly breakouts.* Transition from the ready position into a push-off and streamline as in the preceding item. Begin to dolphin kick, maintaining a tight streamline underwater. Build up your speed for an aggressive kick on the breakout stroke, which you should take just before your back breaks the water's surface. Keep your head in line with your spine as you take your first stroke and begin breathing in the rhythm of the stroke. When you swim butterfly in competition, you must break the surface within 15 meters of the wall.

7. *Breaststroke breakouts.* When you compete in the breaststroke, you are allowed one pull, one breaststroke kick, and one dolphin kick underwater after the start and after each turn. Your head must break the surface of the water before you begin the sweep-in of your next arm pull. Commonly called the *breaststroke pull-out*, this underwater phase of breaststroke creates a smooth transition from the wall into the rhythm of the stroke.

Complete your push-off from the ready position (refer back to number 2 in this list) with a tight streamline. As you feel your momentum slowing, begin the underwater arm pull, which resembles the butterfly pull more than an ordinary breaststroke pull. Press, or sweep, your arms and hands out to a point slightly greater than shoulder-width, holding your palms angled toward the pool walls. Bend your elbows to 90 degrees, open your armpits, and reach deep into the water with your fingertips as you catch the water with your hands and arms for the pull (see figure 8.8*a*).

From this position, sweep your hands in and down toward your feet, maintaining a high-elbow position and a straight body line. After you complete the pull, ride out the momentum in a head-lead streamlined position (see figure 8.8*b*). When you feel your speed decrease, sneak your arms up and over your head, keeping them close to your body, while you lift your heels to begin a breaststroke kick (see figure 8.8*c*).

When you fire the kick, your hands should be streamlined and your body should be approaching the surface (see figure 8.8*d*). Resist the temptation to lift your head up for air, which will drop your hips and slow your momentum. Instead, keep your head in line with your spine and begin breathing with the rhythm of your stroke.

Figure 8.8 Breaststroke breakouts: *(a)* catch, *(b)* ride out, *(c)* bring the arms up, and *(d)* kick.

Once you become comfortable with this traditional breaststroke pullout, add the dolphin kick to the sequence as you complete the underwater arm pull. This kick will add underwater speed while you're in the head-lead position. The key to successful breaststroke pullouts is properly timing the pull, arm recovery, and kicks. If you ride out the momentum from each propulsive movement before beginning the next, you can reduce your resistance and maintain better wall speed and momentum.

Like the flip turn, open turns with a two-hand touch take time and practice to perfect. Focus first on the mechanics of the turn and gradually add speed as you become comfortable. Swimmers sometimes slip into the habit of making one-hand-touch turns for breaststroke and butterfly during workouts. Although they are quicker and take less effort, these turns are not legal in competition and would result in a disqualification. Swimmers are encouraged to complete all their turns legally in their workouts, using every wall as an opportunity to fine-tune the details of the approach, turn, streamline, and breakout.

Individual Medley Transitional Turns

Once you have mastered flip turns and open turns, you can easily progress to the turns used in the individual medley, or IM, events. These events are always swum in the order of butterfly, backstroke, breaststroke, and freestyle, thus requiring three specific turns that transition between strokes.

- *Butterfly to backstroke.* Swim butterfly to the wall, finishing with a full stroke and a two-hand touch. Drive one elbow back ("elbow the robber"), draw your knees up, plant your feet on the wall facing up, bring your other arm over ("call the police"), and push off on your back in a tight streamline. Complete your normal underwater-backstroke-kick sequence and breakout.

- *Backstroke to breaststroke.* Approach the wall by swimming backstroke, marking your full stroke count from the flags to the finish. When you reach the wall, touch it with your hand and rotate slightly onto your side. Pull your knees up and around, plant your feet on the wall, and move your chin from one shoulder to the other. This brings you into the ready position. Push off, streamline, and complete your breaststroke pullout and breakout stroke.

- *Breaststroke to freestyle.* This turn is essentially the same as a breaststroke to breaststroke turn, but you should follow your push-off and streamline with the underwater kicking sequence and breakout for freestyle instead of a breaststroke pull-out.

Perhaps the most challenging part of the individual medley turns is getting comfortable with the transition between the rhythm of the stroke approaching the wall and the rhythm of the stroke departing from the wall. Masters swimming competitions include 100-, 200- and 400-yard/meter IM events, which truly tests swimmers' ability to make stroke transitions and minimize their wall time on the approach, at the wall, and in the streamline and breakout. By mixing turns that transition between strokes into your workouts, you will improve your transitions and add variety to your workout sessions.

FINISHES

Although many swimmers never plan to enter a competition, coaches like seeing quality finishes for every repetition during workouts. If swimmers decelerate into the wall or stop short, they are cheating themselves of the benefits of completing the full distance and perhaps preventing the swimmers behind them from finishing. The following list describes great finishes for both workouts and races.

Single-Hand Touches for Freestyle and Backstroke

- Stretch out as you approach the wall, keeping your head in alignment and your body streamlined to minimize resistance. Maintain your momentum by extending forward and keeping your head down.

- To maintain stroke tempo and speed, do not breathe during the strokes between the flags and the finish.

- Hit the wall fully extended and rotated onto your side, holding your extended arm tight against your ear. Avoid finishing with a half stroke. Practice leading with both your right and left arms during the finish, so that either side will feel comfortable in a race situation.

- Know your stroke count from the flags to the wall for backstroke. Many backstroke swimmers perform a half-dolphin kick with their final stroke to the wall, finishing faster and slightly deeper (8 to 10 inches [20 to 25 cm] at most).

Two-Hand Touches for Breaststroke and Butterfly

- Prepare for your finish well in advance. Set up before you reach the flags by adjusting your strokes so you can carry the momentum of your final stroke to the wall and finish fully extended.

- Keep your head in line with your spine, maintaining forward momentum as you drive your fingertips into the wall under the water line.

In competitions with electronic timing, a timing pad that stops the clock when your fingertips touch is placed on the pool wall underwater. As you finish each of your swims in a workout, imagine stopping the clock by shooting your fingertips into the wall. Look at the pace clock after you finish and then celebrate that fast time!

Whether you are in a workout or a competition, think of the walls as opportunities to gain a little speed with a tighter streamline or a more aggressive push-off. With every approach, you can refine your final strokes to the wall, perfecting the amount of strokes needed to carry your momentum into the turn. Every flip or spin is a chance to tidy up your mechanics and reach the ready position a little more quickly. Every finish is a chance to nail the wall for victory. Since you spend 30 percent of your pool time approaching and departing from walls, you can gain a lot of distance by perfecting each phase of your turns.

Conditioning
for Success

Workout Essentials

There is water in every lane, so it is OK.
> —Ian Thorpe, of Australia and five-time Olympic Gold Medalist,
> on being placed into lane 5 (instead of the faster lane 4)
> as the second place qualifier for a final

Despite the many training aids and gadgets available, swimmers really only need the water and themselves. Every swimmer can relate to the T-shirt that reads, "Instant swimmer: Just add water." Why, then, do swimmers surround themselves at the pool with an assortment of toys and gadgets?

Swimming coaches are continually stepping over stacks of kickboards, hand paddles, and other aquatic goodies. Many of these swimming extras are excellent tools that meet specific needs for both learning and training (see figure 9.1). However, swimmers should understand why, when, and how to use each piece of equipment. This chapter discusses the many pieces of training equipment and how they may or may not fit into your program. Each swimmer has a different set of needs; therefore, each swimmer's toolbox is unique. Consider your strengths, challenges, and goals as you select your own gear.

Figure 9.1 Select the training equipment that fits your needs.

BARE ESSENTIALS

The swimsuit and its related gear are considered the bare essentials, the items pertaining to your personal-care needs while swimming. Several of these items are necessities, and others are purely optional.

Swimsuit After the water, the next obvious swimming essential is a swimsuit. For many, choosing a suit is the first big step to starting a swimming program. The two biggest considerations when selecting a suit are comfort and a design that will minimize resistance as you move through the water. Competitive swimwear manufacturers offer a variety of styles and cuts of swimsuits that are streamlined and comfortable with varying degrees of support and coverage. However, any suit that you are comfortable wearing to the pool is perfectly acceptable.

Goggles Amazingly enough, swim goggles were not designed specifically for competition until the early 1970s. Before that, swimmers could choose between a clunky snorkel mask or living with red chlorinated eyes. Several decades later, swim goggles have evolved to an essential item that very few people would swim without. With the many options of size, fit, and design available, you should easily find goggles that work for you.

When selecting goggles, look for a pair with a leakproof seal that fits comfortably. If possible, try on the goggles to check the fit before you purchase them. Take the goggles out of the package and, without using the strap, position them on your face using a slight amount of pressure. They should hold the suction and stay for a half-second or so before falling off. Small-diameter goggles generally fit swimmers with a small nose bridge or eyes that are deeply set, and the large-diameter designs work well for a wider nose bridge. Goggles with a double strap seem to distribute the pressure more evenly, providing a better fit while you move in the water.

The other critical aspect of goggle selection is visibility. Look for a pair that lets you see peripherally as well as out of the top of the goggles. If you can see in all directions, you will not have to move your head out of alignment to see other swimmers and the walls. Swimmers who use an outdoor pool while the sun is bright may prefer dark-tinted or mirrored lenses. Those swimming indoors in the early morning or late evening hours will get better visibility with lightly tinted or clear goggles. Swimmers with poor vision may select prescription goggles or wear their contact lenses under well-fitted goggles.

Goggles sometimes dry the skin around the eyes, particularly after swimming in salt water or harsh pool chemicals. Coach Jim recommends putting a small amount of petroleum jelly on this sensitive area of the face before putting on your goggles to keep the skin moist and improve the goggles' seal.

Another common problem is that goggles tend to fog up. You might try swishing a little bit of saliva around in each lens and then rinsing them out with pool water. Some swimmers choose one of the many antifog products on the market, while others say that nothing works as well as a quick rinse in a small amount of baby shampoo.

Cap The purpose of a swim cap is to keep long hair contained in a neat package on the head. Without a cap, hair drags through the water and can negatively affect head position and proper breathing. Swimmers who feel cold in the water should consider wearing a swim cap. Like a hat in winter, a swim cap worn in the water helps keep the whole body much warmer.

Swim caps do not keep hair dry or protect it entirely from chlorine damage. In fact, the best way to keep your cap on while swimming is to wet your hair in the nonchlorinated water of the shower before putting on your cap. The water gives you a more secure fit and helps minimize your hair's exposure to chlorine in the pool.

Like goggles, swim caps come in several materials and designs. Most swimmers opt for latex or silicone caps because these materials provide a secure and comfortable fit. The latex cap is the least-expensive choice, but has the shortest life expectancy. Taking good care of a latex cap will extend its life. Dry the cap thoroughly after swimming and put a splash of baby powder inside before storing it. Silicone caps cost more but last longer and do not require as much care. Over time, however, silicone caps stretch out and lose their secure fit.

Although a spandex cap looks like a comfortable option for swimmers, it is much less effective because the fabric is permeable, allowing water to run through it. This causes drag and resistance in the water. These caps also have a shorter life because the pool chemicals cause the spandex to stretch out.

The several styles of neoprene caps offer additional insulation to swimmers who perform in colder conditions, such as open-water swimming. This style of cap must fit securely to keep you warm.

Water Bottle It is easy to forget that you are sweating while swimming. Keep a water bottle at the side of the pool for hydration throughout your workout, particularly if the weather or the pool water is warm. If you plan to swim for more than one hour, you may want to add fuel to your fluids with sports drinks or electrolyte replacements. Use trial and error to find the one that best suits your digestive system.

Earplugs Earplugs are best suited for swimmers who have recurring ear infections or other medical conditions. The most effective style is the soft silicone earplug that can be shaped to fit your ear. The best way to prevent infection is to dry your ears well after swimming. Many swimmers with a history of ear infections use preventive drops to help dry their ears.

Nose Clips Nose clips are common for swimmers who use underwater dolphin kicking as part of backstroke training. Nose clips are best suited for swimmers who have specific allergies triggered by chlorinated, lake, or river water. If you do choose to use nose clips, try the simple clip-on style rather than the strapped style. Shop around until you find the right fit. Nose clips stay more secure if you skip the sunscreen or lotion on your nose.

Sun protection Protecting your skin from sun damage is essential while swimming outdoors in the middle of the day. Select a waterproof variety of sunscreen and allow sufficient time for your skin to absorb it before getting wet. Many swimmers prefer to wear a rash guard made of ultraviolet-protective fabric. Keep in mind that even the tightest-fitting rash guard will add some drag in the water.

Personal care products It's no secret that the chemistry used to keep the pool clear and clean can be damaging to swimmers' skin and hair. Recently, several new lines of personal care products, including body washes, skin creams, shampoos, and conditioners, have come on the market for people who spend time in the pool. These specialty products are optional and subject to individual tastes.

THE TRAINING TOOLBOX

In a typical day at the pool, some swimmers arrive with only a suit and goggles, while others come carrying a small suitcase with an assortment of training gadgets. A discussion of each piece of equipment follows. As you read and build a list for your training toolbox, consider your goals and the types of training you like to do.

Kickboard As perhaps one of the simplest and oldest training gadgets, the kickboard allows you to train your legs while keeping your head out of water and resting your upper body on the board. Since this does not emulate an ideal body position for swimming, many coaches prefer that swimmers kick without the board. However, kickboards are very functional for specific applications.

A kickboard is an effective teaching tool for novice swimmers. It can help you relax and breathe comfortably while focusing on kicking mechanics and listening to the coach. It also makes a great tool if you are learning side breathing and one-arm stroking. Once you become proficient and comfortable with the basics, leave the kickboard on the pool deck to focus on body position while integrating the kick with stroke drills.

Freestyle swimmers use the kickboard for intensive leg conditioning sets. Butterfly and breaststroke swimmers do kicking sets without boards to integrate underwater work and breath control. Swimmers make creative use of the board while kicking backstroke. The kickboard may appear to make a nice pillow, but it negatively affects your body position. If you have back or neck problems, use a kickboard with caution because it puts the body into hyperextension.

Many masters swimmers use the kickboard to socialize. There is no better way to catch up with your teammates than to kick side by side up the pool while discussing your weekend plans.

Fins Perhaps the most fun training tool in the box is a pair of fins. All swimmers, from novice to advanced, can use fins for applications ranging from teaching technique to speed training.

Fins come in all shapes and sizes from short to long, wide to streamlined. The shortest fins look like long fins that have been cut off, leaving them with a blade of only about 2 inches (5 cm). The entire purpose of the fin changes when the blade length is shortened. Longer fins, with their added resistance, help swimmers economize their movement, use less oxygen, and maintain speed. In contrast, short fins maintain some water resistance but require a shallower kick, allowing an increased ability to generate force with the legs. Training benefits include increased oxygen intake, higher sustained heart rate, better body position, and faster swimming.

Swimmers learning the basics often wear longer fins to learn the feel of the proper kicking technique. With fins, they can focus on the flow of energy from the hips through the upper legs, knees, ankles, and feet. Swimmers also use fins for stroke drills and kicking sets focused on stroke improvement. Fins help swimmers concentrate more on their technique than on survival. It is important not to rely on the fins to fix an incorrect body position, but to enhance the learning of a swimmer already well positioned in the water.

Fins can be integrated into all full-stroke swimming styles except breaststroke. Swimming with fins over longer distances makes a great recovery workout for swimmers who are tired from training or working through shoulder soreness. With fins, they stay focused on their technique: keeping a long body line and minimizing resistance as they flow through the water. In addition, swimmers often use the shorter fins for sprint sets to work their legs and swim higher in the water.

Look for fins that are comfortable and lightweight and fit snugly on your feet when you are dry. The longest scuba fins prevent proper kick simulation. If you lack ankle flexibility, don't choose the shortest fins; instead, pick a style that is slightly longer and is more flexible.

Occasionally, breaking in a new a pair of fins requires special treatment. Low-cut athletic socks, petroleum jelly, and duct tape are a few tricks of the trade that protect the skin on your toes and feet. Other swimmers avoid this problem by choosing fins made from a softer material.

Paddles Hand paddles were originally designed to improve stroke technique. Attaching paddles forced swimmers to move their hands through the water using proper stroke mechanics to keep the paddle from falling off. The majority of masters and fitness swimmers use hand paddles for stroke improvement.

Hand paddles range in size from fingertip paddles to paddles the size of dinner plates. For maximum stroke improvement, choose a pair that is no more than twice the size of your hand. Err on the smaller side if you are unsure. Swimmers who train with paddles that are too large are more likely to develop shoulder injuries.

Although paddles will help you improve your stroke, some problems may occur with frequent use. In addition to shoulder injury, swimmers who overuse paddles begin to lose their feel for the water, or their ability to make minute changes in hand angle to maximize stroke efficiency. Look for a pair of paddles with holes in them so that you can maintain the flow of water over the palm of your hand while using them.

Make safety a top priority when you swim with paddles. If there are many swimmers in the lane, or if the lane is narrow, it may be best to leave the paddles in your bag. You can hit another swimmer while wearing paddles if your free-style recovery is even slightly wide.

Pull buoy Pull buoys are foam floats placed between the legs to keep swimmers afloat while they focus on their arms. These pull sets typically include paddles as well, to be used simultaneously.

Like all pieces of training equipment, the pull buoy has its place, but it is often overused. Because it makes the lower body float higher, it becomes an easy solution for swimmers who are not well aligned in the water. Without the pull buoy, the hips and legs would drop under the water. Some masters swimmers are tempted to do all their swimming with a pull buoy.

Training with a pull buoy gives you the opportunity to focus on using the core of your body to set stroke tempo. Keep your legs streamlined behind your hips while you use your core muscles to rotate over your hand in the catch position. Make stroke improvement a greater priority in your pulling sets than speed.

Tempo trainer The tempo trainer is a small gadget that fits on your goggle strap and acts as a metronome. Its audible beep can be set to whatever stroke cadence you desire. It is an excellent tool for rate work in all strokes. Set the tempo slightly higher than your comfortable training pace and swim a short set of 50-yard (50 m) distances. Challenge yourself to maintain the same stroke count through all the 50-yard repeats.

Pace clock The pace clock is probably not an item for your swim bag, but it is an essential tool for swimming workouts. It is a large poolside digital or analog clock positioned to be visible to everybody in the water and the coaches on the deck. The pace clock keeps swimmers synchronized throughout the workout and aids individual swimmers in timing and pacing. Chapter 10, Pool Workouts, discusses the pace clock in great detail.

Tether If you were concerned about missing a swim workout while traveling, worry no more. Several manufacturers now make tethers that you can use anywhere, even in a small hotel pool. The tether has tubing that belts around the waist, keeping you in one place as you swim, even during turns.

Snorkel This gem of a pool toy can be found in almost every elite swimmer's bag of tools. Swimming with a snorkel frees you from worrying about your breathing so that you can focus on body balance; alignment of the head, neck, and spine; and stroke mechanics.

When snorkel shopping, look for a front-mount snorkel designed specifically for swim training. These are more streamlined and better suited to keep your head and neck in proper alignment than traditional snorkels.

Snorkel Training

Over the past decade, the front-mount snorkel has become a favorite training tool of competitive swimmers. This traditional piece of beachgoing gear has been redesigned to provide pool swimmers with a more streamlined ride. The breathing tube firmly attaches and mounts in the front, so the training snorkel creates less resistance and will not pull your head to one side. Furthermore, the adjustable strap fits securely around the head and integrates well with traditional swimming goggles.

When training with a snorkel, you are better able to maintain a constant focus on the mechanics of your stroke without worrying about turning your head to breathe. With all your breathing needs met through the snorkel, you can better maintain a steady head position, which is a key component of moving through the water with minimum resistance. Snorkel-clad swimmers are able to relax and slow down their strokes as they concentrate on balance and body alignment (head in the line of the neck and spine), body rotation, and the catch and underwater pull followed by a relaxed high-elbow recovery (see figure 9.2). Swimmers of all levels can benefit from the opportunity to fine-tune their strokes with snorkel training.

Figure 9.2 Training with a snorkel will allow you to better focus on the mechanics of your stroke.

For first-timers, the snorkel swimming will feel very different than freestyle swimming with side breathing. The following progression of skills takes you through the learning curve quickly and into swimming comfortably and more efficiently.

1. Put your cap and goggles on first and then the snorkel. Use the adjustment to fit the strap comfortably around your head. Some swimmers find that the breathing tube stays more stable when wrapped with a piece of athletic tape where it attaches to the head mount.

2. Seal your mouth around the mouthpiece and practice breathing through the tube, first out of water and then while kicking lightly on the surface of the water. If the adjustment to mouth-only breathing is preventing you from getting comfortable, try using a nose clip.

3. Progress to swimming freestyle for one length of the pool at a time. With each lap, focus on a different aspect of your stroke, beginning with the steady head position and aligned body and progressing through to the catch, follow-through, and recovery. Focus on stroke symmetry in the rotation of your shoulders and extension of your fingertips at the front of your stroke.

4. If water gets into the breathing tube, simply purge it by blowing forcefully into the tube to spout the water out of the top. Once you are comfortable clearing the breathing tube, it's time for flip turns, which will inevitably fill the tube with water. The secret is to save enough air through your turn to purge the water from the breathing tube when you are near the water surface and the top of the tube is above the water.

With time and practice, you will become more relaxed with snorkel swimming and ready to maximize its stroke-improving benefits. The following two simple sets integrate snorkel swimming with nonsnorkel swimming to carry the awareness of core and body alignment into the freestyle stroke.

(continued)

Snorkel Training *(continued)*

Get started with smooth swimming.

8 × 25 smooth freestyle with the snorkel

4 × 25 smooth freestyle without the snorkel

- Rest 10 seconds after each 25.
- Focus on keeping your core stable through all 25s, particularly as you transition to swimming without the snorkel. Repeat the sequence twice.

Progress to turns and longer distances.

3 × 100

- Do 1 and 2 with the snorkel, 3 without the snorkel.
- Focus on maintaining good length in stroke both with and without the snorkel. Count your strokes per length to check yourself.

For many masters swimmers, the snorkel has become the swim toy of choice because they have realized the changes in their stroke and the payback in efficiency and time. At the world-class level, the snorkel is a required piece of equipment and coaches regularly integrate this versatile tool into a variety of training sets. It is worth the time to add one to your bag and see what it can do for you.

MORE GADGETS FOR THE SWIMMER

As you move beyond the basic tools for swim training, you will find that stores sell almost every gadget imaginable. Simple sports watches now take your splits and include a tempo trainer, heart rate monitors keep track of your training levels, and waterproof MP3 players keep you rocking as you stroke. Which gadgets do you really need?

For a number of reasons, swimmers are encouraged to train without a watch. In a group setting, use a pace clock to time swimming repetitions and rests. Using one universal timekeeper, rather than many individual watches, keeps the group synchronized throughout the training sets. A watch on your forearm also creates resistance in the water, making your strokes less effective. However, a watch is a great tool for training in the open water, where a pace clock is not practical.

Another common electronic gadget is the heart rate monitor. This great innovation in training allows you to moderate heart rates while exercising, helping you stay in the zone recommended by your coach or doctor. The monitor measures the heart rate with a chest strap and then displays it on a watchlike wristband. Features range from the basic to the elaborate, including computer-download options. This is a great tool if you are under a doctor's orders to regulate your heart rates during exercise. It also teaches you how to better pace yourself in longer swim sets.

Although music is a great motivator, the waterproof MP3 players are best used when swimming on your own. In a group setting, they can be distracting and make communication challenging. If you decide to swim with music in a lap swim program, watch carefully to see who is coming and going in your lane and around you.

A whole world of software exists for advanced swimmers, ranging from tracking workouts to managing swim teams and events. Swimmers are encouraged to maintain a training log to track their workouts both in the pool and on dry land, using which ever option works best for them—traditional paper notebook, basic spreadsheet layout, or a sophisticated software tracking program that runs on their palm-based device or their home computer.

Finally, there are several excellent videos of swimming technique with narration by many of the world's greatest coaches. Break out the popcorn, invite your swimming friends over, and enjoy these films. Nothing beats putting these visuals into your mind that you can then replay when you are in the water. Members of USMS can borrow these videos through the organization's video-loaner program.

The beauty of this wide selection of training tools and toys is that you can integrate a highly targeted and motivating training program into your workout sessions. No single training tool is the answer; rather, use a combination of tools to build a unique swim program for maximum training benefits. Chapter 10, Pool Workouts, further discusses when and how to use these toys.

10

Pool Workouts

Physical fitness is not only one of the most important keys to a healthy body, it is the basis of dynamic and creative intellectual activity.
   —John Fitzgerald Kennedy

Before you pick up a pencil to draft a training plan, it is essential to understand the fundamentals of physical conditioning and how they apply to swimming. Simply going to the pool and swimming more laps is not enough to improve your fitness and performance. Ideally, you should purposefully plan each pool or gym session to fit into the grand scheme of conditioning your body for your ultimate goal. This chapter teaches you to understand and design goal-specific pool workouts. It begins with a quick lesson in training principles and then moves to their applications for swimming.

CONDITIONING 101

Coaches and trainers continually strive to design training sessions with the ideal *workload,* or the balance of volume and intensity. Each session must fit into the big picture that takes the athlete toward the goal. The individual workouts, the weekly progression of workouts, and the big picture are all based on the following training principles:

Overload Overload, perhaps the most fundamental building block of conditioning, is the progressive increase in workload. Swimmers are constantly challenging their bodies by raising the bar with more intensity or volume. Fatigue sets in when the workload increases past the point where their body has been trained. It is only by gradually stretching the body's limits with increasing overload that training effects are set in motion.

Adaptation Adaptation, or the *training effect*, is the body's response to the overload: an increase in muscle size, strength, and endurance, as well as improved cardiorespiratory fitness. Because adaptation occurs in the recovery period after a high-intensity, or overload, session, you must plan your training weeks carefully to balance intense workouts with recovery or cross-training sessions. Busy and ambitious masters athletes sometimes overlook this critical concept, becoming overtrained, injured, or discouraged.

Specificity The principle of specificity states that adaptation is specific to the swimmers' type of workload. For example, well-trained marathon runners become fatigued after swimming only a short distance because their muscles are adapted to the stresses of marathon training, not swimming. Furthermore, specificity of training happens within each sport. The training plan for 50-meter freestyle swimmers differs dramatically from that of an open-water swimmer or individual medley swimmer.

Reversibility The principle of reversibility is the scientific term for the saying "Use it or lose it." When athletes discontinue training, *detraining* occurs—they lose muscle size, strength, and endurance as well as their level of cardiorespiratory fitness.

Understandably, masters athletes are often afraid to take time off from training, lest they lose their hard-earned level of fitness. However, athletes will not lose their stamina within a few days or even weeks of rest. A detraining study by David L. Costill, director of the Human Performance Laboratory at Ball State University, demonstrated that athletes can reduce the frequency and duration of their workouts by up to one-third over a 15- to 20-day period without a loss in performance. As long as their reduced training load includes some level of intensity, athletes maintain their maximum oxygen consumption, or $\dot{V}O_2max$ (Costill et al. 1985).

Variation Athletes should vary not only the type of their workouts, but also the intensity and the duration. For example, swimmers training to improve their overall fitness level might follow a high-intensity pool workout with a yoga session, which simultaneously allows for recovery and adaptation and builds flexibility and core strength. Swimmers are encouraged to plan creatively to keep their training interesting and maximize their return on each workout.

Periodization Athletes can improve their overall fitness and achieve maximum performances at key events by breaking their overall training plans into small, manageable segments, or *periods*. They can also break down the periods into subperiods for a more focused approach to training.

Masters swimming programs typically divide their annual plans into three or four distinct periods that consider the competition calendars at both local and national levels. Although the majority of club members never plan to compete, all swimmers can benefit from the variety in training that comes with periodization. The periods in the following chart might make up a typical annual plan for a masters program. All the listed seasons could be broken down further into early, middle, tapering, and competition periods.

Masters Swimming Competition Calendar

Season	Common names	Time of year
Short course	Winter, indoor, or short course yards (SCY)	Jan.-May
Long course	Summer, long course (LC), or long course meters (LCM)	May-Aug.
Open water	Triathlon	May-Oct.
Short course meters	Fall, SCM	Sept.-Dec.

Did you know?

As they age, masters swimmers show dramatically less decrease in physical capacity than those who lead sedentary lives. A 1992 study found that men who swim regularly do not show a decline in their swimming performance until their mid-30s (Whitten 2005). Furthermore, this decline was considerably less than the traditional 1 percent loss seen in men who do not train. Masters swimmers do not reach the 1 percent loss per year mark until they reach age 70!

Individualization Masters coaches often remind swimmers that all athletes differ in their training responses and requirements. Swimmers arrive at the pool with their individual strengths, hereditary and physiological factors, ages, levels of experience, and goals. A training plan that works for one athlete may not be appropriate for the next. Successful masters athletes have learned to adapt their training plans to meet their personal needs.

Lap swimmers who swim the same distance every day with the same speed and intensity will not improve their level of fitness. They are simply maintaining their level in a daily program that does not incorporate the training principles. However, the interval-based training described in this chapter is used in organized swim workouts and provides swimmers with opportunities for growth. With this program, swimmers stretch their capabilities through overload training, reap the effects of training through recovery-based sets, and gradually improve their overall levels of fitness through variety, individualization, and periodization.

SWIM SETS 101

If the language of swimmers and coaches baffles you, you are not alone. Workout notation and acronyms vary from coach to coach and club to club, and sometimes even the most experienced swimming veterans do not understand each other. This simple glossary will help you understand the sets and workouts presented throughout this book and will give you a jump start on the language at the pool.

Reps Times Distance Most coaches notate swimming sets with the number of repetitions multiplied by the distance. For example, 4 × 100 indicates that you should swim 4 repetitions of 100 meters. It also implies that you should rest after each 100 meters. However, a set that reads 1 × 400 indicates a continuous 400-meter swim.

Rounds (Cycles) When a particular set of repetitions is repeated, it is called a *round* or a *cycle*. The following are a few samples of sets with more than one round:

3 × [4 × 50]	Swim the set of 4 × 50 three times through for a total of 12 50-meter repetitions, or 50s.
3 × [4 × 50; 1 × 100]	This round is a set of 4 × 50 followed by 1 × 100, and should be done three times.

Send-Off Interval The *send-off interval* of a set indicates how often swimmers begin each repetition. For example, in the set 4 × 100 on 2:00, the send-off interval is two minutes, which means swimmers begin a new 100 meters every two minutes. If they swim the distance in 1:50, then they will have 10 seconds of rest before leaving for the next 100.

Rest Interval (RI) Noted in minutes and seconds or just seconds, the *rest interval* (RI) indicates the specific amount of rest between intervals. For example, 4 × 100, RI = :10 signifies four repetitions of 100 meters with 10 seconds of rest after each 100.

Build When coaches ask you to *build* in a set, they want you to start easily and build speed throughout a designated distance. Here are a few examples:

1 × 300 build	Increase speed from easy to fast over the 300 meters.
3 × 100 build	Increase speed from easy to fast in each 100.
1 × 200 build by 50	Start easily and then switch to a higher gear every 50 meters.

Descend When you *descend* a set, you decrease the time of each repetition, or swim each repetition faster. Here are sample descending sets:

6 × 50 descend 1 → 6	Swim each 50 faster within the set.
6 × 50 descend 1 → 5, 6 all easy	Swim each 50 faster from the first through the fifth, then swim the sixth 50 all easy.
6 × 50 descend 1 → 3, 4 → 6	Swim the first three 50s going faster each time. Return to an easy pace on the fourth 50 and descend through the sixth.

Straight (Even-Paced) Sets In a *straight set*, or *even-paced* set, you should maintain a steady pace throughout all repetitions. For example, in 10 × 100, a swimmer may aim to complete each 100 in 1:30 (1 minute, 30 seconds).

Negative Split A *negative split* swim is when you swim the second half of the distance faster than the first. For example, in a negative split 400-meter freestyle, you should swim the second 200 faster than the first 200.

Distance per Stroke and Stroke Count These two concepts partner together to measure stroke efficiency. The *stroke count*, or SC, is the number of strokes swimmers take over a designated distance, typically one pool length. The fewer strokes swimmers take during a length, the greater the *distance per stroke traveled*, or DPS. Each hand entry into the water equals one stroke.

4 × 75	50 build / 25 DPS	For each 75, build speed during the first 50 and focus on length in the stroke, or DPS, on the third 25.
4 × 100	last 25 of each SC 1	Focus on DPS on the final 25 of each of these 100s by taking one fewer stroke than your normal count.
4 × 50	descend SC 1 → 4	Reduce your stroke count with each 50.

Stroke Rate and Golf *Stroke rate*, or the number of strokes taken per minute, is the third measurement of stroke efficiency. A favorite stroke efficiency set for many masters swimmers is golf 50s. In 5 × 50 golf, you add your swim time to your stroke count for each 25 to come up with a score for each 50. For example, if you swam 22 strokes on the first 25 and 23 strokes on the second 25, and had a time of 50 seconds, your score would be 95 (22 + 23 + 50). Your goal in golf 50s is to decrease your score with each successive 50. Golf 50s are an excellent way to discover the trade-offs between stroke rate and distance per stroke.

Breathing patterns Coaches sometimes specify breathing patterns when working on stroke technique or in open-water sets. Here are sample breathing patterns:

B3	Breathe every third stroke.
BR	Breathe only to the right, or breathe only to your favorite side.
BL	Breathe only to the left, or breathe only to your less-favorite side.
B2R2L	Breathe two times to the right, then two times to the left.

MEASURING AND MONITORING SWIMMING FITNESS

You will only be able to see and understand your improvements in the pool if you have consistent and reliable systems of measurement. Swimming is a completely objective sport with three clear-cut ways of measuring progress: time, stroke rate and stroke count, and heart rate. Although each method provides feedback, the combination of the three gives a complete picture of swimming fitness. Swimmers are encouraged to be aware of their times, stroke rates, stroke counts, and heart rates, so as to be in tune to their progress and attentive to overtraining or fatigue.

Perhaps the most obvious and simplest form of measurement is *time*—how long it takes to swim from point A to point B. Swimmers new to organized workouts will quickly learn how to use the *pace clock*, the large clock adjacent to the pool, which manages the flow of the sets within the workout and provides constant feedback about pace (see figure 10.1). Masters swimmers are reminded to measure their progress by the pace clock, rather than by comparing themselves to the swimmers next to them. The clock provides an objective and consistent measurement that can be compared from swim to swim, workout to workout, and week to week.

Early in the training program, coaches prioritize improving technique and measuring stroke efficiency (DPS). New swimmers should focus on increasing DPS, thereby making each stroke more efficient and reducing their stroke count. In a 25-meter pool, novice adult swimmers typically take 25 or more strokes per length (each hand entry counts as one stroke). Intermediate swimmers have typically improved efficiency to a stroke count of about 20, and the most experienced swimmers take 11 to 17 strokes per length. (If you swim in a 25-yard pool, your strokes per length will be 10% fewer.) Many factors contribute to stroke count, including the quality of streamlines off each wall as well as level of fatigue. As swimmers begin to tire

Figure 10.1 Use a pace clock to keep track of your set times.

in a workout, their DPS decreases and their SC increases. In other words, you take more and shorter strokes. This situation is not ideal, however, and swimmers should train to minimize its occurrence. To maintain the same pace, you must increase your *stroke rate*, or turnover.

You can learn a lot about your fitness by monitoring your heart rate during workouts. As your level of conditioning increases, you should be able to maintain speed at a lower heart rate, and more important, experience a quicker recovery to a resting heart rate. Athletes often use their heart rate recovery time to determine the amount of rest they should take between repetitions to achieve certain training effects. In sprint-oriented sets, swimmers allow their heart rates to recover completely between high-intensity efforts. However, in distance sets, swimmers may allow a rest period of only 10 seconds between lower-intensity swims.

The nature of swimming can make heart-rate training a bit more complicated than dry-land training. Because venous return, or the rate at which blood flows back to the heart, is higher when you're in a horizontal position, your pulse rate during swimming is typically about 10 percent lower than your pulse rate during dry-land training for the same perceived effort. However, swimmers return to a vertical position during the recovery period when they measure their pulse. Heart rate monitors have become very popular with masters swimmers and are the most accurate method of monitoring pulse while exercising. The traditional method of counting your pulse for 10 seconds and multiplying by 6 also works. For the most accurate assessment, swimmers should take a pulse measurement as soon as they complete a swim set.

Before using heart rates to monitor your training, you should understand these key concepts and your own specific target rates.

- Your MHR (maximum heart rate) is based on your age and is an estimate of what your heart rate would be after several minutes of maximum effort. Sally Edwards, exercise physiologist, 14-time Ironman finisher, and CEO of Heart Zones, proposes this formula for calculating your MHR[1]:

$$210 - (.5 \times age) - (.01 \times body\ weight) + 4\ (males\ only;\ females\ add\ 0) = MHR$$

  For example, a 40-year-old male masters athlete with a body weight of 175 pounds would calculate an MHR of 192 bpm.

$$210 - (.5 \times 40) - (.01 \times 175) + 4 = 192.25\ (rounded\ to\ 192)$$

  Keep in mind that the MHR is a theoretical maximum number that varies from swimmer to swimmer. Your heart rate will be about 10 percent lower while you swim.

---

[1] Source: www.sarkproducts.com/sally1.htm; accessed 6/19/08.

- Your RHR (resting heart rate) is your lowest heart rate of the day. Take your RHR before you get out of bed in the morning. This count increases slightly as people age, but decreases significantly for those who exercise consistently. You can learn a lot about your body and your training by tracking your RHR on a daily basis. If your RHR is elevated five or more beats per minute on a given morning and you are not affected by mental stress, you may be overtraining or fighting a cold or other illness. This may be a good day for a recovery workout or a complete rest.

- Your THR (target heart rate) is your heart rate while training. This target, expressed as a percentage of MHR, varies depending on the desired conditioning effect. Sprint sets push swimmers to reach a much higher THR for a shorter duration than in an overdistance training set.

- The final piece of the measurement puzzle that is tightly bound to training intensity, heart rate, and perceived effort is your LT (lactate threshold). This is the level of intensity at which lactate begins to accumulate in your muscles and bloodstream and makes exercise uncomfortable. When you train below the threshold, your muscles are primarily burning fuel *aerobically*, or with oxygen. When you cross over the threshold to a higher intensity, your muscles move to a predominantly *anaerobic metabolism*, or one without oxygen, which is less efficient. When you train aerobically, you can maintain a comfortable pace over a long distance. When you train at a fast and intense rate that is above your lactate threshold, you feel much less comfortable and you tire quickly.

- The key is to find the fastest pace that you can maintain over a distance without accumulating lactate in your blood. The goal of endurance training is to gradually raise that threshold, which allows you to maintain progressively faster paces over longer distances. How do you determine where your LT is? The most accepted method is to use the pace you can hold for a continuous 20- to 30-minute swim. However, new swimmers are encouraged to break this swim into more manageable distances such as 10 repetitions of 50 meters (10 × 50) with a 10-second rest after each repetition. The pace you can hold over the distance is a good approximation of your lactate threshold. Your LT is typically 75 to 85 percent of your maximum heart rate.

One of the biggest challenges new swimmers face is learning to appropriately pace their swimming efforts during a workout session. Improving stroke efficiency and learning to swim in the aerobic zone is the key to success. Swimmers too often begin the workout at a high intensity and then lose steam during the heart of the workout. By warming up gradually and building effort through the one-hour session, you can maximize water time and achieve the desired training effect.

Searching for That Threshold

Here are a few of Jim's favorite sets to test your LT.

Race Pace 50s (see page 116 for more on race pace)

3 × [4 × 50; 1 × 50]

- In the first cycle, swim 4 × 50 at 200 race pace + 2 to 5 seconds.
- In the second cycle, swim 4 × 50 at 200 race pace.
- In the third cycle, swim 4 × 50 just under 200 race pace.
- Swim the 1 × 50 easy for all cycles.
- RI = :10 after all 50s.
- Add an extra 2:00 rest between cycles.

Descending Distance and Time

In 3 × 300, descend 1 → 3, RI = :30.
Swim 1 × 100 easy, RI = :40.
In 3 × 200, descend 1 → 3, RI = :20.
Swim 1 × 100 easy, RI = :30.
In 3 × 100, descend 1 → 3, RI = :10.
Swim 1 × 100 easy.

INTERVAL TRAINING AND ENERGY ZONES

Before the 1950s, no universally accepted method for training swimmers existed. Throughout the years, coaches experimented with different strategies, but none brought together all of the training principles that we now consider essential to good training. Not until the 1956 Olympic Games, when the previously mediocre Australian team dominated the medal race, did the world begin to think about training swimmers differently. The Australians took the concept of *interval training*, already accepted and used by track athletes, into the water. Instead of swimming long distances at low intensity, they were swimming repetitions of shorter distances at a higher intensity with short recovery periods. The Australian swimmers demonstrated the advantages of overload and the adaptation response.

Coaches like Doc Counsilman began to use interval training to prepare swimmers for specific events by varying the distance of each repetition, the number of repetitions, the duration of the rest, and the intensity of the effort. With this creative and highly configurable method of training, coaches soon began training their swimmers at varying intensities, or in *energy zones*. These clearly defined zones allowed coaches to target workouts for individual swimmers and provided the variation necessary for the overall training plan. Specificity, variation, periodization, and individualization all came into play as the world of swimming training was revolutionized.

Although a variety of energy zone systems have been defined, this book recommends the simplicity of the system of four energy zones presented by USA Swimming (see table).

Four Energy Zone System

Energy zone	Set duration	Rest or work to rest ratio	HR (% of max)	Types of training
Aerobic	Variable	10-30 sec rest	≤ 80	Recovery, overdistance, or slow-interval sets
Aerobic / Anaerobic mix	8-40 min	15-60 sec rest	80-100	Endurance, fartlek or speed-play, or fast-interval sets
Anaerobic	2-15 min	2:1-1:4	90-100	Race pace, goal sets
Sprint	1-2 min	1:3-1:4	100	Sprints

Adapted, by permission, from M. Skinner and D. Whitney, 2004, *Energy categories*. [Online]. Available: www.usaswimming.org/USASWeb/DesktopDefault.aspx?TabID=67&Alias=Rainbow &Lang=en [July 8, 2008].

Within each of the four energy zones, there are several types of swimming training sets. The lines between these zones are gray, allowing for some crossover between energy systems in any swimming set.

Organized workout groups for adults take advantage of interval training's ability to target specific energy zones. In fact, most coaches organize masters swimming workouts by grouping swimmers into lanes by their aerobic *cruise interval*, or *lane base*. Swimmers' cruise intervals are the send-off intervals in which they can comfortably swim 10 × 100 with about 10 seconds rest between repetitions. For example, the swimmers in the 1:50 lane swim will swim each 100-yard (or meter) repetition in about 1:40 and then leave again when the clock is at 1:50, giving them a 10-second rest. Some of the swimmers in the lane may be faster or slower, thus getting more or less rest on the 1:50 send-off. In the novice lanes, cruise intervals are typically based on comfortably swimming 10 × 50 with 10 to 20 seconds rest. Masters coaches often vary the intensity, or the energy zone, of a set by specifying an interval higher (more rest) or lower (less rest) than cruising. Swimmers must learn their own cruise intervals and how to use the pace clock as their training program begins to include more types of swimming sets.

TRAINING SETS OF SWIMMERS

One of the most creative parts of a coach's job is designing workouts that continually change things up to target the various training zones. These workouts must fit into the big picture of the training plan to allow for recovery and adaptation. With good planning, you will thrive on the variety as your level of conditioning gradually improves, moving you closer to your goals. The following list of types of training sets includes those favored by most masters programs.

Recovery Sets Most swimmers look forward to recovery sets. They provide the opportunity to recover from high-intensity work while focusing on low-heart-rate, aerobic swimming. Recovery sets are an ideal time to focus on stroke mechanics, body position, and the fine points of turning and streamlining.

Here is a sample recovery set:

6 × 100

- On odd-numbered 100s (1, 3, 5): Swim 50 catch-up drill / 50 freestyle, max DPS.
- On even-numbered 100s (2, 4, 6): Swim 50 freestyle / 50 backstroke, focusing on great turns.
- RI = :10 to :15.

Overdistance Sets If you're preparing for longer distances and open-water events, intersperse overdistance swims into your training program. These confidence-building swims vary in length, depending on your goal, from 500 to more than 2000 yards or meters. Focus on maintaining a low heart rate (60 to 70 percent of MHR) and a steady pace; pay attention to technique in your strokes, turns, and streamlines.

Endurance (Slow-Interval) Sets Endurance-training sets, the foundation of general aerobic conditioning, are typically a long series of repetitions at a moderate intensity with short rest breaks of 10 to 20 seconds. The goal of endurance training is to gradually increase the speed at which you can swim aerobically, or to raise your lactate threshold.

Here is a sample endurance set:

15 × 100

- Freestyle swim at a steady pace.
- On cruise or RI = :10.
- Novice lanes reduce the distance to 50s or the number of repetitions to 10.

The duration of the set should be 20 minutes or longer with the heart rate in the aerobic zone (60 to 75 percent of MHR) to improve aerobically.

Fartlek (Speed-Play) Sets Both fun to swim and excellent for conditioning, fartlek sets provide a mix of aerobic conditioning and speed. The element of variation in stroke rhythm and speed in these sets make them ideal for preparing for the unique challenges of open-water swimming.

Here is a sample fartlek set:

2 × 500

- Freestyle swim the 500-meter distance continuously, making speed changes at various points as indicated.
  1. 125 easy / 25 fast / 100 easy / 25 fast / 75 easy / 25 fast / 50 easy / 25 fast / 25 easy / 25 fast
  2. 25 easy / 25 fast / 25 easy / 50 fast / 25 easy / 75 fast / 25 easy / 100 fast / 25 easy / 125 fast
- RI = 1:00 (after each 500)

Note that you should swim only at a pace you can maintain for the duration for the distances marked as "fast." As a guide, complete the easy lengths at 60 to 70 percent MHR and the fast lengths at 70 to 80 percent MHR.

Fast-Interval Sets With a work-to-rest ratio as high as 1:1, fast-interval training demands a much higher level of intensity than slow-interval training and rallies more of an anaerobic effort with each repetition. The goal of fast-interval sets is to improve endurance and speed. The focus shifts from *quantity* to *quality*.

Here is a sample fast-interval set:

6 × 100

- Freestyle swim with excellent effort (80 to 85 percent of MHR).
- RI = 1:00 after each 100.

Race-Pace Sets As you prepare for competition, race-pace training becomes a critical piece of the big picture. Race-pace training allows you to experience the effort required to swim at your target pace. These confidence-building sets are critical for developing a keen sense of pace before competition.

Often, race-pace sets are designed with *broken swims*, where the total distance is broken down into smaller distances with rests. The following sample broken swim profiles a swimmer preparing to complete a 200-meter freestyle in a time of 2 minutes 40 seconds (2:40). By breaking the total distance into four 50-yard swims, the swimmer can complete the pieces at, or very close to, competition pace and can watch the time of each 50 by using the pace clock. The goal is to swim each 50 at the same pace, which would be 40 seconds each (2:40 ÷ 4 = :40).

4 × 50

- Freestyle swim, at 200 race pace (90 to 100 percent of MHR)
- Send-off interval = :55.

The fixed send-off interval of 55 seconds gives the swimmer 15 seconds rest between 50s and plenty of time to read the clock.

A second, and perhaps more common, method of doing broken swims is to swim the 200 meters taking exactly 10 seconds rest after each 50. After the swim, subtract the 30 seconds rest (3 stops at 10 seconds each) from the total time of your 200 for your broken-200 time. Because you may not be leaving at a convenient mark on the pace clock each time, this method makes it a bit trickier to track your 50 splits. However, this is typically how broken swims are done when a coach is available to time the splits and the rests.

Goal Sets and Repetition *Benchmark sets* (also called *goal sets* or *test sets*) assess swimming fitness levels. The rest duration is sometimes as much as three times the swim duration, so these sets allow for best-effort swims (90 to 100 percent of MHR), followed by complete recovery. The following table shows a variety of the goal sets used by the Dallas Aquatic Masters with modifications for every level of swimmer. Because of the very high intensity of these sets, you should begin with only a few repeats and gradually, over several weeks, build up to the entire set. Furthermore, you should allow several days of recovery workouts after goal sets.

Sample Goal Sets

	50s	75s	100s	150s	200s	Distance (straight time trials)
Advanced	16 × 50 on 1:30	10 × 75 on 2:00	8 × 100 on 2:30	5 × 150 on 3:00	4 × 200 on 4:00	750-800
Experienced	12 × 50 on 1:45	8 × 75 on 2:30	6 × 100 on 3:00	4 × 150 on 4:00	3 × 200 on 5:00	600
Novice	8 × 50 on 2:00	5 × 75 on 3:00	4 × 100 on 4:00	3 × 150 on 5:00	2 × 200 on 6:00	400-450
Triathletes and open-water swimmers[1]	6-10 × 200 on 3-6 min	4-7 × 300 on 4-7 min	3-5 × 400 on 5-8 min	2-3 × 800 on 10-15 min	1 × 2000	2000-2400

[1] Triathletes and open-water swimmers swim goal sets with longer distances to better prepare for their specific races.

Sprint Sets Although sprint sets are favored by sprinters, every swimmer in the pool can benefit from the power-specific sprint training sets. With repetitions of 12.5 to 100 meters, less than 500 total meters in the set, and work-to-rest ratios as high as 1:1, the intensity of these sets is demanding.

Here is a sample sprint set:

12 × 25

- Freestyle swim with the fast portions at all-out race effort (95 to 100 percent of MHR).
- Begin odd 25s with a dive, do 12.5 fast / 12.5 easy.
- Begin even 25s with a push-off, swim fast with a turn at the finish.
- RI = 2:00 after each 25.

By changing the distances, the effort, the rest interval, and the number of repetitions, you can create an infinite number of swimming sets that target a variety of heart rates and energy zones. Furthermore, within any organized swimming workout, you can tailor any given set for your own skill level and goal.

PACE CLOCK BASICS

In organized swimming workouts, the pace clock becomes the metronome of the workout, telling swimmers when to swim, how fast they swim, and how long to rest. All swimmers keep an eye on the clock as they stay in rhythm with the prescribed set and abreast of their pace. Because of its critical role, learning how to use the pace clock should be a priority for new swimmers. This section looks at three ways that the pace clock is used for managing swimming sets in order of complexity: *fixed-rest sets*, *straight intervals*, and *varying-rest intervals*.

Fixed-Rest Sets The simplest use of the pace clock in swimming is a *fixed-rest set*, which designates a specific amount of rest. The following warm-up set uses a fixed rest to help you focus more on technique than on finishing in any particular time or interval.

8 × 50   25 stroke drill / 25 swim; RI = :10

In this set, the swimmers complete eight repetitions of 50 meters, with the first 25 of each a stroke drill, the second 25 swimming, and an RI of 10 seconds after each 50. As swimmers complete each 50, they will look to the clock, rest for exactly 10 seconds, and then leave again for the next 50.

A second application of a fixed-rest set is a broken swim, as described in the race-pace sets in the previous section. Broken swims are typically done later in the season as swimmers begin training specific to racing.

Straight-Interval Sets When coaches say, "Six 50s on the minute," they have just given the swimmers a *straight-interval set*. In this set, written as 6 × 50 on 1:00, swimmers complete six repetitions of 50 meters, leaving the wall for a new repetition every minute. Assume that they begin swimming the first 50 when the second hand of the pace clock is on *the 60* (sometimes called *the top* or *the up*). They will leave for the second 50 exactly one minute later, on the 60 again, and so on until all six 50s are finished.

Things get slightly more complex when the interval is not a convenient amount of time. For example, if the interval were changed to 1:10, then the departure time (the location of the second hand on the clock) would change with each 50. Again, assuming that the swimmers begin the first 50 on the 60, then the second 50 would begin when the clock's second hand is on the 10 (1:10 later), the third 50 would start on the 20, and so on. The following table shows how swimmers figure their swim times, rest, and departure times for 6 × 50 on the 1:10.

Sample Straight-Interval Set

50 meters	Departure time: leave on	Arrival time: come in on	Swim time	Rest time until the next 50 meters
1	60	55	55	15
2	10	5	55	15
3	20	15	55	15
4	30	24	54	16
5	40	30	50	20
6	50	35	45	–

Varying-Rest Sets A variation on the straight set is a *varying-rest set*, in which the interval changes (ascends or descends) between repetitions. The following table reviews the pace clock departures and swim times for the following set:

4 × 100   1st 100 on 2:20, then descend interval by :05 each 100

Sample Varying-Rest Set Using the Pace Clock

100 meters	Departure time: leave on	Interval	Arrival time: come in on	Swim time	Rest time until the next 100 meters
1	60	2:20	60	2:00	20
2	20	2:15	15	1:55	20
3	35	2:10	30	1:55	15
4	45	2:05	35	1:50	–

Although it sometimes seems overwhelming at first, swimmers quickly catch on to pace clock math and learn to appreciate its role in adding variety to swimming sets. Make the pace clock work for you with these tips for success.

1. *Make sure you can see the clock.* If visibility is obscured because of poor or fogged goggles, replace them or clean them using your saliva or a defogging solution, available through most swim shops. If you cannot see the clock because of visual impairments, you can either wear contact lenses under a pair of well-fitted goggles or wear a pair of prescription goggles.

2. *Start sets on the top or the bottom.* If you consistently start each set on the 60 or the 30, it will be easier for you to keep track of the number of repetitions. As you leave on each repetition within a set, remember where the second hand is on your departure, what the interval is, and begin to think ahead about when you will leave for the next repetition.

3. *Know your pace and forget the minute hand.* By knowing what your pace per 50 is and in what time you expect to swim a repetition, you will be able to anticipate where the second hand will be when you finish each swim. Assume that you maintained a pace of about 1:00 per 50 on the descending interval in the previous set example. If you leave on the 60 and return on the 60 after swimming a 100, you know without looking at the minute hand that your time for the swim was 2:00 (2 × 1:00 per 50). If you come in on the 5, then your swim time is 2:05, and if you come in on the 55, your swim time is 1:55.

4. *Peek at your pace.* Assuming that the pace clock is conveniently positioned on the pool deck, you can monitor your pace by peeking at the clock on a breath either going in or coming out of a turn. If you know exactly where you expect the second hand on the clock to be, you can take a good look at the clock with just a glance.

5. *Adjust intervals as necessary.* Swimmers who are barely able to catch their breath between intervals and have no time to read the clock should remember that it is OK to move to a lane moving at a more suitable pace and a more relaxed interval. If you are on your own and struggling with an interval, simply adjust the interval so that you can focus on technique.

By using one central clock for the entire pool, rather than individual wristwatches, all the swimmers in any lane or group of lanes stay synchronized. If there is more than one pace clock at the pool, the second hands of the clocks should be synchronized so that swimmers can keep tabs on their pace from any position in the pool.

Swimming even the simplest sets with a pace clock can become confusing when you are trying to catch your breath. Do not hesitate to adjust your interval or work with your coach to find the appropriate interval for you. Remember that it is better to increase your RI to maintain proper stroke technique and DPS than to swim with poor technique on a set interval.

WHAT IS YOUR CRUISE?

The simplest and most common way for swimming workouts to be organized is by using cruise, or lane base, intervals to group swimmers of similar abilities. In any one workout, you may find lanes ranging from a 1:15 100-meter cruise to over 2:00 100-meter cruise. The beauty of this system is that there is a lane for every level of swimmer who wants to jump into the action. Novice swimmers may start with 50s.

Your cruise interval is the send-off interval in which you can comfortably swim 10 × 50 (or 100) with about 10 to 15 seconds of rest. If you are unsure what that is, use this basic swim set to figure it out. Again, novices may do 3 or 4 × 50s and work up to 10 × 50, then try a shorter set of 100s.

1. *Swim.* Begin by swimming a 1000-meter distance broken into 100s with 10 seconds of rest after each 100. Swim the 100s in the fastest pace that you can consistently maintain. Your pulse rate at cruise speed should be 70 to 80 percent of MHR and definitely under your lactate threshold. If you're just starting out, try 10 × 50 as an alternative to the 100s. Again, if you're a novice swimmer, start with a 300 to 500 broken set with 50s instead of 100s.

2. *Get your time.* A clearly visible pace clock or waterproof wristwatch will allow you to rest for precise intervals as well as record the total time of the swim, including the rests.

3. *Do the math.* Add 10 seconds to your total time (to account for the rest after the tenth 100) and then divide by 10. This is your average time for each 100-meter swim plus the 10-second rest. Round up to the nearest 5-second increment and you have your own masters cruise interval!

As your training progresses, swim 10 × 50 (or 100) on your cruise interval every few weeks and challenge yourself to maintain a faster pace over the 50s or 100s as your fitness improves. When your cruise interval begins to feel too easy, add more 100s to the set. When you are getting more than 15 seconds of rest on your cruise interval, it is time to reduce it by 5 seconds.

With each lane assigned a cruise interval, the masters swim coach can give several lanes of swimmers the same set of instructions more efficiently. For example, each lane, depending on their cruise interval, will interpret the set *5 × 100 on cruise* slightly differently. Coaches can specify variations on cruise as illustrated in the following sample sets.

3 × 200 on cruise	3 × 200 on your 100-cruise × 2
4 × 50 on cruise	4 × 50 on your 100-cruise ÷ 2
2 × 100 on cruise – :05	2 × 100 on your 100-cruise – 5 seconds
3 × 200 on cruise + :10	3 × 200 on (your 100-cruise × 2) + 10 seconds

Note that in the last example you add the 10 seconds *after* you calculate the 200 cruise interval.

When you arrive for a workout session overtired or in need of a recovery workout, swim in a lane at a more relaxed cruise interval than you normally would. Conversely, if you're looking for a challenge, step up and try a faster cruise interval at some workouts.

FREQUENTLY ASKED QUESTIONS

By understanding the answers to these commonly asked questions, you can take a sensible approach to your own training program.

How far should I swim in a workout? During practice, focus more on your level of intensity than on the distance you swim. Although many masters swimmers seem to believe that swimming farther means improved fitness, the quality of your swimming is actually more important than the quantity.

The typical masters workout is structured to provide one hour of swimming for participants with a variety of experience levels. The total distance of the workout will vary from approximately 1500 to 3500 meters depending on the skill level, but the quality and intensity of the workouts will be very similar. Although workouts longer than one hour are not practical for the busy family and work schedule of typical adult swimmers, certain situations do warrant longer sessions, such as preparing for a long-distance open-water event or triathlon. On the other hand, shorter sessions are often more appropriate for novice swimmers.

How often should I come to workout? Masters swimmers should work out in the pool three to five days each week. Although one or two times each week is better than none, you may become frustrated over a long period when you do not experience improvements in endurance or power. Swimming more than five days each week can lead to burnout and potential injury and does not allow time for the critical component of cross-training.

Swimmers are encouraged to cross-train at least once each week with activities such as running, cycling, hiking, Pilates, yoga, and strength training. Training programs that mix variety and recovery with intensity will bring the highest gains.

What types of training should I emphasize? The aspect of variety in training continues in the pool. Coaches like to pride themselves on keeping the workouts creative and different. All swimmers, regardless of stroke or event specialty, can improve endurance and keep workouts interesting by training to some degree in all four strokes and keeping all facets of training sets in their repertoire—overdistance to sprint, broken swims to breath control sets. Swimmers who are training for a specific event, such as a triathlon, open-water, or pool competition, will tailor their training with more event-specific sets as the season progresses, but will continue to make variety a priority.

How hard should I swim in a workout? How hard you swim really depends on your level of fitness and your goals. If you're a new swimmer, focus on technique and gradually build cardiorespiratory endurance with a goal of comfortably completing the one-hour practice session. Only after you reach this first milestone should you begin to turn up the intensity for key parts of the workouts.

If you want to improve speed and power, you need to include more of what the American College of Sports Medicine calls *vigorously intensive aerobic exercise*, which creates a substantial increase in heart rate. Examples out of the water are running faster or up hills, and examples in the pool are sprint sets, goal sets, and race-pace training. Well-designed masters programs offer a variety of workouts with opportunities to step up the intensity, as well as recovery-based, lower-heart-rate aerobic training.

These are the main ingredients—the training principles and how they are applied in swimming sets. Mix these with dry-land training to improve strength and flexibility, and with cross-training for variety and you are on your way to creating your own road map to success. Chapter 13, Make Your Plan for Success, offers guidelines on moving these concepts into a plan designed specifically for you and your goals.

Dry-Land Training

Dry-land training is more responsible for the advances in swimming over the last twenty years than anything else. I do as much training out of the pool as I do in the pool.

> —Gary Hall Jr., five-time Olympic gold medalist
> and founder of the Race Club

No training plan is complete without some work outside of the pool, or what swimmers call *dry-land training*. Coaches encourage swimmers at every level to do some dry-land work for increased strength and flexibility. Swimmers in every successful collegiate program profit from a variety of out-of-pool exercises, such as cycling, plyometrics, yoga, and Pilates. Triathletes, who must balance their swimming with two land-based sports, have long known the benefits of variation in training. Masters swimmers who invest even a small amount of time each week in dry-land work will gain improved muscular endurance and stroke efficiency.

DRY-LAND TRAINING GOALS

Although improving flexibility and building strength are the two main goals of a dry-land training program, two additional often-overlooked benefits are variety and injury prevention. Going to the gym, cross-training in a different sport, or participating in a group exercise class will add variety and interest to your weekly training program. Using your muscles in a different way and working a greater range of motion will make you fitter and more resistant to injuries.

How Flexible Are You?

Use these three simple tests to assess your flexibility for efficient swimming.

1. Stand with your back and heels against a wall. Raise your arms outward from your sides until they are parallel to the ground. Bend your elbows to 90 degrees so that your forearms are pointing forward while the back part of your arms press up against the wall. From this position, slowly move your arms up over your head, maintaining contact between the wall and your triceps. Ideally, you should be able to raise your elbows above your shoulders to have the flexibility required for proper freestyle and butterfly technique.

2. Lie down on your back. Lift your arms above your head, holding one hand on top of the other with your palms facing up and your elbows locked. Squeeze your shoulders up to your ears while keeping your arms flat on the ground, and hold that posture. This streamlined position is the most efficient way to cut through the water with minimum resistance.

3. Kneel on the ground and sit on your ankles, pressing the tops of your toes, your feet, and your shins into the ground. Sit up with a straight back. If this position is difficult or uncomfortable, you have limited ankle flexibility for efficient freestyle, backstroke, and butterfly kicks.

One reason that flexibility decreases with age is that people become less active and don't put their muscles through the same range of motion they did when they were younger. Before they started a swim program, very few masters swimmers needed to move their shoulders up to their ears or extend their arms and hands over their heads for 45 minutes.

STRETCHING

Since flexibility is critical to improving swimming, the most essential element of any dry-land program is a safe and thorough stretching routine. Flexibility decreases with age, due in part to changes in connective tissue, but more from reduced activity. Furthermore, sitting at a desk or working on a computer accelerates this natural process. A regular stretching program can both maintain and increase your flexibility, bringing you improvements in your swimming and all your athletic endeavors.

While there are several types of stretches, this chapter discusses only a few key static and dynamic stretches. Warm up before the workout with dynamic stretches, and cool down at the conclusion of your workout with static stretches.

Do the following three dynamic stretches on the pool deck before your workout. Make the movements in these stretches long, slow, and within your range of motion. The goal of these exercises is to relieve tightness while increasing pliability in the muscles.

• *Arm circles.* Stand tall with good posture and extend your right arm upward. Next, slowly move the arm backward in a circle, feeling the stretch through your shoulder and upper back. Keep your arm straight and your elbow soft and relaxed. Place the fingers of your left hand on the front of your right shoulder to stabilize it throughout the movement (see figure 11.1). Focus on the backward motion to contrast with the typical forward motion of this joint in daily activities. Circle 5 to 8 times per arm.

Figure 11.1 Use opposite hand to ensure anterior stabilization.

Figure 11.2 Keep your weight over your right foot as you lower your left knee toward the ground.

• *Walking lunges.* From a standing position, stride forward with your right foot, bending your right knee to 90 degrees and dropping your left knee toward the ground (see figure 11.2). Maintaining continuous motion, stand up again and bring the left foot forward and the right knee down to the ground. Take 10 to 16 lunges (5 to 8 per leg). Position your hands on your hips or behind your head for an extra challenge. Stay focused on excellent upper-body posture throughout this hip flexor stretch.

• *Side lunges.* Stand with your feet set wide apart and alternate lunges to either side. As you lunge to the right, drop your body over your bent right leg and keep your left leg straight (see figure 11.3). Lift your toes up for a deeper stretch. Repeat 5 to 8 times per side to stretch the adductors and hips.

Figure 11.3 Keep your left leg straight as you shift your body weight over your bent right leg.

As you cool down from your workout with the following static stretches, avoid the temptation to rush by focusing on proper breathing, which will enhance the stretch. Take a deep breath through your nostrils and expand the abdomen (not the chest) at the deepest point in the stretch, then lean into the stretch a little more as you slowly exhale through your mouth. This slow abdominal breathing relaxes your muscles and allows them to lengthen more.

- *Latissimus dorsi (upper back)*. Begin on your hands and knees in a crawling position. Sit back on your heels, keeping your palms stationary on the mat and your arms straight (see figure 11.4). If you are not feeling this stretch in your upper back, slowly slide your hands forward. Hold the stretch for 30 seconds. Walk your hands to the right and hold for 30 seconds, then do the same on the left side.

Figure 11.4 Keep your arms straight and your palms stationary as you sit back on your heels during the latissimus dorsi stretch.

Figure 11.5 Press your arm against the wall and lean forward to feel the stretch in your chest.

- *Pectoralis (chest)*. Bend your elbow to 90 degrees, raise your arm so that your upper arm is parallel with the ground, and place the inside of your forearm against a door frame, pole, or wall (see figure 11.5). Keeping your forearm planted, lean forward to feel the stretch in your chest. Hold the stretch for 15 seconds and repeat three times per side.

- *Triceps*. Stand facing a wall diagonally with your left side close to the wall, and place the back of your flexed left elbow on the wall (see figure 11.6). Lean your arm, armpit, and body toward the wall to feel the stretch in your triceps (the back of your upper arm). Hold the stretch for 15 seconds and repeat three times per arm.

Figure 11.6 Raise flexed arm overhead as you lean into wall to stretch triceps.

- *Gastrocnemius (calf muscle).* Stand facing a wall and place your palms against the wall at shoulder height. Place one leg behind you, several feet from the wall, and keep it straight as you press the heel to the ground. Bend the knee of your front leg and gradually lunge, or lean forward, toward the wall until you feel the stretch in your calf, or your gastrocnemius muscle (see figure 11.7a). Hold the stretch for 15 seconds and repeat three times per leg.

  The soleus muscle is partnered with the gastrocnemius muscle, and you can stretch it from this same position. Instead of leaning in toward the wall, lower yourself as though you were going to sit down, bending your back leg and keeping your heel on the ground (see figure 11.7b). Again, hold each stretch for 15 seconds and repeat three times per leg.

Figure 11.7 *(a)* Gastrocnemius stretch and *(b)* soleus stretch.

- *Hamstring.* Stand facing a step or a low bench and place one heel on it, keeping your toes pointed up and your knee straight. Stand tall, then slowly hinge at the hips, lowering your chest toward your extended leg until you feel the stretch in the back of your thigh (see figure 11.8). Be sure to keep the knee straight, your toes up, and your spine extended (not hunched). Hold for 15 seconds and repeat three times per leg.

Figure 11.8 Keep your back straight as you slowly lean forward until you feel the stretch in the back of your thigh.

- *Quadriceps, shin, and ankle.* Stand near a wall or countertop that can be used for balance. Bend one knee, grab your foot with the hand on that side, and draw the heel of your foot toward your buttocks (see figure 11.9). The knee of your bent leg should be aligned with, or just slilghtly behind, your standing leg. Hold the stretch for 15 seconds and repeat three times per leg.

Figure 11.9 Holding foot of the flexed leg, feel the stretch in the quadriceps, shin, and ankle.

Figure 11.10 In half-kneeling position, lean forward stretching hip flexors.

- *Hip flexors.* Kneel on one leg with your other knee in front of you. Keep your eyes focused forward. Hold your torso upright and move forward until you feel a stretch in the front of your hip (see figure 11.10). For a deeper stretch, slide your front foot forward and drop your back leg lower. Hold the stretch for 15 seconds and repeat three times per side.

After stretching consistently two or three times per week for several weeks, you will begin to see improvements in your range of motion. Be patient with stretching and try not to rush your progress by overstretching, which can injure your muscles. Proper stretching leaves you relaxed and feeling good. If you are sore after stretching, you need to lower the intensity. Yoga practitioners recommend listening to relaxing music while stretching to settle your body into a relaxed state and to encourage you to move through your stretches slowly.

You can enhance your stretching program with regular massage, which helps to lengthen your muscles, break up knots in their fibers, and improve your circulation. In fact, a massage just before stretching prepares your muscle fibers to lengthen. If you can't have a full massage, you can achieve a similar effect by using a foam roller (see Cool Toys for Dry-Land Training on page 132). If you receive professional massages, ask your therapist to focus on muscle groups specific to swimming.

STRENGTH TRAINING

Whether you are training simply for greater fitness or with a specific competitive goal, you should add a strengthening program to your training. Until recently, swimmers limited their strength building to what they believed to be the critical swimming muscles—shoulders, triceps, back, and some leg muscles. However, coaches now know that swimmers achieve the best results, such as faster swimming, fewer injuries, and improved muscle balance, by training all of the stabilizing and reciprocal muscles in a full-body routine.

One of the primary areas of focus for swimmers in a strengthening program is the midsection, or core, of the body. Swimmers with strong core muscles retain their body position and their stroke technique better over longer distances and at faster speeds. As Coach Jim says, "The stronger your abdominals are, the faster you'll swim."

When talking about strength training, most swimmers visualize a traditional gym setting with weight-training equipment. However, weight training is just one of several options for your strength training program. You can work on a basic strength building program almost anywhere, including home, in a hotel room while traveling, or on a pool deck with friends. By using bands, balls (see Cool Toys for Dry-Land Training on page 132), your own body weight, and a little creativity, you can exercise all of the major muscle groups without ever going to a gym. Health clubs and YMCAs typically offer group exercise classes that focus on building full-body strength using bands, hand weights, and similar pieces of equipment. If you don't have the time or motivation to spend hours in a gym, these options will allow you to benefit from a strengthening program.

Another popular and coach-approved choice for swimmers is Pilates, a strength training program developed by Joseph Pilates in the 1920s. This exercise method has gained approval of athletes at all levels. Pilates emphasizes stabilizing and strengthening the abdominal, lower-back, hips, and buttocks muscles, or what Joseph Pilates called the *powerhouse* of the body. Like yoga, Pilates is a mind–body program that focuses on slow and controlled movements, rhythmic breathing, and quality over quantity. If you have limited time and want the best return on your time, you can choose one or two Pilates sessions each week for strength and flexibility training. The improving balance, strength, and flexibility in the core muscles will help you improve your water skills as well.

If you choose weights for strength training, consult with a strength training coach or a personal trainer and read some of the excellent books that detail the facets of weight training and illustrate proper form. It is essential to understand when and how to bring the many goals of weight training, including muscular endurance, strength, and power, into your program. With the right resources, you can develop a program that meets your specific needs and complements your swimming.

Whether you are on the pool deck or in a gym, your strengthening program should follow a few essential guidelines to help you achieve the best results and reduce the risk of injury. Always begin with a warm-up of 10 to 15 minutes, which can include a short jog, the use of a cardio machine such as an elliptical trainer, or any cardiovascular exercise that raises your heart rate into an aerobic zone (60 to 70 percent of MHR). After the warm-up, move through the workout from the largest muscle groups (abdominals) to the smaller, more specific ones (arms). Finally, scheduling 10 minutes to relax and stretch your muscles at the conclusion of your session will reduce any soreness you may feel the next day.

Cool Toys for Dry-Land Training

Athletes who do their dry-land training in a gym have the luxury of selecting from a variety of equipment, such as hand weights, full weight machines, and balls of every size and weight. If you're looking to train at home without building a small gym, there are many options. You can complete a full-body workout with just a few pieces of basic training equipment, such as the four listed here. As with all training, begin with just a few repetitions before building up, paying attention to good form.

Stability ball This amazingly versatile piece of equipment is known by many other names, including Swiss ball, balance ball, and exercise ball. This big round toy uses the many muscles of the body's core to maintain balance in any exercise. For example, while doing a traditional abdominal crunch, you will use your middle and lateral abdominal muscles, back muscles, hamstrings, and hip flexors to stabilize your body on the ball. The many stability ball exercises illustrated on Web sites, books, and videos make it easy to add variety to your dry-land training.

Exercise bands Use bands, which are available in varying thicknesses, to provide resistance while exercising through any range of motion. A few examples of exercises with bands are internal rotation, external rotation, and rowing from the basic strength training program listed in the next section of this chapter. Select thicker bands that will provide more resistance to work larger muscles. Reserve the thin bands for the smaller muscles of the shoulders.

Medicine balls Medicine balls, available in all weights and sizes, add challenge and variety to your workouts. When you throw a medicine ball to the ground, in the air, or back and forth with a partner, you strengthen your upper extremities while challenging your balance and core. Choose a lightweight ball for more explosive movements that increase the speed of muscle contraction, which leads to greater power. Look for ideas for medicine ball training through the Internet, books, and videos.

Foam roller Although these are traditionally favored by runners, more and more swimmers now use foam rollers. These hard foam cylinders help relieve tight muscles by applying the pressure of your body weight to sore areas as you roll across it. You can benefit by rolling your upper-back and latissimus dorsi muscles. Similar to a deep muscle massage, rolling just prior to stretching will result in a more effective stretch.

BASIC STRENGTHENING PROGRAM

The following program of six exercises provides an introduction to strength training and an opportunity to get a jump-start on a more comprehensive program. If you have time, expand on this program to target all your major muscle groups and work them in a variety of ways. Use the following table as a guide for gradually building your strengthening program.

Sample Guide for Strengthening Program

Week	Number of sets	Number of repetitions per set
1-2	1	10-12
3-4	2	12-15
5-6	3	15-20

- *Warm-up.* Schedule 10 to 15 minutes to use a cardio machine, take a brisk walk, or go for a light jog to move your muscles and raise your heart rate.

- *Front plank.* The standard position for front plank looks like a push-up, except your forearms are placed on the mat with your elbows bent at 90 degrees. Make each hand into a fist and place them on the mat pinky-side down. Elevate the body to a plank position, holding your upper arms squarely under your shoulders, keeping your head in line with your spine, and curling your toes up to maintain footing on the mat (see figure 11.11). If this position is too challenging, modify it by placing your knees on the mat. Draw your shoulder blades down (as if to put them in your back pockets) and pull your navel in toward your spine. Hold this plank position for 15 to 30 seconds.

Figure 11.11 The front-plank position strengthens your upper body as well as your core muscles.

As you progress, add hip twists to the plank to recruit your oblique abdominal muscles. Keeping your spine in alignment, alternately tip your left and right hips. Begin with 5 repetitions per side and build up to 15 per side.

- *Side plank.* Lie on your side, bend your elbow to 90 degrees, and place your forearm and elbow on the mat. Elevate your body to form a side plank position, maintaining a straight line from your head down your spine to the point of contact on the mat—either your knees (modified) or your feet (see figure 11.12). You may place your opposite hand on the mat for support, but as you progress, try to rest it on your side or raise it perpendicular to the mat. Maintain the plank position for 15 to 30 seconds.

Figure 11.12 The side-plank position is a test of overall core strength.

- *Y-lift.* Lie facedown, extend your arms over your head, and place them flat on the mat to the sides in a Y shape. Pull your shoulder blades down, as though you are putting them in your back pockets, and squeeze them together. Raise your arms off of the mat and then lower them, maintaining good form and control during both the up-and-down movements (see figure 11.13).

Figure 11.13 With arms extended outward and thumbs pointed upward, raise arms off the mat.

- *L-lift.* Lie facedown on an exercise bench or on the corner of a bed with both arms hanging down. Squeeze your shoulder blades back and down, lift your elbows up, and bend them to a 90-degree angle. Your upper arms should be parallel to the ground and your forearms should be perpendicular to the ground, creating a pair of Ls (see figure 11.14a). From this position, rotate your arms at the elbow until your forearms are parallel to the ground (see figure 11.14b), then lower them again, keeping the movement smooth and controlled. This exercise stabilizes the shoulders, strengthens the rotator cuff, and improves scapular strength to aid muscle movement.

Figure 11.14 L-lift with *(a)* forearms perpendicular to the ground and *(b)* forearms parallel to the ground.

- *Internal and external rotation.* Fasten a sport cord to a railing at approximately the same height as your elbows. Stand an arm's length away from the railing with your right side facing it and hold the band with your right hand. Begin with your elbow flexed to 90 degrees and held close to your side with the knuckles of your hand facing the railing (see figure 11.15a). While keeping your elbow at your side, slowly pull the band inward toward your stomach, then slowly release it back out toward the railing. This process rotates the shoulder internally.

Continue holding the band with the right hand with your right elbow bent to 90 degrees and tucked against body, but turn around so that your left side is toward the railing. Your right forearm will be resting across your abdomen. Slowly pull the band away from your abdomen out to the side, and then slowly release it to its original position. This process rotates the shoulder externally.

Repeat the internal rotation exercise on the left side, followed by the external rotation (see figure 11.15*b*).

Figure 11.15 *(a)* Internal rotation on the right side and *(b)* external rotation on the left side.

- *Rowing.* Fasten a sport cord to a railing. Stand facing the railing and grab one end the sport cord with each of your hands. Step back so that your arms are straight and the sport cord is taut. Stand up straight with your shoulders pulled back and down, then pull your elbows back, keeping your palms facing down (see figure 11.16*a*). Turn your fists over so your palms face up and slowly release the band as your arms straighten out again (see figure 11.16*b*). Rowing exercises strengthen your upper back, triceps, and biceps.

Figure 11.16 Rowing with sport cord.

- *Cool-down.* Schedule 10 to 15 minutes to stretch and relax after completing your workout. This is the ideal time to stretch your muscles.

Most swimmers feel the effect of a strengthening program after 6 to 8 weeks of consistent biweekly sessions. Be patient and consistent with your effort and you will see results.

VARIETY

Because of the popularity of triathlons and group exercise classes offered through YMCAs and health clubs, cross-training has now become a household word. The secret is out—training in another sport or activity will complement your primary sport by exercising your muscles in a different way and adding interest and variety to your weekly training schedule. This book cannot address the endless list of cross-training options. However, this next section discusses a few of the most popular cross-training choices for adult swimmers.

Running, jogging, and power walking all work the cardiorespiratory system and bring an additional weight-bearing component to fitness programs. Coach Mo, who is primarily a runner, advises her swimmers to begin any type of running, jogging, or walking program gradually on soft, level surfaces. You can reduce your risk of injury by investing in a supportive pair of shoes designed specifically for running or walking. Over time, running and jogging can reduce hip and leg flexibility, so if you cross-train on the roads or trails, be sure to schedule time to stretch afterward.

Coach Jim cross-trains with a bicycle to build his aerobic stamina and increase his leg strength for a stronger kick in the pool. Swimmers who choose to bike discover that it gives their overworked shoulders a chance to rest. Make sure you size your bike to the proper fit or consult a professional to recommend what are the best options.

Swimmers of all levels are discovering the amazing benefits of yoga, which include relaxation, improved core strength for balance and stability, breath control, and flexibility. Yoga is similar to Pilates but adds a spiritual component and teaches you how to simultaneously work some muscles and relax others. Yoga isolates and works only the muscles needed for a particular pose, an essential skill for fluid swimming strokes. Another critical element of yoga that also helps in the pool is relaxed and controlled breathing. Coach Jim, an avid yoga fan, says, "The lungs are taught to expand fully, thus increasing flow of oxygen to the body and providing more fuel for the muscles used in swimming." Swimmers with tight muscles will benefit from the increased flexibility that comes with practicing yoga.

Health clubs, YMCAs, and community centers typically offer classes that may include yoga, Pilates, and weight workouts. Any of these classes are great options for swimmers on the go. If you decide to try a class, introduce yourself to the instructor on the first day and explain your goals. These classes are often very social and can fit easily into a regular routine.

The key to combining cross-training with your fitness program is to introduce new exercises gradually and to vary the intensity. Look at each day of your week and decide which days work best for the kind of workout you are considering. You might choose a yoga class to relax your muscles the day after a high-intensity sprint set rather than a leg-intensive running workout. With a little creativity and planning, you can put together a weekly workout schedule that maximizes your training time, provides interest and variety, and keeps you motivated.

Coach, My Shoulder Hurts

Repetitive errors in stroke mechanics are the primary cause of swimming injuries. Almost all swimming injuries develop over a long period and result from exaggerated stress on the intrinsic structures of the joint.

The most common swimming injury is bicipital tendinitis, caused by a straight-arm pull and dropped elbow in freestyle. Think of your arm as a lever and of the front of your shoulder as its fulcrum. Straightening your arm during the pull lengthens the lever, which places stress on the shoulder. If your arm is in the high-elbow position, your upper arm becomes a shorter lever, which places less stress on the shoulder.

Most swimmers who develop tendinitis from this stroke error say that their pain is most intense early in the underwater phase of the pull. Swimmers with a straight-arm pull place the biceps tendon in an unfavorable position for enduring stress that makes them more vulnerable to irritation. Inversely, swimmers with proper arm and elbow technique during the pull exert the maximum strength of their large girdle muscles, which places less stress on the biceps tendon.

Stay focused on technique as you tire, especially if you have shoulder problems. Don't rush the early part of the underwater phase of the pull, bend your elbow, and keep it high throughout the pull to avoid shoulder problems.

INJURY CARE AND PREVENTION

Even swimmers with great attention to stroke technique and a carefully planned training program sometimes get injured. The secret to getting through an athletic injury is to react quickly with a rehabilitative plan, which includes resting the muscle or joint, rebuilding it through strength training and stretching, and taking steps to prevent reinjury. Athletes who are disciplined in their rehabilitative care and who stay positive work through injuries quickly and successfully.

The following list of tips on surviving injury is based on years of athletic and coaching experience.

- *Listen.* When your body alerts you to an injury, immediately stop and listen. By paying attention to the first signals of pain, swimmers' injuries would be less complicated, their recovery time would be reduced, and their training plans would be less disrupted. Although this point seems obvious, swimmers sometimes ignore the pain and continue swimming in a state of denial until they cannot lift their arms up.

- *Rest.* Rest the injured area by choosing a different activity for a few days. If you a have shoulder injury, you can focus on your legs with a kicking-only pool workout. Other options include cross-training favorites such as bike riding, cardio machines, Pilates, and yoga.

- *Ice.* Although it is not always convenient to use, ice is the most effective anti-inflammatory. Holding a bag of ice on an injury for 10 to 15 minutes a few times each day, particularly after exercise or massage, reduces inflammation significantly.

- *Consult a professional.* If the pain continues after a few days of rest, seek the advice of a physical therapist (PT). An experienced PT can create a personalized plan of recovery that will get you back in the pool quicker than if you simply waited for the injury to heal. With a comprehensive PT program that includes stretching, strengthening, massage, and ice, you can return to the pool stronger and more resistant to future setbacks.

- *Massage.* Massage is an effective way to bring blood flow back to the injured area and is often part of physical therapy. Occasionally, getting a deep-tissue massage from a qualified professional helps athletes work out muscle pain that signals the start of an injury.

- *Focus on the positives.* Keep a positive attitude and stick with your training plan as much as possible. Use cross-training alternatives for cardiorespiratory conditioning and take the opportunity to explore Pilates or yoga. Swimmers who have always wanted to improve their kicking can put in the extra effort on the legs while resting their shoulders.

- *Make a prevention plan.* This is perhaps the most important tip for athletes who want to get off or stay off the injured list. Ask yourself how the injury occurred. If you were simply doing too much too soon, you should form a plan for a more gradual buildup. If it is a problem with your stroke technique, consult with your swim coach or a qualified instructor on how you can improve your stroke efficiency and reduce injury-provoking stress.

If you gradually build into and maintain the stretching and strengthening program presented in this chapter, you will be more resistant to injury. Using the internal and external rotation exercises with a low-resistance band, a high number of repetitions, and the your available range of motion will make you less susceptible to shoulder injuries. All prevention plans should include core strengthening exercises.

Generally, if you actively participate in a dry-land program that includes cross-training, strength training, and stretching, you're less likely to become injured. However, if you do become injured, you're also more likely to recover quickly. The benefits of dry-land training, particularly improved core strength and balance, better position you for a successful, injury-free training program that will provide variety and motivation for many years.

A well-designed long-term training plan will include one or more dry-land components. Until recently, swimmers often overlooked the benefits of dry-land exercises for their training. A well-designed strength and flexibility program creates a more fluid and streamlined body line in the water and improves power through the stroke, which makes you more efficient both in the pool and in the open water. Variety in training, such as cross-training in other sports or taking organized fitness classes, is crucial for avoiding swimming injury, overtraining, and burnout. Keeping your swim training a priority and wrapping in these other elements can become a balancing act, but the result, a whole-body training plan, will keep you swim-fit for life.

Open-Water Training

Open-water swimming is swimming in its purest form—it's just you and the elements.

—Steven Munatones, USA Swimming open-water coach and former open-water world champion

Evidence shows that ancient peoples were swimming long before the first hole was dug for a pool. Cave drawings dating back to 4000 BC depict swimmers doing a variant of the crawl stroke. Swimming was one of seven agilities required for knights in the Middle Ages. In the mid-1800s, Native Americans used an early version of the crawl stroke to win a challenge against the British, who were swimming breaststroke.

The open water—lakes, rivers, bays, and oceans—continue to intrigue us. The sheer beauty of these bodies of water entices many swimmers to relax in the elements. Others enjoy the unstructured feel of swimming without the limits of walls and lane lines. Many are drawn to the challenge of swimming across a specific distance, such as a river, lake, or channel crossing. More than 1000 swimmers have crossed the English Channel since Matthew Webb made the first swim from England to France in 1875. For those who are so inclined, open-water competitions offer a variety of distances in a diverse set of water conditions, ranging from calm lakes to ocean breaks.

This chapter begins with the basics of safety and relaxation in the open water. The uncontrolled nature of the open water is inherently riskier and requires swimmers to understand and be prepared for the water temperature, currents, depth, and other conditions. The second section of this chapter discusses the differences between pool and open-water swimming, including stroke rate, length, and navigation. You should first gain confidence in the skills specific to open water in the deep end of a pool before venturing out.

SAFETY FIRST

Moms and coaches offer the same safety advice: Use your common sense, and never swim alone. The following guidelines will get you started safely in your open-water endeavors. Ultimately, successful swimming in nature's elements is about understanding the water conditions, knowing your own personal abilities, and using good judgment.

Swim With Supervision

Swim in groups, or as your camp counselor used to say, "Buddy up!" If the group includes novice swimmers or anyone new to open water, recruit additional experienced swimmers to come along. Stick together while swimming; even if you must slow down, wait or circle a slower swimmer.

The best option is to swim with lifeguard supervision or with an escort boat. Many beaches and lakefronts provide open-swimming areas beyond the recreational swimming area but still under lifeguard supervision. These situations are excellent for open-water swimming training. If you will be outside of a supervised area, have a friend accompany you in a boat to assist you when you are tired, make you more visible to other watercraft, aid with navigation, and provide you with fluids and food as needed.

Understand the Water Currents

Be absolutely sure that you understand the conditions of the water you are diving into. This section outlines some questions to consider.

Is there a current? Even the most experienced open-water swimmers can have trouble swimming against a strong current, so you must consider the direction and strength of currents before getting wet. Swim against the current first so you can take advantage of the current's push on your return, when you might be more tired. Currents are affected by many factors, including wind, gravity, and the changing tides in tidal zones. If you are unsure of the current's direction, check with a lifeguard or waterfront staff member.

Continue to monitor the current while you are swimming, since its direction and strength can change quickly. Experienced swimmers may be able to gauge the current's direction by feeling for increases and decreases in water flow. Observe your speed as you pass a reference point such as the ocean bottom or a landmark. The direction in which anchored boats point also indicates current.

Can you spot a rip current? If you plan to swim in any body of water with changing tides, such as an ocean or a large lake, you should know how to spot a rip current and what to do if you are caught in one (see Why Rip Currents Form on facing page).

Are the tides going in or out? Check local tide charts to understand daily high and low tide measurements. A change in tides can mean a change in the direction of the current.

Why Rip Currents Form

Waves travel from deep to shallow water and break near the shoreline. When waves break more strongly in some locations than others, circulation cells form that are known as *rip currents*: narrow, fast-moving belts of water traveling away from the shore.

How to Identify Rip Currents

Look for any of these clues:

- A channel of churning, choppy water
- An area with a noticeable difference in water color
- A line of foam, seaweed, or debris moving steadily seaward
- A break in the pattern of incoming waves

Any of the preceding clues may indicate the presence of rip currents, but they can also occur without presenting these signs. The average beachgoer has difficulty identifying rip currents. For your safety, be aware of this major surf-zone hazard. Polarized sunglasses make the rip current clues easier to see.

Swimming Out of a Rip Current

If you find yourself in a rip current, follow these guidelines for swimming to safety.

- Remain calm to conserve energy and think clearly.
- Don't fight the current. Swim out of the current in a direction parallel to the shoreline. If you are unable to swim out of the rip current, float or calmly tread water.
- Attempt to swim toward the shore only when you are out of the current.
- If you are still unable to reach shore, draw attention to yourself: Face the shore, wave your arms, and yell for help.

If you see someone in trouble, ask a lifeguard for help. If a lifeguard is not available, have someone call 9-1-1. Throw the victim something that floats and call out instructions on how to escape. Remember, many people drown while trying to save someone else from a rip current.

Adapted from National Weather Service, 2005, *Rip current safety*. [Online]. Available: http://www.ripcurrents. noaa.gov/overview.shtml [July 7, 2008].

Monitor Water and Weather Conditions

When you venture into the open water, you must understand the environmental and weather conditions. Unlike the controlled and consistent water of a pool, open water in lakes, rivers, and streams changes daily, even hourly, with shifts in the weather. Open-water swimmers must be aware of the conditions and weather forecast for their chosen area. You can answer many of the questions on this list by watching weather reports, consulting tide charts, and talking to local waterfront authorities.

What is the temperature of the water? Make hydration a priority when you swim in warm water, particularly on a warm day. On the other side of the spectrum, cold-water swimmers should be aware of the symptoms, treatment, and prevention of hypothermia. Know your water temperature tolerance and don't put yourself in dangerous situations.

What are the conditions at the water's bottom? Are there rocks? Does the ground drop off gradually or quickly? If you understand the surface of the water's bottom, you will be better prepared to make safe entries and exits. This awareness is particularly important for swimmers participating in open-water competitions who must get in and out of the water quickly.

Hypothermia

You risk becoming hypothermic when your body heat escapes faster than you can produce it and your body temperature drops below normal (98.6 °F; 37 °C). Hypothermia sets in when the body temperature reaches 95 °F (35 °C), which can happen very quickly in cold-water conditions. Because the body loses heat more quickly in water than in air, you can become hypothermic in almost any body of open water. Therefore, you should be aware of the symptoms, the treatment, and—most important—the prevention of hypothermia. Swimmers with hypothermia are often unaware that they are exhibiting symptoms, so swimming partners should stay close together and observe one another.

Symptoms of Hypothermia
- Uncontrollable shivering
- Lack of coordination
- Slurred speech
- Slowed breathing and heart rate
- Pale skin
- Blue lips, ears, or hands
- Confusion, difficulty with reasoning and judgment
- Drowsiness or stupor (in severe states)

Treatment
- Get out of the water and remove wet clothing.
- Warm the body with towels and blankets, particularly the neck, armpit, and groin areas.
- Warm the body's core with hot drinks.
- In cases of severe hypothermia, carefully monitor heart rate and call 9-1-1.

Prevention
- Dress for cold-water conditions with gear such as a wet suit, a neoprene cap, two swim caps, or neoprene booties.
- Swim in groups and watch each other.

Is seaweed present? Small sprays of seaweed are part of the open-water experience and are, at most, an annoyance. Avoid large beds of seaweed, such as kelp. If you find yourself in an uncomfortable amount of seaweed, don't try to kick it off or your ankles and feet may become tangled. Swim straight out to find clearer water.

Is the water clear? The water will not be particularly clear at the ocean break, since the breaking waves pull up sand from the bottom. This is natural and the water past the break should be clear. However, for one reason or another, some bodies of water are less clear than others. This can be particularly disconcerting for new swimmers, since they may have difficulty seeing their hands underwater as they swim.

A deep reddish brown coloring to the water could indicate a *red tide*, or an algal bloom. Algae, specifically phytoplankton, accumulate rapidly in these areas. Some swimmers have experienced respiratory and skin irritation from swimming in these conditions, but these areas are typically not banned.

Is the water clean? Most beaches provide a water report on a weekly, if not daily, basis to ensure the safety of swimmers, surfers, and other water enthusiasts. Look for information about your chosen swimming area through your local weather service or waterfront staff.

Are jellyfish around? If you are swimming in an area where jellyfish have been reported, wear a wet suit to protect yourself from being stung. If you brush up against a jellyfish and get stung, swim back to shore and consult a doctor. Most jellyfish encounters simply leave a rash at the site of the sting, but some species can be quite toxic to humans.

What are the weather conditions? Weather conditions can affect whether you swim and where you swim. While you are swimming, keep an eye on the weather and look for changes in wind, incoming fog, or storms. Variations in wind speed and direction can affect swells and currents. Deep fog diminishes visibility, which can make any swimmer disoriented. In addition, if you cannot see anything, then nobody can see you, including watercraft operators and other swimmers. Lightning and thunder, indicators of an electrical storm, are warnings to stay out of the water until the threat has passed.

Are you visible to traffic? Are you swimming in an area shared by boats, jet skiers, or other water vehicles? Always make yourself visible with a brightly colored swim cap. If watercraft might be in the area, you must stay close to an escort boat.

You will have a great open-water experience if you understand the water conditions and use good sense. Look for resources about water safety and the specific rules and regulations for your local beaches and swimming areas. The Internet is a valuable tool for learning more about tides, water temperature, and swell conditions.

Big Fish Stories

Fear of sharks has kept many pool swimmers from testing the ocean waters. The 1975 blockbuster movie *Jaws*, featuring a series of shark attacks in a small beach community, provided vivid images that convinced many people that ocean swimming should be left to the big fish. However, the actual chance of being attacked by a shark is very small. You take a greater risk while driving to and from the beach. According to the International Shark Attack File (ISAF), located in the Florida Museum of Natural History, the low number of shark attacks indicates that these big fish do not feed on humans by nature. Most shark attacks are simply due to mistaken identity.

In 2007, there were 71 reported unprovoked shark attacks on humans worldwide and only one fatality, which is significantly lower than the 2007 fatality rate for bee stings and snake bites. ISAF director George Burgess says, "It's quite spectacular that out of hundreds of millions of people worldwide spending hundreds of millions of hours in the water in activities that are often very provocative to sharks, such as surfing, there was only one incident resulting in a fatality." The number of shark attacks has been increasing, which is a reflection of the rise in aquatic recreation and the improved documentation of attacks over the past few decades. However, the fatality rate has been on a downward trend, due in part to improved beach safety, medical response to attacks, and increased public awareness. To avoid the very low risk of an attack, Burgess advises swimmers to seek safety in numbers and stay with their group. "Sharks, like all predators, tend to go after solitary individuals, the weak and the infirm, and are less likely to attack people or fish in groups" (Keen 2007).

DRESS THE PART

As with a trip to the pool, you'll want to pack a bag with all the specific tools for open-water swimming. Here is a quick list of open-water essentials.

1. *Brightly colored swim caps.* You should pack more than one, in case you rip the first or someone in your group forgets a cap.

2. *Dependable goggles.* You will not want to deal with foggy or leaky goggles while swimming in open water where visibility is a priority. Be sure you have a dependable pair and a spare set that have been adjusted for a good, comfortable fit. See chapter 9, Workout Essentials, for more information about design, fit, and defogging tips for goggles.

3. *Wet suit.* Manufacturers of wet suits have kept up with growing enthusiasm for open-water swimming and triathlon sports. The newest designs feature increased shoulder mobility for freestyle swimming and lighter, denser neoprene for added buoyancy, speed, and warmth. Look for a tight yet comfortable fit through the shoulders, neck, and torso. Because swimming is the only way to truly judge a wet suit's fit, many triathletes and open-water swimmers choose to rent a variety of designs before purchasing one.

4. *Earplugs.* In cold-water swims, earplugs may help keep you warmer but will decrease your ability to hear what is going on around you.

5. *Watch.* Although watches are not recommended for pool swimmers, open-water swimmers should wear a watch to keep track of their swimming time.

6. *Sunscreen.* Sun protection is a must for outdoor swimmers. The Skin Cancer Foundation recommends reducing lifetime sun exposure by applying sunscreen year-round, even on cloudy days, to give skin the best chance at long-term health. Sunscreen is even more important in the open water because the sun reflects off the water and directly onto swimmers' skin (www.skincancer.org/prevention/year-round-sun-protection.html).

7. *Chafe control.* Salt water, tight-fitting suits and wet suits, and the repetitive nature of swimming can all create chafing around the neck and arms. Marathon open-water swimmers often rub lanolin, a natural water-repellent lubricant, on the skin in high-friction areas. A cheaper, readily available option is petroleum jelly. You can also find several other easy-to-apply products in convenient sticks and tubes that prevent or minimize the effects of chafing.

8. *Fluids and food.* If you will be swimming for over one hour, it is essential that you drink periodically. Keep your fluids on your escort boat or in a place you can return to, such as a dock or beach area. For longer swims, add calories to your drink or eat energy bars. Tuck gel packets loaded with carbohydrate and electrolytes into your suit to consume on the go. Long-distance swimmers learn through trial and error what their own personal nutritional intake should be.

9. *Towel and warm clothing.* When you get out of the water, particularly after cold-water swims, get dry and warm quickly. Prepare by packing a large towel or blanket and a set of warm clothes.

On arriving home after each swim, repack your bag and assess what else you might need. Over time, this equipment list will evolve into a packing list tailored for your personal preferences and needs.

RELAX

Swimmers who are not just a little bit anxious about diving into the open water for the first time are rare. Compared to a crystal-clear pool with the guidance of the painted black line and the lane lines, the blackness of a lake, river, or ocean is intimidating. Swimmers wonder where they are going and who else might be sharing the water with them.

To gain confidence and relax in nature's swimming pools, begin by educating yourself about the local waters and their potential risks. The previous section discusses ways you can minimize your risks and maximize your experience. You will feel much less anxious if you understand what you are dealing with.

If you first master basic swimming skills in a pool, you will be able to venture into the local swimming hole with self-assurance. Focus on the relaxation, body position, and breathing skills from chapter 3, Develop Your Water Sense. Practice skills specific to the open water in the pool before heading into the elements, including adjusting, taking off, and putting on your goggles in deep water while floating on your back or treading water. Test out your wet suit to get comfortable putting it on and taking it off, and to see how it feels when you are swimming.

If you're a novice open-water swimmer, enter the water slowly, particularly if you're unfamiliar with the bottom. Allow your body to acclimate to the temperature change. Then begin swimming close to the shoreline at a comfortable pace, concentrating on exhalations and breathing comfortably. Focus on a goal for each swim: to reach a particular buoy or landmark, to swim for a specific number of minutes, or improve time or technique over a given course.

Although a wet suit might seem constricting, it is an amazing flotation device and can give you a tremendous feeling of confidence for open-water adventures. Some swimmers find that loosening the neck of the wet suit helps them relax and breathe more easily. If you normally swim with fins in the pool, bring them to the open water. Fins and other swim aids are not allowed in competitions but are perfectly acceptable if your only goal is to enjoy and relax in nature.

Every swimmer who dives into oceans, rivers, and lakes wonders about the water's natural inhabitants. Rest assured that the fish are much more intimidated by you, particularly if you are in a group, than you are by them. To put your mind at rest, simply ask the local lifeguards and waterfront staff what types of fish are in the water.

By getting in the open water on a consistent basis and slowly increasing the length of each swim, you will build the same level of confidence outdoors that you have in the pool. The unstructured nature of open-water swimming is a refreshing change and a great complement to pool swimming. The rewards for you and your training program are worth the time that you invest getting comfortable in this environment.

BREATHING AND STROKE PATTERNS

The technical aspects of the freestyle stroke in open water are similar to those in a pool. If you're a new swimmer, avoid the common mistakes of breathing too little and kicking too much early in the swim, which lead to fatigue. Stroke rate and arm recovery will vary somewhat in the open water.

In the open water, breathe early and breathe often. Breathing every third stroke in the freestyle simply does not provide enough air exchanges to maintain steady effort over a long distance. Very few competitors in Olympic freestyle distance events (800 meters to 10K) breathe every third stroke. They do, however, breathe on both sides throughout the event to keep up with the competition and to maintain symmetry and balance in their strokes. Distance swimmers typically alternate two to four right-side breaths with two to four left-side breaths or, when training in a pool, mix one length of right-side breathing with one length of left-side breathing.

Although all swimmers should learn to breathe comfortably on either side, or bilaterally, the practice is crucial for open-water swimmers and triathletes. There are situations, when swells, wind, or choppy water inevitably prevent you from breathing on a certain side, forcing you to use the other. Breathing on the side parallel to the shoreline helps you navigate and keep an equal distance from the shore. Confidence in bilateral breathing prepares you for any open-water situation and helps prevent neck and shoulder fatigue in longer swims.

The extra buoyancy of the wet suit and high density of salt water make open-water swimming a real treat if you struggle with body position. Riding higher in the water, you will enjoy a higher distance per stroke and a somewhat lower stroke rate. Another difference is that the neoprene in the wet suit constricts the arm and limits bend in the elbow on the arm recovery. In the open water, you may opt for a higher, more loping stroke that keeps the hands free of the choppy water.

Because oceans, lakes, and rivers lack the familiar walls of the pool for rest stops, keep a relaxation phase in your stroke cycles: riding out each stroke, working from the core muscles, but maintaining a relaxed and rhythmic flow through the water.

Keep your kicking light and rhythmic, picking up the pace only to pass another swimmer in a race situation or to make a strong finish. Triathletes, in particular, should manage the use of the legs to pace properly for the bike ride and run that follow the swim.

GET IN, GET AROUND, AND GET OUT

New skills to learn for the open-water venue include entering, exiting, and navigating through the water without the luxury of lane lines and a black line painted on the bottom. You can learn and practice most of these skills, which are vital to open-water training sessions, before heading to the beach.

Successful entries and exits begin with understanding the terrain of the water's bottom. Are there rocks, plants, or coral? Does the ground drop off gradually or quickly? In competitions, swimmers aim to move through the shallow section out to the deeper water as quickly as possible.

If you have smooth ground for your entry, first run through the surf holding your knees high to clear the incoming wave break. As you run, swing your heels to the outside of your knees to keep them free of the waves (see figure 12.1).

Figure 12.1 Keep your knees high as you run through deep water.

As soon as the water level reaches your midthigh area, start *dolphin diving*, or surface diving through the water toward the bottom, leading with your hands and cradling your head between your arms in a streamlined position. When you reach the bottom, pull forward with your hands and draw your legs under you (see figure 12.2*a*), using them to push up to the surface (see figure 12.2*b*). Then, dive forward again. Continue leading with your hands and diving through any approaching waves. You can extend your underwater time by grabbing the sand or dirt at the water's bottom and pulling your body forward. In deeper water, experienced swimmers extend their underwater time during the dolphin dive by doing an underwater pull similar to a breaststroke pullout combined with a dolphin kick. Practice this skill in the shallow end of a pool, preferably waist deep, until you are confident.

When the water gets deep enough for swimming, go for it. The key to successful water entries is to keep your momentum; do not stop. Run with high knees, dolphin dive, and then swim, staying focused on your goal of reaching the deeper water. In a race situation, focus on the first buoy.

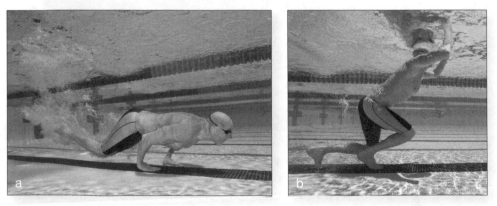

Figure 12.2 Dolphin diving: *(a)* reaching the bottom and *(b)* pushing back to the surface.

When exiting the water, you repeat the motions from the entry in reverse order. When you reach water that is waist level, begin to dolphin dive; when you reach water that is just above your knees, stand up and high-knee run out to the beach. When swimming in an ocean or a large lake, you will be able to ride the push of the waves coming into the shore. With good timing and the right wave, you can be carried all the way to the sand.

A lake, river, or ocean bottom that contains large rocks, plants, or coral will require more caution in entering and exiting. It may be safer to wade and then swim through the shallow areas, keeping an eye out for obstacles. When exiting water with a less-than-ideal bottom, many competitors swim until they beach themselves, then stand up and run out. This works very well in situations where silt or mud covering the water's floor makes for unsteady footing.

Swimming a straight course in open water is more challenging than working with a black line below you and lane lines beside you. The key to navigating through nature's waters is to have a visible set of buoys or land-marks to guide you and a sighting technique that does not disrupt the flow of your stroke. Sighting means taking a peek ahead at a predetermined target while you are swimming.

The cleanest and least disruptive style of sighting in the freestyle is a *peek-breathe* pattern. As you set your arm up for the catch at the front of the stroke, lift your head forward and up enough to clear the water with your goggles crocodile-style and take a quick look at your target (see figure 12.3*a*). As your arm continues through the underwater phase of the stroke (see figure 12.3*b*), turn your head toward that same side for your breath (see figure 12.3*c*). When sighting, your arm cycle should be one continuous motion that merges with the flow and rhythm of the stroke.

Choose landmarks that you can see with a quick peek. If you can't spot a buoy on the water, select a larger, more visible landmark in the same line. Large trees, buildings, and

Figure 12.3 Peek-breathe pattern: *(a)* At the front of your stroke, lift your head crocodile-style for a look at the target. *(b)* As your arm continues through the under-water stroke phase, *(c)* turn your head toward the same side for a breath.

land formations are easily visible, stationary landmarks. Begin by sighting every six to eight strokes and adjust this number higher or lower depending on how well you are staying on your line. It is good to know how well you can swim straight and which direction you tend to veer so you can make adjustments as you go. Because breathing to only one side can affect stroke balance, symmetry, and direction, pick a breathing pattern that uses both right and left sides. Switch to single-side breathing only when the conditions require it.

Open-water swimming is growing in popularity. Many waterfronts now keep a line of buoys available for swimmers to hone their skills as they traverse the shoreline and enjoy the freedom of swimming without walls, turns, and chlorine. Swimmers of all levels regularly compete in sanctioned open-water events with a variety of distances. Triathlons continue to bring land-loving athletes into waterfront venues. Chapter 15, Competing in Open Water, builds on this chapter by outlining strategies for preparing for and swimming in open-water events.

New swimmers and veterans of the open seas are driven by both the challenge and the simple beauty of swimming in oceans, lakes, and rivers. As you take on this challenge and build your confidence, your open-water swims will soon become some of your most memorable swimming experiences.

Make Your Plan for Success

I swam the race like I trained to swim it. It is not mathematical. I just let my body do it. It is a lot easier if you let your body do what it is trained for.

—Ian Thorpe, five-time gold medalist, 2000 and 2004 Olympic Games

Whether you are training for a specific competition or to achieve a higher level of fitness, a well-thought-out training plan will be your road map to success. With your months and weeks clearly charted out in your plan, you can complete your daily training with the confidence that you are on track to safely achieve your goals. Furthermore, the time you spend training will be more efficient, saving you from training aimlessly and risking injury or burnout.

Chapters 11 and 12 reviewed the principles of training and how they translate into pool workouts, dry-land training, and open-water swimming. Think of these principles as the map and the training plan as the road you plan to take. By choosing the route carefully from among the different paths to get to your goal, you can create a personal plan that will bring the desired results.

This chapter begins with a list of necessary qualities for a successful training plan, and then continues with monthly and weekly planning. You may want to chart your own personal route as you read. Although many swimmers like their plans detailed down to the day, others prefer to work from a rough draft. Regardless of your style, you should consider in advance what mixture of elements is right for you and your goals.

QUALITIES OF SUCCESSFUL PLANS

Several factors can contribute to the success or failure of a training plan. Training with a plan that is not appropriate can hinder your motivation and ultimately lead to injuries, setbacks, or burnout. Unsuccessful training plans are almost always missing one of these important qualities:

- *Start smart.* Every successful training plan begins with an honest assessment of current fitness, training history, age, and history of injuries. Coaches first assess an athlete's swimming *base*, or the amount, quality, and intensity of recent swimming training. They next consider the level of fitness in other sports, such as running, cycling, weight training, or Pilates. An adult new to swimming will start at a different point from an adult who has been lap swimming and is moving into a masters program.

- *Build gradually.* The general rule for building distance is to add a maximum of 10 percent to the total weekly distance from one week to the next and to add a maximum of 10 percent to the total distance of the longest workout from one week to the next.

- *Set interim goals.* Small milestones along the way to a bigger goal give you opportunities to measure your improvement and build confidence in the training plan and in yourself. For example, you might first build up to 30 minutes of workout time, then plan to increase the length of your workout in increments of 15 minutes. Many athletes plan small milestones like learning a new stroke or a flip turn, or swimming on a new base cruise interval. Smaller goals are incredible motivators and make it easier to achieve the long-term goal.

- *Make it interesting.* Training plans that provide variety in and out of the pool are quite simply more interesting and motivational. Furthermore, the right blend of dry-land training and cross-training helps improve strength, balance, and flexibility, which also makes you more efficient and faster.

- *Allow for rest.* Every successful training plan includes recovery workouts and rest days to give the body time to rebuild after periods of stress. Continuous training without designated rest and recovery days, or *overtraining*, leads to sports injuries and burnout. Overtraining and its effects can completely derail a training program, leaving you discouraged and unmotivated.

- *Allow for changes.* Athletes who make effective training plans allow time for their commitments outside of the pool and the gym, such as career, family, religious communities, and social activities. As you plan weekly and daily schedules, be honest with yourself about striking a balance between your training, your other priorities, and getting adequate sleep.

Set yourself up for success by making sure your new training program has all of these qualities before you begin. Don't be afraid to scale back or modify the plan to make it work for you and your life.

THREE TRAINING PHASES

Chapter 10, Pool Workouts, describes how athletes typically break down training plans into smaller, more manageable pieces through a process called periodization. The calendar of masters swimming competitions is designed with three or four seasons per year, allowing you to organize training to prepare for events within those periods. The periods are further divided into subperiods, or phases, to better address your needs as they change throughout your training. The transition from one phase of training to the next must be gradual, allowing you to adapt to the changing stresses. This chapter divides training plans into three phases: base and technique, endurance and strength, and tapering and racing.

Phase I: Base and Technique

In phase I of training, the focus is on improving technique and building an aerobic base. New swimmers are encouraged to train in this phase longer than more advanced swimmers, keeping a higher focus on technique and base building. The goal of this phase is to gradually increase weekly distance with slow-interval and overdistance sets. Focus on stroke technique in this phase, paying attention to body position, relaxed breathing, long strokes, streamlines, and proper turns. Phase I is an ideal time to introduce a stretching and core strengthening program that will complement your work in the pool and can be used throughout your entire training schedule. Consistent effort in phase I of the plan prepares you for the increased intensity of phases II and III.

Phase II: Endurance and Strength

Phase II features higher-intensity swimming. The focus is on swimming faster over longer distances by increasing your lactate threshold. When fast-interval, endurance, speed-play, and goal sets are properly mixed with recovery sets and dry-land training, you can reach a new level of fitness. This chapter also introduces sprint and power sets: high-intensity sets which are essential for fast swimming. As you move into phase II, you should gradually increase the amount of high-intensity swimming, vary your weekly schedules with dry-land activities and cross-training, and allow time for recovery. Many athletes, particularly triathletes, devote every fourth week in their training plans to adequate rest and recovery.

Many noncompetitive masters swimmers train almost exclusively in phase II, enjoying the many benefits of a high level of fitness. The conditioning, stress relief, and social aspects of masters swimming motivate them to stay in the water.

Phase III: Tapering and Racing

Phase III focuses on race-specific training: pacing, broken swims, starts, and turns. This phase is for swimmers who are training for specific events.

Swimmers with a good understanding of their goals, including specific events and performance targets, are better able to focus their training during this phase. For example, swimmers who understand exactly how they want to pace their 200-meter freestyle, including their estimated 50-meter split times, can craft more effective workouts than their teammates with less-detailed goals. Likewise, swimmers training to participate in a 1-mile (1.6 km) open-water race will be more successful if they study the course layout, determine their desired completion time, and tailor their workouts for that goal. For this reason, swimmers at every level are encouraged to set race-specific goals before, or during, this phase of training.

The final part of phase III, the taper, is a one- to three-week period of reduced distance and lower-intensity swimming that encourages full recovery for optimal performance in competition. Several factors influence the length of the tapering phase:

- *Age.* Because recovery time increases with age, older swimmers require a longer tapering period than younger swimmers.
- *Sex.* Men typically require a longer tapering period than women.
- *Size.* People with more muscle mass require a longer tapering period.
- *Event.* Sprinters should have a longer tapering period than distance swimmers.
- *Number of events.* The more events swimmers plan to do, the longer they should taper. For example, swimmers planning to compete in more than five events in a three-day competition will taper for longer than those planning to compete in a single event on one day.
- *Base.* Swimmers who have invested training time early, giving them a higher level of base conditioning, will benefit from a longer tapering period.
- *Size of event.* Swimmers training for a big event at the end of the season often choose to participate in at least one smaller midseason competition. They should schedule a mini taper of two or three days for the midseason meets and a major taper of two to three weeks for the final competition.

Several factors outside of the pool can affect the success of an athlete's tapering phase, including a strong positive outlook, a high-quality diet, sufficient rest, and low stress. It can be difficult for adults with busy careers and families to attain this stress-free ideal, but it is worth striving for. When you have invested months in preparation for a competition, nothing feels better than showing up on the morning of the event rested and ready to perform.

WEEKLY PLANNING

When structuring your training plan, first determine the length of the program and then divide the time into three phases. The number of weeks that you spend on the various training phases depends on several factors, including swimming experience, initial fitness level, age, specific event (distance, sprint, open-water, triathlon), and the total length of the training plan.

Next, you prepare weekly workout schedules within each phase of training. If you have many things to juggle each week, you might not know when to schedule specific workouts. The following guidelines for smart weekly scheduling can simplify this piece of the planning:

- *Swim three or four workouts each week.* Three or four swimming workouts per week are ideal if you're very busy and are seeking a healthy variety in training. Swimmers who do fewer than three pool workouts each week find it difficult, if not impossible, to improve. More than four weekly workouts are recommended only if you're preparing for long events.

- *Alternate types of workouts.* If possible, schedule similar workouts several days apart to allow your body time to recover. Separate your swimming and cross-training workouts with one or two days and your strength training workouts with two or more days.

  Furthermore, alternate the intensity of your workouts. For example, follow a rigorous cross-training day with a low-intensity workout day, such as swimming or stretching. Likewise, follow a high-intensity swim with a more relaxed activity.

- *Prioritize your swimming.* Most masters swim programs publish their daily and weekly workout schedules to designate what type of training swimmers can expect on any given day. This menu of workouts can help you create your own weekly plan. Select three or four workouts that fit your goals, write them into your plan, and schedule your dry-land training on alternating days.

- *Rest.* Schedule one full day of rest in your week to let your body recover. If you are not comfortable with a day of inactivity, schedule one day in your week with a light activity such as stretching, a yoga class, or easy cross-training.

The following four tables, each based on a 16-week training plan, provide guidelines for modifying the length and focus of each training phase for various types of swimmers. The sample schedules depict a typical week for each phase. As you sketch out your plan, remember that there is not a universal training plan. Your plan will be uniquely yours, designed to match your schedule and your life.

16-Week Training Plan Guidelines: Novice Swimmer

Experience level: Limited   **Goal:** Improved fitness

	Phase I	Phase II	Phase III
	7-9 weeks	7-9 weeks	0 weeks
Overview	In the beginning of this phase, spend as much as 85% of pool time focusing on stroke drills and technique. The goal is to relax while swimming over longer distances and to build a greater aerobic base. As technique improves, spend 40-50% of the time on technique and 50-60% on swimming. Begin with workouts 30 min long and gradually build up to 60 min. Alternate swimming workouts with stretching, strengthening, and cross-training for full-body fitness.	One of the three pool sessions should feature aerobic base conditioning, and the other two should feature higher-intensity workouts, such as endurance, fast-interval, fartlek, speed play, sprinting, or goal sets. Increase level of intensity gradually in order to adapt to the stress. Dry-land stretching becomes even more critical in this phase to facilitate muscle recovery and training adaptation.	If not planning to compete, don't use phase III.
Sample weekly schedule[3]	**Mon:** 30-60 min swimming: aerobic and technique	**Mon:** 60 min swimming: aerobic and anaerobic mix	
	Tues: 30-60 min cross-training[1]	**Tues:** 30-60 min cross-training[1]	
	Wed: 30-60 min swimming: aerobic and technique	**Wed:** 60 min swimming: aerobic and anaerobic mix	
	Thurs: 60 min strengthen and stretch[2]	**Thurs:** 60 min strengthen and stretch[2]	
	Fri: 30-60 min swimming: aerobic and technique	**Fri:** 30-60 min swimming: aerobic with sprints	
	Sat: 30-60 min cross-training[1] 30 min strengthen and stretch at home	**Sat:** 30-60 min cross-training[1] 30 min strengthen and stretch at home	
	Sun: Rest	**Sun:** Rest	

[1] Cross-training includes any dry-land cardio activity, such as bike riding, walking, or dancing.
[2] Strengthen and stretch includes Pilates, yoga, circuit-training classes, or your own at-home program.
[3] See appendix for sample swimming workouts for each category.

16-Week Training Plan Guidelines: Lap Swimmer

Experience level: Lap swimming only   **Goal:** First masters competition

	Phase I	Phase II	Phase III
	3-5 weeks	6-8 weeks	4-6 weeks
Overview	Expand base fitness level with a focus on aerobic swimming and technique, including stroke efficiency, negotiating the walls, streamlined position, flip turns, and making legal turns in all strokes. If not already in a strengthening program, gradually begin one for added core strength and flexibility. Cross-train for variety and full-body fitness.	One of the three pool sessions remains aerobic base conditioning, and the other two feature higher-intensity workouts, such as endurance, fast-interval, fartlek, speed play, sprinting, or goal sets. Increase level of intensity gradually in order to adapt to the stress. Dry-land stretching becomes even more critical in this phase to facilitate muscle recovery and training adaptation. Follow high-intensity swimming days with recovery days or low-intensity days. Select events for competition. Know the race distances and goal times before entering the race-specific phase III.	Narrow the focus to individual events, goal paces, race starts, and race finishes. Make race-pace sets a regular part of high-intensity workouts. Include adequate time for rest, recovery, and stretching to stay healthy for competition. Assess meet results and make changes in training if necessary. Focus on basic core strengthening exercises and stretching during dry-land training.
Sample weekly schedule[3]	**Mon:** 30-60 min swimming: aerobic and technique	**Mon:** 60 min swimming: aerobic and anaerobic mix	**Mon:** 60 min swimming: aerobic and technique
	Tues: 30-60 min cross-training[1]	**Tues:** 30-60 min cross-training[1]	**Tues:** 30-60 min cross-training[1]
	Wed: 30-60 min swimming: aerobic and technique	**Wed:** 60 min swimming: aerobic and anaerobic mix	**Wed:** 60 min swimming: aerobic and anaerobic mix
	Thurs: 60 min strengthen and stretch[2]	**Thurs:** 60 min strengthen and stretch[2]	**Thurs:** 60 min strengthen and stretch[2]
	Fri: 30-60 min swimming: aerobic and technique	**Fri:** 60 min swimming: aerobic with sprints	**Fri:** 60 min swimming
	Sat: 30-60 min cross-training[1] 30 min strengthen and stretch at home	**Sat:** 30-60 min cross-training[1] 30 min strengthen/stretch at home	**Sat:** Swim meet or 60 min swimming: anaerobic
	Sun: Rest	**Sun:** Rest	**Sun:** Rest and stretch

[1] Cross-training includes any dry-land cardio activity, such as bike riding, walking, or dancing.
[2] Strengthen and stretch includes Pilates, yoga, circuit-training classes, or your own at-home program.
[3] See appendix for sample swimming workouts for each category.

16-Week Training Plan Guidelines: Masters Swimmer

Experience level: Skilled   **Goal:** Improved 100-meter freestyle

	Phase I	Phase II	Phase III
	3-5 weeks	6-8 weeks	5-7 weeks
Overview	Initial base-building phase focuses on technique and recovery from the previous season's competition and high-intensity training. Add a weight training program or some extra dry-land work to build core strength and flexibility in preparation for phase II. Cross-training is integral for variety and a high level of fitness.	Raise the intensity level with more anaerobic, sprint, and power workouts. Workouts can include endurance, fast-interval, fartlek, speed-play, sprint, or goal sets. Dry-land stretching becomes even more critical in this phase to facilitate muscle recovery and training adaptation. Follow high-intensity swimming days with recovery days or out-of-the-pool days. Aim for 3-5 weekly swim workouts. Leg-intensive kicking sets provide a good anaerobic workout that doesn't tax the shoulders and provides a big payback in the competitive venue.	Narrow the focus to individual events, goal paces, race starts, and race finishes. Make race-pace sets a regular part of high-intensity workouts. Include adequate time for rest, recovery, and stretching to stay healthy for competition. Assess meet results and make changes in training if necessary. Focus on basic core-strengthening exercises and stretching during dry-land training. If involved in a weight-training program, eliminate heavy lifting and focus on maintaining core strength and power through plyometrics and medicine ball exercises. Running and other leg-intensive cross-training activities are discouraged in the weeks before big events.

	Phase I	Phase II	Phase III
	3-5 weeks	6-8 weeks	5-7 weeks
Sample weekly schedule[3]	**Mon:** 30-60 min swimming: aerobic and technique	**Mon:** 60 min swimming: aerobic/anaerobic mix	**Mon:** 60 min swimming: aerobic and technique
	Tues: 30-60 min cross-training[1]	**Tues:** 30-60 min cross-training[1]	**Tues:** 30-60 min cross-training[1]
	Wed: 60 min swimming: aerobic and technique	**Wed:** 60 min swimming: anaerobic	**Wed:** 60 min swimming: anaerobic
	Thurs: 60 min strengthen and stretch[2]	**Thurs:** 60 min swimming: aerobic and technique 60 min strengthen and stretch[2]	**Thurs:** 60 min swimming: aerobic and technique 60 min strengthen and stretch[2]
	Fri: 60 min swimming: aerobic and technique	**Fri:** 60 min swimming: aerobic with sprints	**Fri:** 60 min swimming: aerobic with sprints
	Sat: 30-60 min cross-training[1] 30 min strengthen and stretch at home	**Sat:** 30-60 min cross-training[1] 30 min strengthen and stretch at home	**Sat:** swim meet or 60 min swimming: anaerobic
	Sun: Rest	**Sun:** Rest	**Sun:** Rest and stretch

[1] Cross-training includes any dry-land cardio activity, such as bike riding, walking, or dancing.
[2] Strengthen and stretch includes Pilates, yoga, circuit-training classes, or your own at-home program.
[3] See appendix for sample swimming workouts for each category.

16-Week Training Plan Guidelines: Triathlete

Experience level: Limited   **Goal:** 1-mile (1.6 km) swim

	Phase I	Phase II	Phase III
	4-6 weeks	5-7 weeks	4-6 weeks
Overview	In the beginning of this phase, spend as much as 85% of pool time focusing on stroke drills and technique. Relax while swimming and breathing over longer distances and build a greater aerobic base. As technique improves, spend 40-50% of the time on technique and 50-60% on swimming.	Increase speed and distance with workouts such as endurance, fast-interval, fartlek, speed-play, sprint, and goal sets. In particular, the fartlek and speed-play sets simulate the open-water swimming experience.	Focus training on the unique aspects of open-water swimming in preparation for competition. If possible, practice water entries and exits in conditions similar to the intended competition.
	Novice triathletes should begin with workouts 30 min long and gradually build up to 60 min.	Increase the level of intensity in workouts gradually in order to adapt to the stress.	Triathletes with an extensive swimming background can reduce swimming days to two per week to ease schedule.
	While balancing training hours between three sports, triathletes with limited swimming experience, should aim for three pool sessions weekly.	If weather and water conditions allow, move one of the weekly swims to the open water.	Balance races with recovery and rest days. Mondays, after a big training or racing weekend, are an ideal day for an easy swim. If you have a more rigorous weight-training program, reduce time in the gym but continue to focus on core strength and power exercises, such as plyometrics.
	While focusing on technique, swim in the controlled environment of the pool rather than in open water.	Dry-land stretching becomes even more critical in this phase to facilitate muscle recovery and training adaptation.	

	Phase I	Phase II	Phase III
	4-6 weeks	5-7 weeks	4-6 weeks
Sample weekly schedule[3]	**Mon:** 30-60 min swimming: aerobic and technique	**Mon:** 60 min swimming: aerobic/ anaerobic mix	**Mon:** 60 min swimming: aerobic and technique
	Tues: Cross-training[1]	**Tues:** Cross-training[1]	**Tues:** Cross-training[1]
	Wed: 30-60 min swimming: aerobic and technique	**Wed:** 30-60 min swimming: aerobic with sprints	**Wed:** 30-60 min swimming: aerobic and anaerobic mix
	30 min strengthen and stretch[2]	30 min strengthen and stretch[2]	30 min strengthen and stretch[2]
	Thurs: Cross-training[1]	**Thurs:** Cross-training[1]	**Thurs:** Cross-training[1]
	Fri: 30-60 min swimming: aerobics and technique	**Fri:** 30-60 min swimming: aerobic/ anaerobic mix	**Fri:** 30 min swimming: aerobic with (limited) sprints
	Cross-training[1]	Cross-training[1]	
	Sat: Cross-training[1] 30 min strengthen and stretch at home	**Sat:** Cross-training[1] 30 min strengthen and stretch at home	**Sat:** Race or cross-training[1]
	Sun: Rest	**Sun:** Rest	**Sun:** Rest and stretch

[1] Cross-training includes any dry-land cardio activity, such as bike riding, or running.

[2] Strengthen and stretch includes Pilates, yoga, circuit-training classes, or your own at-home program.

[3] See appendix for sample swimming workouts for each category.

Dallas Aquatic Masters' Weekly Plan

In general, masters programs post the theme, or focus, of their daily workouts in advance. You can select the workouts that best fit your preferences and goals. Furthermore, you can move to a faster or slower lane to increase or decrease intensity in any workout.

This typical weekly schedule from the Dallas Aquatic Masters offers swimmers a complete spectrum of workouts.

Typical 7-Day Masters Program

Mon	Middle and distance freestyle	Endurance, slow-interval, and over-distance freestyle sets, some kicking and pulling sets
Tues	Athletes' choice	Sprinters: Long warm-up followed by a high-intensity sprint set
		Distance and open water: Open-water simulation (no lane lines) in pool with a buoy-marked course, or an overdistance swimming set mixed with speed play
		Strokes and IM: Aerobic, technique, option of working on fly, breaststroke, backstroke, or IM
Wed	Freestyle sprints	Aerobic, building to anaerobic; goal set of 25s and 50s
Thurs	Strokes and IM	Same as Tues
Fri	Variety	A relaxed effort mixture of swimming, pulling and kicking sets, and cruise intervals
Sat	Freestyle sprints	Similar to Wed, but add more 50s and 100s
Sun	Athletes' choice	Sprinters: Long warm-up followed by a high-intensity sprint set
		Distance and open water: Open-water simulation (no lane lines) in pool with a buoy-marked course, or an overdistance swimming set mixed with speed play

DAILY PLANNING

Most swimming coaches design their own workout templates with the main set neatly sandwiched between warm-up and cool-down sets. Depending on the day, the main set may be aerobic, anaerobic, or sprint, and power. The goal in workout design is to provide the appropriate blend of swimming and technique work that will prepare the swimmers to perform their best in the main set. When you consider all that is accomplished in one hour, you can appreciate the efficiency of the masters swimming workout.

If you are training without the luxury of a coach's planning, you should take the time to plan your time in the water. You might begin with the following template to schedule an hour that flows smoothly.

Suggested Template for Workout Design

Warm-up	5 min	Reserve this time for stretching and easy swimming (freestyle or backstroke), focusing on slowly loosening up your shoulders, back, and legs.
Stroke drills	12-20 min	This structured set that mixes stroke drills with swimming is both an extension of the warm-up and an opportunity to focus on technique. Maintain a low heart rate as your muscles warm up. You might use your fins to focus on stroke length and efficiency.
Minisprints	6-10 min	This transitional set brings the heart rate up in preparation for the main set. Choose either swimming or a mixture of swimming and kicking.
		If you plan on doing a power or sprint set, extend the length of this set to give your muscles more time to prepare for the intensity.
		If your main set will be a distance set, add some pace 50s to help your body to settle into your target pace. During phase II and III of training, use this time to fine-tune your starts, turns, streamlines, and relay hand-offs while you are fresh.
Main	15-40 min	This is the heart of the workout, where you spend the majority of your pool session. Depending on your training focus for the day, you might work on aerobics, aerobic and anaerobic mix, anaerobic, or sprint and power.
		Aerobic sets should be at least 20 min long and may be as long as 40 min for overdistance swims. High-intensity sets should be 15-20 min long, with a 30 min maximum.
Clean-up	0-20 min	If time allows, add a set that complements the main set such as a dedicated kicking set, which is ideal for sprinters and IM swimmers. Another option, particularly after a high-intensity set, is to refocus on technique with an aerobic-based set or drills.
Cool-down	5 min	Cool down with easy swimming to reduce postworkout soreness. This is an excellent opportunity for static stretching.

Over the past several years, the Internet has become an amazing resource on swim training. You can find workouts for novice swimmers, world-class swimmers, triathletes, and competitive masters swimmers on the Web. Although some online workouts will be appropriate for you, you may need to adjust others to meet your needs. You can also copy and paste Internet sets you like into your own workout template for something new. In time, you will be amazed by the variety of challenges you can bring to the pool.

Signs of Overtraining

Athletes who do not properly balance the stresses of training with sufficient rest risk overtraining, or burnout. Unlike normal fatigue from daily training efforts, the symptoms of overtraining persist for weeks and cannot be resolved with a few days of rest. Overtraining can completely derail your workout schedule, so it is essential to understand the symptoms and take precautions to avoid it. The following are common symptoms of overtraining:

• Fatigue, even after a few days of rest
• Persistent muscle soreness
• Elevated resting pulse
• Loss of appetite
• Decrease in performance
• Loss of enthusiasm
• Lowered resistance to colds and illnesses

If you have any of these symptoms, you should rest for three to five days. When you return to training, build up your workload and intensity gradually and make adjustments to the training plan to avoid a relapse.

TIPS FOR SUCCESSFUL TRAINING

Whether young or old, novice or experienced, and regardless of how simple or elaborate the training plan is, for many athletes the road ahead can look long and daunting. These training tips from winning athletes and coaches can help make your journey both successful and rewarding.

Keep a Log Most world-class swimmers keep a journal of their daily training for reasons that also apply to adult masters swimmers. Training logs encourage you by reminding you what you have accomplished, and they help you identify which training patterns and workouts worked for you. Observing how you feel during workouts and your resting heart rate each morning helps you anticipate sickness, injury, or overtraining. These insights can help you avoid or minimize illness, injuries, and their resulting setbacks. Tracking weekly mileage allows you to build up distance and intensity gradually. By logging performances in workouts, you can see improvements, notice plateaus, and make any necessary adjustments to training.

You can make your log as detailed as you want in a notebook, on your computer, or in your daily calendar. Find a system that works for you. Typical log entries include the date, hours of sleep, your resting heart rate (taken before you get out of bed), details of your swim workout (with whom, distance, intensity, swim sets and times, how you felt, stroke tips from your coach), and details of dry-land training (stretching, strengthening, cross-training). The following is an example of how Coach Jim organizes each daily entry in his weekly training log.

Goals this week:					
Date:			Hours of sleep:		RHR:
M O N D A Y	Swim workout				Cross-training / Dry land
	AE	AE/AN	AN	SP	

Train With Partners If you aren't able to attend a structured adult workout at a YMCA or local pool, you might share your pool time with a friend with a compatible schedule. Even swimmers who train at different speeds can make adjustments to swim together. The accountability of meeting a partner makes your training more consistent and more fun.

Be Flexible Remember that your training plan is just a plan. Plans change when necessary to accommodate family obligations, careers, illness, or injury. Because swimmers' lives are usually so busy, training programs that play out exactly as planned are very unusual. Make your training plan flexible, and let minor adjustments further personalize your training plan to fit your time and your life.

Eat Like a Champion Years of research support the connection between a balanced diet and athletic performance. The American College of Sports Medicine links sufficient intake of good nutrients with maintaining body weight, replenishing glycogen stores, and building muscular and supporting tissues. Complementing your training with good nutrition helps your body perform to its highest potential.

Your training maps out your route and begins your journey. At this point, it is perfectly normal to feel overwhelmed by the task and the weeks of work ahead. Remember that each week of your plan is designed to build gradually into the next. What lies ahead will be less intimidating when you reach that step in your program. Begin your first week by focusing your energy on daily training, and allow the momentum and your confidence to build. Maintain perspective by both focusing on small weekly goals and keeping sight of your long-term goals. Ride out the bumps in the road by being flexible with your workouts and prioritizing effective sleep habits and nutrition. As your body settles into the rhythm of the training weeks and you build strength, endurance, and confidence, settle back and enjoy the journey!

IV

Competition

Competing in Pool Events

This was my first swim meet and being part of a team of other first-timers (many of whom are triathletes) made it unforgettable. . . . I arrived a completely clueless newbie and I left a competitive swimmer with official times. It was a thrill to be a part of this.

—Mike Weklser, on his first masters swim meet

Swimmers who are new to competitive swimming quickly learn that a masters swim meet is much more than a venue for testing your swimming skills; it is an opportunity to see new places, meet new people, and be a part of a team in a relaxed and stimulating atmosphere. Like masters workouts, swim meets attract swimmers of all ages, abilities, and experience levels who are motivated by the challenge of competition, the camaraderie of others, and a passion for swimming.

This chapter begins by examining the fundamentals of masters swimming competitions. It also covers what you should expect on the day of the meet and strategies for a successful experience. With a better understanding of what lies ahead, you'll be more relaxed and confident in training.

SWIM MEETS: THE BASICS

Masters swim meets vary considerably in size and scope, giving you the opportunity to select a meet that matches your experience level and goals. Swimmers with competitive experience often find the atmosphere at masters events less intense than the high school and club competitions of their youth. Adults with full lives focus less on winning and more on simply enjoying the lifelong sport of swimming with friends and teammates. The best choice for first-time competitors is a small, low-key event, which provides a good introduction to meet venues and an opportunity to get comfortable with the flow of the action. Here is a sample of typical meets for adult swimmers.

- *Intraclub meets.* Many teams offer intraclub meets, or *time trials*, where all the competitors are from the same club. Intraclub meets let swimmers have a go at a swim meet without making a major time commitment.
- *Relay and themed meets.* Relay-only swim meets, in which swimmers compete as a team, are low pressure and fun. All novice swimmers are encouraged to jump in on these opportunities.
- *Local invitational meets.* Like all-comers track meets, invitational swim meets are open to any masters swimmer. If the meet is sanctioned by United States Masters Swimming (USMS), then the only requirement is that swimmers be registered USMS members. In some areas of the United States, local masters meets attract more than 100 swimmers and run for most of the day, while other meets have fewer swimmers and run for only a few hours. These meets are an excellent way to gain competition experience and meet others who share an interest in swimming.
- *Regional championship meets.* These meets are also typically open to all adult swimmers. Several organizations, including USMS, the YMCA, the National Senior Games Association (NSGA), and International Gay and Lesbian Aquatics (IGLA), hold regional, zone, or state championship meets. These meets have more competitors and are usually scheduled over a two- to three-day period.
- *National championship meets.* These meets are larger than the regional meets and draw a more competitive crowd, but they remain open to all swimmers.
- *World championships.* Every two years FINA (Fédération Internationale de Natation), the international governing body of swimming, hosts the masters world championships, a weeklong competition that draws masters swimmers from all over the globe.

Many factors can influence your choice of meet. You should get your feet wet at a smaller, local event before setting your sights on a big championship meet. Consider these questions as you scan the meet calendar:

- *Convenience.* Does it fit into your schedule? Will the meet run a few hours or is it an all-day, or several-day, commitment?
- *Meet level.* Are you comfortable with the level of competition in this meet? Is it appropriate for your level of experience?
- *Events.* Does the meet offer the event or events that you like to swim?
- *Travel.* Is it far away? If so, can you afford the time and money to travel?
- *Team.* Are your teammates going?

Meet organizers provide an information sheet detailing every aspect of the meet, including a list of events and the registration process. Before computer systems were used to organize swim meets, competitors entered by completing an entry card for each event they wanted to swim. Now, swimmers typically list their names, events, event numbers, and entry times on one consolidated entry form. Your entry time is an estimate of your swimming time for each event. You can make an estimate based on practice times or time in a previous meet, or you may simply enter no time (NT). Although some meets require that entries be made in advance, others allow *deck entries*, or entries made on the day of the meet. Again, the meet information sheet specifies these details.

As the meet entry forms come in, organizers consolidate the information with software designed specifically for managing swim meets. Swimmers' entry times are used to *seed* them in *heats*, or place them in groups, for each event. Within those heats, swimmers are further seeded into lanes; the faster swimmers are in the center lanes and the slower swimmers are in the outer lanes. The heat and lane assignments are posted by order of event on the day of the meet.

Throughout the meet, an announcer updates participants on the progress of the meet by announcing which events and heats are in the water. As you approach your assigned lane, check in with the volunteer timer assigned to that lane. As each heat ends, the timers record the time of the swimmers in their respective lanes. These results are sent back to the main organizational desk where the results of all the heats within that event are compiled, printed, and posted. The results often include swimmers' split times.

To prevent meets from running too long, meet organizers choose the most efficient way to seed the events. In smaller meets, all the swimmers in an event are often seeded together by speed, regardless of sex or age. The resulting heats of swimmers of similar abilities provide the best opportunity for each swimmer to be motivated by competitors in the adjacent lanes. However, when the results are compiled, the swimmers are sorted by sex and then into five-year increment age groups for awards. Therefore, a 55-year-old swimmer who finishes sixth in a heat may still be the winner for that event in the 55- to 59-year age group.

Championship meets, such as USMS Nationals and the FINA World meets, seed the heats within an event according to sex and age. These large meets must simultaneously run two different *courses*, or pool venues, to finish the events every day. *Heat sheets* are printed for every event, which list the names and entry times for all swimmers as well as their heat and lane assignments. Meets of this size require an amazing number of volunteers and months of planning to manage the many logistical details.

Meets also have officials who oversee the activity in the pool to ensure that the heats run smoothly and in accordance with the rules of the sport. The deck referee and the starter work together to call swimmers to the block, give the starting commands, and recall heats if false starts occur. Judges are positioned at the sides and ends of the pool to observe swimmers' strokes and turns. If you are navigating through a swim meet for the first time, ask meet officials or one of the many volunteers on and around the pool deck for help.

Rule Adjustments for Masters

In general, the rules for masters swimming competition are the same as those in all USA Swimming competitions. The notable exceptions are for the starting procedures, relay events, and the butterfly stroke.

- *Starts.* In an effort to accommodate swimmers of all ages and skill levels, masters competitions allow swimmers to start their events from the starting block, the edge of the pool, or in the water. Furthermore, masters competitions require swimmers to position one foot at the front of the starting platform, the edge of the pool, or the wall of the pool, before the "Take your mark" command. Swimmers who choose to start in the water must have at least one hand in contact with the wall or starting block.

- *Relays.* As in the individual events, masters competitors may choose to start their leg of a relay event in the water. Swimmers who choose this option should notify the official before entering the water. In addition, after finishing their leg of the relay, masters swimmers who cannot exit their lane quickly are allowed to rest at the finishing end of the pool, staying clear of other swimmers and the electronic timing equipment. When all the teams in the heat have finished swimming, swimmers may exit from their lane or from a ladder.

- *Butterfly.* Although it is not considered the most efficient way to swim the butterfly, USMS rules permit swimmers to use the breaststroke kick for the butterfly competition. The rules state specifically, "The breaststroke or whip kick may be used exclusively or interchangeably with the dolphin kick while doing the butterfly stroke at any time during the race. Only one breaststroke or whip kick is permitted per arm pull, except that a single breaststroke or whip kick is permitted prior to the turn and the finish without an arm pull. After the start and after each turn, a single breaststroke or whip kick is permitted prior to the first arm pull [as part of the underwater pull out]" (United States Masters Swimming 2008).

PLANNING FOR SUCCESS

The key to a positive swim meet experience is to be both focused and relaxed. Coach Jim attributes much of his success to striking the perfect balance between these two critical components of competition. For Jim, relaxation comes with focusing on details such as breathing, streamlining at the start and turns, pacing, controlling the kick, and maintaining stroke rhythm and rate. He builds a plan that details exactly how he will swim every stroke.

Jim goes to a swim meet with a plan for the entire event, including when and how he warms up, what and when he eats, and what he packs in his bag. A detailed plan for the day leaves fewer unknowns and allows Jim to relax and confidently swim the races he has prepared for. Your training plan has given you the physical conditioning and the confidence to swim your race, and now your swim-meet plan will carry you through the event successfully. If you are preparing for your first swim meet, this chapter will help you picture what to expect and make your plan for success. As you gain experience and make adjustments to details such as your packing list or your warm-up, your plan will become personalized like Jim's. As the details fall into place, you will find it easier to relax and focus on swimming your best.

Before the Meet

In the weeks leading up to your event, your training plan will take you through a taper period, focusing on a reduced workload and more details specific to the race. You must get sufficient rest to have a successful tapering period, which can be a challenge for busy masters swimmers. Far too many swimmers arrive at the meet exhausted from working overtime for days to clear their calendars so they can attend the meet. Swimmers are instead encouraged to plan to reduce their workloads in the weeks preceding a big meet so they can be rested, focused, and primed for a great experience.

As your workload in and out of the pool gets lighter, you should begin to adjust your body rhythms for the day of the event. This may be as simple as waking up a little earlier and swimming before you start your workday to simulate the time of day that you will do your meet warm-up. If you are traveling to a different time zone, consider the change in your sleep patterns and make reasonable adjustments. These minor changes to your schedule will prepare your body for a seamless transition to a relaxed and focused competition day.

It is not too early to start making a list of all the things you'll need to pack for your race day. The extensive list that follows includes almost everything swimmers have brought to meet venues. Some items are essential and others are just nice to have. The venue, the weather, how long you expect to be there, and your personal preferences will influence what you bring.

- *Swimsuits.* If you have an extra swimsuit, you can opt to put on a dry suit after your warm-up swim. Swimmers who choose to race in a high-tech competition suit typically warm up in the morning with a different suit and then don the fast suit for their race.

- *Goggles.* Always bring a spare set of your favorite goggles in case you break or misplace the first pair.

- *Swim caps.* As with the goggles, have a spare!

- *Towel.* You will use your towel many times during warm-ups, races, and cool-downs. Carry an extra if you want a dry towel when you hit the showers at the end of the day.

- *Warm clothes.* Sweats or a swim parka are essential for warming up your body between swims. Cold feet are less sensitive to the water and therefore less efficient, so remember to bring socks and shoes to keep your feet warm. In addition, you will want a complete set of dry clothes at the end of the day when you are done wearing your swimsuit.

- *Nutritious food.* You must stay hydrated and energized through the day for a good experience. Bring a water bottle, a light lunch, and snacks that you can eat between events. Select foods that you normally eat—the day of the meet is not a day to try something new.

- *Chair.* A comfortable deck or beach chair will help you relax throughout the day. Furthermore, you will have more options for places to sit at the pool venue.

- *Sun protection.* Bring sunglasses, sunscreen, an umbrella, or a tent. In an outdoor venue, the swimming pool and the surrounding cement deck act as giant reflectors magnifying the intensity of the sun. Protect yourself from sunburn.

- *Sleeping bag.* Bring a sleeping bag if you want to relax or nap in a quiet area between swims at an all-day meet.

- *Pencils, highlighter, paper.* A highlighter is useful for marking up heat sheets and having a paper and pencil makes it easy to record your times, splits, and notes about your races.

- *Something to do.* If you'll be at the meet all day, you may want to bring the morning paper, a good book, or your knitting needles.

As the day of the meet grows closer, grab a bag and begin putting things inside that you plan to bring. Packing your bag and gaining control of the logistical details in advance will clear your mind and allow you to relax, get good sleep, and focus on your swimming.

Day of the Meet

As you awaken to the sound of your alarm on the morning of the meet, remind yourself to stay relaxed and focused. You've prepared physically with weeks of training, you've packed your bag, and you're ready for a great day. Allow sufficient time in the morning to eat, do a few stretches, have your coffee, travel, and park the car. Your goal is to arrive at the meet venue unrushed, on time, relaxed, and in control.

Once you arrive at the pool, remember these three words of advice from Coach Jim: *Get comfortable early*. Here are five easy steps for getting settled at the meet venue:

1. *Get the lay of the land.* The pool area will be busy with meet officials, swimmers, and volunteers. Take it all in, noting the location of the registration and check-in areas, the locker rooms, the deck area, and the pool (or pools).

2. *Park your stuff.* Find a place out of the sun where you can store your bag and set up your chair. Do you want to be in the thick of the action with a close view of the pool or do you prefer a quiet area away from the noise?

Shave Down or Suit up?

Legendary Australian swimmers Murray Rose and Jon Henricks rocked the swimming world when they arrived at the 1956 Melbourne Olympic Games with their body hair shaved. Five gold medals later, the other competitors were certainly taking a look. In 1960, Rose and Henricks moved to Los Angeles to swim with the University of Southern California, bringing their prerace ritual with them. It did not take long for "shaving down" to catch on in the United States. Today, the phrase *taper and shave* is used to describe a swimmer's preparation for a big meet.

When Rose dove into the water shaved, he reported an immediate sensual awareness of the water (Spawson 1992). This heightened feel for the water and the sensation of being slippery and fast are the effects swimmers look for when they take to the shower with a razor on the final day before a critical competition. Although many swimmers suspected that it was merely a psychological advantage, a 1989 study (Sharp and Costill 1989) demonstrated that, when shaved, swimmers do achieve more distance per stroke from a reduction in active drag forces, thus decreasing the physiological cost of swimming. The feeling of hypersensitivity to the water is most likely the result of shaving off the outside layer of dead skin cells, leaving a fresh layer of new sensitive cells. The ritual of shaving down is part of meet preparation for swimmers of every level, including masters. It is not unusual at championship meets to see hairless arms and legs on both female and male swimmers all looking to experience a smoother ride and perhaps even shave a few tenths of a second off their times.

Swimming was not to be the only sport left out of the technology age. Swimsuit manufacturers have been busy designing a suit that will move a swimmer through the water with less resistance, raising the slippery, fast, shaved feeling to another level. Early speed suit designs improved on the fabric, creating more of a second skin that was likened to swimming naked. Suits have since evolved to a variety of designs from full-body suits to *jammers*, or shorts, styles. The result of these dramatic advances in suit technology is faster swimming and much debate. Swimmers report feeling lighter, faster, and more like a torpedo in the technical suits as they squeeze their bodies into them for big competitions and critical meets. Critics are fearful that the suits bring an unfair advantage to the sport, perhaps even providing added buoyancy that assists individual swimmers differently. Researchers are finding it hard to keep up with the advances in technology and quantifying the effects. Nevertheless, masters swimmers have jumped into the action as well, sporting all varieties of the fast new suits and enjoying the gains in speed, even if those gains are only psychological.

After months of training, fine-tuning your technique, and perfecting your race details, it seems only natural to polish off your taper with the added boost of the shave, the high-tech suit, or both. For swimmers at the world-class level, these tactics can mean the difference between making the Olympic team and watching on TV or standing on the awards podium and watching from the stands. For many masters swimmers, the shave and the suit are indeed part of their meet preparation and a fitting cap on all their hard work. Masters competitors agree that it's fun to feel fast, and the shave and the new suit can only make the ride better.

3. *Check in.* Most local meets require swimmers to check in for their events on the morning of the meet. Although you may have registered in advance, you must complete the check-in procedure when you arrive at the meet. The meet information sheet will list check-in details. The meet organizers only seed the heats for each event with those swimmers who have checked in to ensure a quicker, more efficient meet.

4. *Warm up.* As you approach the pool for your warm-up, look for signs that designate the speed and the activity in each lane. Some lanes will be labeled as kicking only, others may be one-way sprints, and others will specify easy, medium, or fast speeds. Select one that suits you and begin your warm-up (see Meet Warm-Ups on facing page).

5. *Get warm and dry.* After your warm-up, rinse off and put on warm, dry clothes. If you are scheduled to swim in an early event, you will want to don your competition suit. Remember to keep your feet warm with shoes and socks.

As the day progresses, you will find yourself falling into a routine for each of your swims. Before the start of each race, get wet in the warm-up area with the goal of getting loose and focused for your race. Sprinters will do as little as 4×25, while distance swimmers will consider a longer prerace dip. As the start grows close, position yourself behind your block and stay focused on the details of your race—the start, turns, streamlines, and how the first 25 or 50 meters will feel. After your swim, go back to the warm-up area for a cool-down. Use this time to loosen up your muscles and work out some of the tightness from the race. Congratulate yourself on the swim, get dry and warm, hydrate and snack, and relax until your next race.

With experience, you will find yourself falling into a routine that works for you, with specific details on eating, warming up, and cooling down for each event. Remember to do the things that help you relax and focus.

After the Meet

At the conclusion of the meet, find the posted results and take notes on your times and splits, if applicable. Consider these results and your feelings about each swim as you plan your future training. Your coach will want to know how you felt during each swim and how you think you could improve. Did you lose momentum on the turns? Did you start too fast or too conservatively? What would you do differently if you swam it again? And most important, how can you train to better prepare for the next meet?

Finally, while the meet is still fresh in your mind, make adjustments to your packing list. Did you have enough suits and towels? What did you prefer to eat? Over time, you will perfect this list with the items necessary to create your perfect space at a swim meet.

Meet Warm-Ups

Although the warm-up pool at a swim meet can appear to be in complete disarray with people coming and going in every lane, swimmers who have focus and a plan can have a good warm-up swim. Swimmers who choose to warm up earlier will enjoy less populated lanes than those who join the rush toward end of the warm-up period. Regardless of when you arrive, begin by looking for a lane that is moving close to a speed that fits you, then slip in feet first and begin circle swimming.

The following sample meet warm-up works for most swimmers and can be personalized as you gain more experience.

Sample Meet Warm-Up Routine

1 × 500	Get warm with easy aerobic swimming or a mixture of stroke drills and swimming. Familiarize yourself with the pool walls and the position of the backstroke flags if you will be swimming IM or backstroke.
2-3 × 100 + 50	Build each 100 m, beginning at 60% of your race pace and finish the last 10 m at race pace. Swim 50 m recovery after each 100 m, then rest for 1 min before beginning another 100 m.
2-3 × 100 + 50 **or** **2-3 × 50 + 25**	If warming up for events longer than 200 m, swim 100s here, using the pace clock at the side of the pool to settle into race pace. Sprinters should choose the 50s option, building from 60% of race pace to 100% of race pace in the final 5 m. Recover by swimming an easy 25 m between 50s or an easy 50 m between 100s. Rest well between sets.
1 × 100	Do an easy swim, kicking drill, or stroke drill.
2 × 25	Breakouts: Push off with maximum effort, break out, and swim 4-6 fast strokes, then swim easily to the finish. Focus on maintaining a streamlined body position and a balanced stroke.
2 × 25	Builds: Build from 60% of your race pace to 100% of your race pace. Focus on maintaining your stroke length and rate as your speed increases, keeping your kick small and under control, and finishing with your head down and a long stroke.
Starts	If a starting lane is available, do a few starts to get comfortable with the blocks. As in the breakout 25s, focus on your underwater streamlines, breakout, stroke rhythm, and your desired pace.
1 × 100-200	Relax with an easy swim, kick, or stroke drill.

While you brag to your buddies about your accomplishments the day after the swim meet, rest and replenish your body with fluids and healthy food. Soon your friends will be asking when the next meet is and what they should pack.

As you will discover, the swim meet experience is less about exercise than the pursuit of your perfect swim. Whatever your stage of life, you are really racing against yourself and your own times and performances. Coach Jim cannot replicate his performance at the 1976 Olympic Games, but he continues to thrive on the challenge of competing at new and different levels in masters swim meets every year. Jim and thousands of other masters swimmers keep their packing list handy as they look forward to next opportunity to step onto the blocks to compete.

Coach Jim delivers instruction and encouragement to his swimmers between swim sets.

In the Mind of a Champion

Despite his busy schedule as a contractor and father of two, 1988 Olympic gold medalist Richard Schroeder continues to look forward to his daily swim. Although he does not compete regularly, every few years he steps up on the blocks at a masters competition and shows that he has not lost his gift for being an incredible racer. A three-time national masters champion and three-time masters world record holder, Richard has clearly mastered the concentration required to perform at his best. Here is what Richard is thinking about when competing in his signature stroke, the breaststroke:

"I step onto the starting block with no distractions, thinking only of the task at hand and my game plan. Worrying about other swimmers, sore muscles, and fatigue only adds negative energy.

"At the start, I streamline on my entry and through the pull-down, riding out the speed as long as possible. This is critical, as this is the fastest part of my race and it cannot be rushed. After the breakout, at the start, and after every turn, I build up my turnover for the first four strokes to maximize the catch and establish a rhythm. This keeps me from spinning my wheels with the excitement of the race.

"Walls are opportunities. I time the turns before I cross under the flags and then accelerate the intensity going in and out every wall. On the push-offs, I explode off the wall with a tight streamline to maximize my pull-down, just like the start—with lots of speed! As I approach the final wall, I focus on maintaining maximum pace without losing efficiency. At the finish, I think of punching through the wall. Remember that no one has trained as hard as you, and your hard work will pay off.

"I worked on all of these points not only in the pool at practice and meets, but also through endless hours of mental visualization to help solidify the concepts."

Competing in Open Water

The open-water training really gave me a great aerobic base. I felt like I was in better shape than I had ever been before.

—Chip Peterson, on winning the 1500-meter freestyle
at the U.S. Nationals just two and a half weeks after winning
the 10K World Open-Water Championships, August 2005

Open-water competitions date back to the beginning of Olympic history. In the 1896 Athens Olympics, competitors swam 100-, 500-, and 1200-meter races in the heavy surf and 55 °F (13 °C) water of the Bay of Zea. At the Paris Olympics in 1900, five downstream races were held in the Seine River, including a 4-kilometer swim. Open-water competition returned to the Olympic venue in the 2008 Beijing Games with a 10-kilometer event in the canoe basin. This long distance event is a perfect fit for the Olympic Games, since it complements the swimming events the way that the road marathon complements the track events.

One of the oldest and most beloved open-water competitions for masters swimmers is the La Jolla Roughwater. This San Diego–based event is one of an increasing number of events that cater to both youth and adult swimmers. The race started in 1916 and attracted over 1000 swimmers who competed in distances ranging from 250 yards to 3 miles (5 km). The beauty of the La Jolla Roughwater and other open-water events is that, unlike swim meets, you do not need to schedule a whole day or weekend to swim. The entire event can take only a few hours, including the check-in, warm-up, and cool-down.

With the proper training and preparation, participating in open-water competitions can be both fun and gratifying. Set yourself up for success by selecting an event and creating a plan that is suited to your experience, your available training time, and your abilities. This chapter discusses some of the factors to consider in race selection and what to expect on the day of the event. It presents competition strategies that help both novice and experienced swimmers prepare for the unique conditions of open water with both pool and open-water workouts.

PREPARE FOR THE EVENT

Like runners, open-water swimmers have the luxury of browsing through various event schedules and finding events suitable to their strengths. Races vary not only in distance, but also in water conditions—warm water or cold water, salt water or fresh water, flat water or choppy ocean water. First-timers might want to get their feet wet with a smaller, low-key event. Experienced swimmers might be ready to step up for longer distances or more challenging conditions.

As you set your goal, consider your current level of fitness and the amount of time you have to dedicate to training and preparation. Make your goal challenging yet attainable. Share your goal with your coach, who can help you develop a training plan. Be flexible when setting your goal times, since there are so many uncontrollable factors in open-water swimming, including water and wind conditions.

Once you have selected an event, familiarize yourself with the details such as water temperature, the starting and finishing procedures, and a course description. All these should be detailed in the event information. If you understand these finer points, you can make your training more targeted and you will feel more confident at the starting line.

Many swimmers and triathletes first consider the temperature of the water when selecting an open-water or triathlon event. The water of a typical lap pool is 78 to 81 °F (26 to 27 °C). The more the water temperature for your event varies from this norm, the more you must understand your own tolerance for colder and warmer conditions.

In cold-water conditions, you may choose a wet suit. The rulebook of USA Triathlon, the governing body of the sport of triathlon, indicates that swimmers may choose to wear a wet suit in water 78 °F or colder. When the conditions allow, most triathletes take advantage of this option, reaping the benefits of the wet suit's added buoyancy and speed. Outside of triathlons, wet suit guidelines vary for open-water swims. Although many events allow them in colder conditions, wet suit–clad swimmers are sometimes considered ineligible for awards or put into a separate division. Swimmers are encouraged to decide whether or not to compete with a wet suit early in their training cycles. This allows them to either train in the suit or acclimate their bodies to colder water if they decide not to wear one. Over time, you can train your body to handle the cold water by gradually building up your exposure time with each successive swim.

As in cold-water conditions, swimmers training for an event in warm water can prepare themselves by training in warm conditions. Some events allow competitors to remove their swim caps after the race starts to keep their bodies cool. Take advantage of any opportunity to hydrate yourself before, during, and after the swim.

THE TRAINING PLAN

The ideal training program for open-water swimming includes both pool and open-water training. If both venues are available, a mix of approximately 80 percent pool training, with an emphasis on technique and pacing, and 20 percent open-water training is recommended. The primary focus of the latter should be on the unique challenges of open water, including water entries, navigation, buoy turns, and finishes. These training percentages can vary depending on swimmers' goals, strengths, weaknesses, and personal schedules.

Each venue provides different opportunities to focus on the many nuances of swimming and competing in water without stable conditions and lane lines. Pool training occurs in a controlled environment where swimmers can replicate given distances and measure time and stroke rate improvements. The pool is also an excellent venue for learning and developing open-water skills, such as sighting and drafting. Open-water training allows swimmers to enhance these skills in various water and weather conditions.

For many swimmers, accessing open water for training can be a challenge, particularly in the colder months. Rest assured that many swimmers compete in open water without regularly training outside of their home pool. There are many ways to bring the unique aspects of open-water swimming into your pool workouts.

DEVELOPING AND TRAINING OPEN-WATER SKILLS IN THE POOL

The structured setting of the pool is an ideal environment for honing your open-water skills and racing strategies while measuring your pacing, heart rate, stroke rate, and other training targets. As swimmers prepare for triathlons and open-water events, they mix these skills into pool swimming sets in a variety of training zones.

Swimming Straight Swimming in a straight line without the reference of pool lines and markings is a developed skill. Most swimmers have a dominant pulling arm that causes them to drift in one direction. Knowing which direction you drift and correcting your stroke accordingly is the key to swimming straight.

186 Mastering Swimming

An excellent and very simple set for focusing on direction is to swim a 4 × 25 with your eyes closed. Be sure that the lane is clear of swimmers before you begin. Experiment with left-side breathing and right-side breathing, since your preferred breathing pattern can affect your stroke efficiency and direction. Consider these aspects of your stroke: head position (Is it steady?), core rotation (Do you move symmetrically on both your left and right sides regardless of your breathing pattern?), and hand entry (Are you entering too wide or too narrow?). Ask a coach to assess your stroke to correct any drifting to the left or right.

Sighting Chapter 12, Open-Water Training, discusses why sighting with the peek-breathe method is the most efficient way to spot your target buoys and landmarks with minimum disruption to your stroke cycle. Even if you do swim in a straight line with your eyes closed, you will need to sight in open water to stay on course, since currents, swells, tides, and even other groups of swimmers can move you off your line.

There are many ways to bring sighting into your pool workouts, such as in this overdistance set:

5 × 300

- Sight on the first and fourth 50 of each 300.
- Descend 300s 1 → 5.
- RI = :20.

Select your target before you swim. If you are swimming a short course (25 meters), you will need a target at each end of the pool. Place a tennis ball at the water line or select a large building or tree beyond the pool. Sight every fourth or sixth stroke and focus on maintaining your stroke rhythm and keeping your stroke rate consistent through the swims.

This fartlek, or speed-play, set incorporates sighting into fast-paced swimming:

3 × [4 × 25; 4 × 100]

- Swim the first 25 of each set of 25s with a head-up freestyle, crocodile, or water-polo-style stroke. Keep your eyes focused on a point in front of you.
- Sprint and sight in the recommended peek-breathe style on the remaining 25s.
- Descend each set of 100s 1 → 4, swimming the fourth in each round faster.
- Rest 5 to 10 seconds after each 25.
- Rest 10 seconds after each 100 or repeat them with a comfortable send-off interval, such as on cruise + :05.[1]
- Rest an extra 15-30 seconds after the fourth 100 in each round.

[1]Refer to chapter 10 for an explanation of cruise intervals and how they are determined.

Get out quickly on the 4 × 25 and sprint aggressively, as though you are headed to the first turn buoy. Settle back in the 100s and find a rhythm, breathing pattern, and pace that you can maintain and build on through the race.

Breathing Establishing a comfortable breathing pattern is critical for swimming long distances in open water and the pool. In open water, you will not always have the luxury of selecting a breathing side, since waves and swells may prevent you from breathing on a particular side. For this reason, you should incorporate breath control and a variety of breathing patterns into your pool workouts. This sample breathing set can be mixed into a longer set or done alone as a shorter set.

6 × 100

- Freestyle swim, focusing on stroke symmetry.
- Odd 100s: Breathe for 25 to your right side only / 25 to your left side only / 25 alternating two right side breaths with two left side breaths / 25 breathing every fifth stroke.
- Even 100s: Breathe in your favorite pattern, descend 1 → 3.
- Swim all 100s on cruise. Maintain a steady stroke count throughout the set.

Successful bilateral breathing takes time, but it is well worth the effort when you can dive into the open water knowing that you can comfortably and confidently breathe in any situation.

Pacing The most successful open-water swimmers have mastered the ability to adjust their pace to the unstructured nature of an open-water race. Whether you start the race in the middle of the pack or approach conservatively from the side, your heart rate will be elevated as you experience the energy and excitement of the start. It's critical that you ride that initial peak and then settle into a steady rhythm that you can maintain and build on through the race. You may have other opportunities to speed up and settle back during the race as you swim around buoys, pass other swimmers, or encounter currents, swells, or tide changes. If you can simulate these changing conditions with speedplay or fartlek training in your pool workouts, you will be better prepared for them in a competition.

This sample freestyle set is about 1 mile long (1.6 km) and includes a variety of techniques for speed play.

3 × 50

- Swim with the fastest possible send-off interval, or with RI = :05.
- Sight on a target while swimming the first 25 of each 50.

2 × 200

- Settle back into a steady rhythm.

- Keep your stroke count steady as you alternate swimming 25s breathing to the left side with 25s breathing to the right side.
- Swim on cruise + :10 or with RI = :20.

5 × 100

- Descend 100s 1 → 5 from 75 percent effort to 85 percent effort.
- Swim on cruise.

2 × 200

- Repeat the preceding technique for 2 × 200.

3 × 50

- Swim fast to a great finish.
- Use the fastest possible send-off interval, or RI = :05.

Stroke Rates Open-water swimmers often depend on increasing their stroke rate, or turnover rate, to pick up speed. Rather than muscling the water, relax your arm recovery and pick up your tempo with your kick. Think like a marathon runner—quick, light, and rhythmic. Keep this focus, for example, when you descend the 5 3 100 in the previous sample set.

As you settle back into the 200s, ride out each stroke for a longer time and find a rhythm that emphasizes stroke length. Swimmers who wear wet suits find that the added flotation allows them to naturally ride out each stroke for more distance. If you plan to compete in a wet suit, capitalize on this significant advantage.

Crowd Control In practice, recruit other swimmers to simulate the crowded conditions you may encounter in an open-water swim. Although swimming close to others can initially be somewhat intimidating, over time, swimmers learn to go with the flow and use the energy of those around them. You will come into contact with other swimmers in open water, and the best way to become comfortable with it is to simulate the crowd with your friends in the pool. In masters workouts, swimmers do six to eight 25-yard (25 m) sprints with three people across in each lane. Swimmers should sight once or twice in each length. Ideally, each group of three swimmers will be immediately followed by another group of three.

Buoy Turns Swimmers can recreate the open-water experience in the pool by taking out all the lane lines and adding a few buoys. They then sprint in packs to and around the buoys. This method is excellent for learning to round buoys efficiently and getting comfortable with the technique in a crowded situation. Swimmers can add to this drill by looking for, sighting on, and sprinting toward a target after they round the buoy.

A proper buoy turn resembles a partial corkscrew stroke. Take an arm stroke of freestyle, then an arm stroke of backstroke, then another stroke of freestyle as you perform a scissor-like leg movement. This technique may be unsafe if there are too many swimmers in the area, in which case you can simply round the buoy with shorter, somewhat choppy, freestyle strokes.

Since it is not always practical to remove all the lane lines, you can also practice your open-water turns by making a normal turn in the pool before you reach the wall. This practice makes you more comfortable resuming your speed without the luxury of a wall. For example, swim 1 × 600, executing all of the turns in the deep end of the pool just inside of the backstroke flags. Vary your style of turning to become comfortable with both the corkscrew style and the freestyle stroke-around style.

Drafting Drafting, or swimming in the bubbles and the wake created by swimmers in front of you, is legal and prevalent in open-water events (see figure 15.1). If you can position yourself behind a faster swimmer, you can gain an advantage by swimming in their draft. A 2003 study, "Drafting Distance in Swimming," concluded the ideal drafting position is 0 to 50 centimeters, or 20 inches, behind the lead swimmer. Swimmers in this position can reduce drag by up to 21 percent. When drafting, the swimmers increased their stroke lengths and reduced both their perceived exertion and heart rates (Chatard and Wilson 2003). As in cycling races, open-water swimmers cluster in packs to benefit from the draft of the other competitors.

Figure 15.1 Drafting behind another swimmer can help gain speed in open water races.

You can easily practice drafting with your friends in the pool. If you leave the wall in one-second intervals, instead of the customary five, you will position yourself to enjoy the draft of the swimmer ahead of you. This sample team pursuit set gives all the swimmers in a lane the opportunity to draft as well as lead:

1 × 800

- Send off in 1-second intervals.
- At each 100, the first swimmer moves to the side, allows the others to pass, and then jumps back in at the end of the line.
- When you are the leader, challenge yourself to step up the pace.
- When you are drafting, stay with the pace of the swimmer in front of you.

Experiment with your position by swimming at the hip of the swimmer you are drafting. The key is to stay close while maintaining your own space, which requires awareness and confidence. You can gain both by practicing first in the pool and then in the open water.

Dolphin Diving The shallow section of the pool is a great place to practice entering the water with the dolphin-diving techniques from chapter 12, Open-Water Training. Try this sample set, which starts and ends in the shallow end:

6 × 50

- Begin each 50 with 1 to 2 dolphin dives, and then sprint the remainder of the first 25.
- Swim easy on the second 25 of each 50.
- RI = :15.

Once you are comfortable with the dolphin dives, experiment with an underwater pull and a dolphin kick to extend the distance you cover underwater.

Overdistance swimming You should get comfortable with the distance of your planned swim in a pool before you tackle that distance in the open water. At 1- to 2-week intervals leading up to your event, designate one pool workout for a longer, overdistance swim. Focus on finding a rhythm and pace that you can maintain comfortably. Start with a distance that you know you can swim and then gradually increase it.

Know Your Equipment There is no better place to test out your equipment than in the comfort of a pool. You must have a comfortable and reliable pair of goggles that do not leak and provide the necessary visibility. If you plan to wear earplugs, as many open-water swimmers do in cold water, first test them for comfort and fit in the pool. For safety, all open-water swimmers are required to wear a brightly colored swim cap. Those who do not normally swim with a cap may need time to adjust to swimming with their heads covered.

Bring your wet suit to the pool and get comfortable putting it on, swimming in it, and taking it off. A weekly pool swim in your wet suit allows you to adjust your stroke for the added buoyancy and the reduced mobility in your shoulders and arms. Another benefit to testing your wet suit in the pool is that you will know exactly where to apply products to prevent chafing before you dive into the open water.

Fueling If you are planning a lengthy swim and will need to refuel during competition, you should simulate this in your pool swims. An incredible number of race-ready gels and fluids with various amounts of carbohydrates, proteins, and electrolytes are available. You should test a few out in training to learn what you and your body prefer. Take the time to find one that works for you, then train with it by tucking the gel packets in your suit and asking your escort boat to have your water bottles at the ready.

Sample Pool Workout
for Open-Water Swimmers

Warm-Up

1 × 200

Swim easy, then switch at the wall.

10 × 50

RI = :10

1-3: Kick, descending 1 → 3.

4-6: Do a stroke drill, emphasizing stroke length.

7-9: Swim, building each 50.

10: Swim easy.

Main Set

15 × 100: Freestyle swim[1]

1-2: Swim fast, on cruise + :05, sprint and sight on the first 25 of each 100.[2]

3, 4, 5: Swim at a moderate, steady effort, settle into your stroke rhythm, on cruise.

6, 7, 8, 9: Swim at a moderate effort, breathe with the following pattern: 50 right side / 50 left side, on cruise + :05.

10, 11, 12: Swim 50 pick up / 50 easy, hold stroke, cruise.

13, 14, 15: Descend 1 → 3 to a maximum effort finish, cruise.

Cool-Down

8 × 25

Drag your fingertips on odd 25s.

Focus on excellent technique and relaxation.

Total: 2400 yards or meters

[1]Swimmers training for distances of 4K or greater should consider swimming this set as 200s instead of 100s.

[2]Alternatively, this set can be done with fixed rest as follows: Rest 5 seconds after each of the first two 100s, then 10 to 15 seconds after the remaining 100s.

OPEN-WATER WORKOUTS

Swimmers who are fortunate enough to have access to a river, lake, ocean, bay, or other local swimming hole should add open-water workouts to their training plans. These venues are ideal for building your confidence in the open-water skills you have learned in the pool, making you better prepared for the race-day experience.

This chapter's open-water workouts focus on racing skills, including entries, exits, negotiating buoys, drafting, maneuvering in crowds, and beach runs. Every race presents a different set of water and weather conditions; no two races are the same. Purposeful open-water workouts will give you the confidence you will need to handle most open-water situations.

The following open-water drills and sets can be tailored to fit the size of your training group and your waterfront situation.

1. *Swimming straight.* Select a buoy or a landmark and swim toward it without sighting. After 10 strokes, look up and check your direction. Make adjustments and then swim 20 strokes before checking your direction. Continue to make adjustments and build up to 50 strokes. Rotate which swimmer of the group is swimming blindly, so that every team member remains in sight.

2. *Sighting.* A primary skill for successful open-water swimming is selecting a target to sight on. Waves and other swimmers can block your view of buoys sitting on the water's surface. Think big when you select your target. What else is in the line of the buoy? A land mass, a large building, or even a lifeguard tower positioned in the same line as the buoy may be a more visible target.

   When training in open water, learn to quickly locate landmarks in various weather conditions so you can sight with confidence as you swim.

3. *Drafting.* Swim in a tight formation with your teammates to simulate crowded racing conditions and gain comfort with pack swimming. You will all swim faster if you use others' drafts.

   Indian sprints, a favorite open-water drill that incorporates both drafting and speed play, begins with 3 to 4 swimmers positioned in a line. The last swimmer picks up the pace, sprints by the group, and then assumes the lead position. As this swimmer settles into the front, the next one in line does the same by sprinting into the lead, and so on. After just one round of this challenging drill, every swimmer should be convinced of the benefits of drafting.

4. *Turning.* Buoys and floats help swimmers become comfortable with open-water turns. Swim around the buoy in a group and race back to a designated spot (see figure 15.2). As you come around the buoy, quickly readjust your line of sight to the next buoy or landmark, assess the position of the sun, find your stroke rhythm, and settle in. With practice, maneuvering buoys and turns will be less disruptive and more automatic in your long swims and races.

5. *Finding your line.* After rounding a buoy in a race, swimmers find the next buoy and set a line of sight on it. This drill is a fun way to work on this essential part of navigating through open-water races. Place a teammate or friend on the beach with a flag or brightly colored towel. As the group swims out to a buoy or designated spot, the teammate relocates to another position on the beach. After rounding the buoy the group of swimmers must locate, then sight and sprint toward the person on shore.

Courtesy of Mo Chambers

Figure 15.2 Swim close to the buoy to save time on turns.

6. *Entries, exits, and beach runs.* Getting in and out of the water quickly and comfortably are two components of open-water swimming that cannot be simulated in the pool. Therefore, if it is possible, you should include these aspects in all of your open-water workouts.

No two race starts are the same. The position of the other competitors, the surface of the bottom, the size of the waves, and the angle of the sun may all change the conditions. Rehearse running into the water and dolphin diving in close proximity to your training partners. Start several times, then add a sprint to a designated buoy or landmark.

If you are training for an open-water event that finishes on the beach, you will want to practice swimming in, standing up, and running up the beach. You may need time to master this skill, so take it slowly at first and then add speed. Many competitors swim a fantastic race but get passed by others on the dash up the sand. Investing a little time on your water exits and beach runs can pay off with a great finish to your race.

The most successful swimmers carefully plan their open-water training to consider all of the details of the race. Although it is tempting to just slip into your wet suit for an easy swim with your friends, your time would be better spent on a structured workout that focuses on these critical race points. It will be more challenging, but it will also be more fun and you will be better prepared for your next open-water or triathlon swim.

Sample Open-Water Workout

This sample workout, which includes entries and exits, is designed for a course with buoys set parallel to a sandy beach. Try this with a group of swimmers close to your pace.

Warm-up Take a light jog on the beach, stretch, then take an easy swim out to the first buoy and back. Check the bottom surface as you go in and out to make sure it is clear for dolphin diving.

Buoy 1 Make a fast beach entry (high-knee run, dolphin dive, and swim) and then sprint to buoy 1. Keeping the buoy on your right shoulder, make a 180-degree turn around it and then swim easy back to the shore and rest for one or two minutes.

Buoy 2 Make a fast beach entry (high-knee run, dolphin dive, and swim) and then sprint to buoy 1. Keep the buoy on your right shoulder, make a 90-degree turn, and then settle into a moderate pace as you swim toward buoy 2. Keeping buoy 2 on your right shoulder, make a 90-degree turn and swim toward the shore. Build your pace for a fast finish, water exit, and sprint in the sand back to your starting position on the beach (in line with buoy 1). Again, rest for one or two minutes.

Buoy 3 Make a fast beach entry (high-knee run, dolphin dive, and swim) and then sprint to buoy 1. Keep the buoy on your right shoulder, make a 90-degree turn, and then settle into a moderate pace as you swim past buoy 2 toward buoy 3. Keeping buoy 3 on your right shoulder, make a 90-degree turn and swim toward the shore. Build your pace for a fast finish, water exit, and sprint in the sand back to the starting position on the beach (in line with buoy 1) and rest.

Continue to add more buoys or repeat this sequence starting at buoy 3 and working back toward 1. Switching direction will allow you to practice turns with the buoy on your left shoulder and experience the water conditions (current, tides, swells) from the opposite direction.

PLANNING FOR SUCCESS

A successful open-water experience comes not only from proper training, but also from having a race-day plan that considers all the logistics of the venue, the weather, and your personal needs. In the days leading up to the event, start packing your bag essentials such as warm clothes, a towel, and a few pairs of goggles. Have a cooler at the ready to fill with fluids and your favorite post-swim snacks. Plan a light evening the night before your swim to ensure plenty of quality sleep. The more logistics that you can control before race morning, the more time you give yourself to focus on your swim. As you read through this section on what to expect before, during, and after your swim, build a picture of how your race day will go and make your own plan of success.

Before the Event

Although at times the weeks or months of training seem long, the morning of the event always seems to come up quickly. A lot happens in the hours between the moment when your alarm clock goes off on race morning and the moment when the starting gun is fired. Use this critical time wisely to improve your overall experience.

Many swimmers ask what should they eat on the morning of the event. The day of the race is not the time to experiment with something new, so stick with food that has been successful for you. Most swimmers prefer something light with a mixture of carbohydrates and protein, such as a bagel with peanut butter or an energy bar. Use your weeks of training to determine what works best for you.

Day of the Event

Arrive at the event early to orient yourself to the venue and find your way to the check-in area. Assuming you have preregistered, you will be assigned a race number and given a brightly colored cap. You may also be assigned to a *wave*, or heat, of swimmers whom you will start with. By breaking the competitors into smaller groups, typically by age, and sending them off in two- to five-minute intervals, the race start becomes more controlled and less hectic. Race volunteers will mark your body with your race number on your legs, arms, shoulders, and swim cap so you can be identified in the water and when you reach the finish line. Swimmers who register for the swim on the day of the event should go first to a registration table and then to the body marking area.

Once the administrative details are behind you, it's time to get a look at the swimming course. Take some time to study the map of the course, which is typically posted on a board. Is the start in the water or on the beach? Note how many buoys there are and if they are directional buoys or turn buoys. Directional buoys are positioned to guide you along the straight-aways and, unless otherwise directed, you may swim to either side of them. Turn buoys, in contrast, indicate a change in direction and the race instructions designate which side of the buoy you must be on. For example, if you are to make a right turn at a buoy, the race instructions may read, "Keep the buoy on your right shoulder." As you stand by the water and look at the course layout, note the size, color, and shape of each buoy.

The best way to ease the normal preevent jitters and prepare for a great swim is to get in the water for a short warm-up. Perhaps the biggest mistake that open-water swimmers can make is to skip this opportunity to get their muscles warm, acclimate to the water, and check the bottom surfaces in both the starting and finishing areas. The warm-up is also an ideal time to adjust your goggles, swim cap, and wet suit, if you're wearing one, for a comfortable and secure fit. Fill your wet suit with water by pulling the neck of the suit open slightly as you go underwater. Your body will warm the water trapped in your wet suit, and if your suit fits well, cold water should not trickle in again during the swim. Loosen up your shoulders as you swim and sight in the line toward the first buoy. Is there a larger landmark behind it that is easier to see? Go to the finishing area and scout a landmark that you can use for sighting while swimming the final leg toward the finish line. When the beach is full of people, banners, and activity, you might not know exactly where to go on that final stretch. If you do your homework in the warm-up, you can step up to the starting line with fewer unknowns, ready to swim the race you've trained for.

As the start of the race grows closer, swimmers will begin to gather at the starting area. The race director typically takes advantage of the captive audience awaiting the start to announce race logistics, finishing instructions, or any other last-minute details. In the minutes just before the start, the competitors in the first wave will begin to position themselves for the first leg of the race.

As you watch the first waves of swimmers, you will be able to see the many strategies that swimmers use at the start. The faster and more competitive swimmers will center themselves for a straight-line attack on the first buoy, consequently putting themselves in the thick of the crowd. They will set an aggressive pace early to join one of the packs that forms as the swimmers approach and round the first buoy. Experienced swimmers aim to position themselves in the fastest pack of swimmers and stay there throughout the swim. If they draft within a pack swimming slightly faster than their own pace, they can essentially be pulled to a faster finishing time than they could have made on their own. Swimmers with the right training, ability, and experience should use this excellent strategy.

Two good choices for less experienced swimmers are to start from the outside and take a wider line toward the buoy or to simply wait until the crowd leaves and start behind them. Both of these starting strategies keep newer swimmers out of the chaotic crowd rushing to the first buoy. Swimmers who use these approaches can better control their heart rates and swimming pace from the start of the race. Mike Collins, accomplished open-water swimmer, Ironman Triathlon finisher, and head coach of Multisports Orange County and Nova Aquatic Masters in southern California, recommends that new swimmers "relax first, then consider merging into drafting with others." Breathe often, resist the temptation to kick too hard, and settle into a steady stroke rhythm.

As you approach and round the first buoy, you may find opportunities to swim closer to others and benefit from their draft. The best situation is to find swimmers who can pull you to a faster pace. Move around swimmers who are swimming slower than you and position yourself close to those who are swimming slightly faster. You will be pulled along at their speed without working any harder. This is exactly what the lead swimmers are doing!

In the Mind of a Champion

The vast majority of open-water swimmers are quite content with one-, two-, or maybe three-mile adventures. However, there are a few that seem to have no limits. Meet 37-year-old Chris Derks, who swims far and fast! As a five-time All-American open-water swimmer, Chris has won the USMS 5K National Open Water Championship and the Great Chesapeake Bay Swim (4.4 miles) in his shorter outings. He is also a four-time winner of the 24 Mile Tampa Bay Marathon Swim and a two-time winner of the Manhattan Island Marathon Swim (28.5 miles) He also placed second in the 1995 Atlantic City Around-the-Island Marathon Swim (22.5 miles). In 2001, Chris successfully crossed the English Channel. Swimmers who spend that many hours in the water have a lot of time to think. Chris shares with us how he maintains his focus while swimming and racing.

"Throughout every race I swim, my number-one priority is what I call effort management. From the start until the point that I feel I am close to the finish, I ask myself, 'Can I keep this pace up for × number of hours?' If there is any doubt, I relax and slow down.

"Because I haven't settled into a nice groove yet and swimmers are still tightly packed, the first part of the race is the hardest. I try not to think too much about what is going on around me and again, I remind myself to settle down and relax. Going out too fast can be dangerous. As they say, 'slow and steady wins the race.'

"Effort management becomes more challenging when I am in a tight race with other swimmers. I constantly evaluate what is going on around me. Has my competition gone out too fast? Do I need to give chase now, or can I wait and pick up the pace later? Is my lead big enough? It is very easy to get demoralized if your competitors get large leads early, but I have to remember that most of my races take hours, so I need to be patient and stay relaxed.

"I try not to think too much about the finish. A watched buoy never arrives! I let myself take a peek at the finish only as I get closer or when finishing is certain. If the finish is beyond the horizon, there is no use in looking for or thinking about it.

"Finally, I do the math in my head about when I'm going to finish. Based upon where I am and how long I've been in the swim, I can usually figure out how much longer I have until I finish. The changing weather and water conditions can affect my calculations, as they did in the English Channel. Based on my time and location two-thirds of the way through the swim, the escort boat and I had figured on finishing around 7 hours 30 minutes. However, we encountered a strong current in the final mile (1.6 km), which took 45 minutes to negotiate, bringing my finish time to 8 hours 32 minutes.

"Unlike with pool swimming, the benefits of concentrating on perfect technique can be wiped out instantly if you get rolled by a wave or are stuck swimming into the wind. I make relaxation and a consistent, long stroke rate a priority.

"Because of the duration of my events, hydration is clearly a make or break factor. I know from experience that dehydration leads to cramping, which leads to survival mode, which means it's too late. Without proper hydration, I cannot push myself to my limits and swim the race I am trained to swim. To avoid this critical error, I hydrate early and often in my races.

"Bottom line—I'm primarily focused on my hydration, effort management, and winning."

As you approach a turn buoy, begin to position yourself within your group. Do you want to make a tight turn on the inside of the group or would you prefer to avoid the congestion with a wider turn? With few exceptions, the top competitors choose the shortest path by making a tight turn close to the mark, risking a possible thrashing from other swimmers' arms and feet. However, many swimmers opt for the longer path around the crowd to minimize disruption to their rhythm. After rounding the buoy, settle back into your rhythm and sight a few times to get a line on your next target. If you are swimming with a group of swimmers who are consistently on line, you may choose to sight less often. If you find that you are veering off your line, sight more often and make adjustments.

After rounding the final buoy, set your sights on the finish line, which you found during your warm-up and now have a perfect line on. Build your tempo and pick up your kick to make a strong finish. Dolphin dive through the shallow water, start to high-knee run as soon as the bottom allows it, and continue to the finish line for a well-deserved celebration.

After the Event

What you do immediately after the race affects your muscle recovery and general wellness in the following days. Begin with a short, easy swim and some light stretching to relax your muscles and reduce any future soreness. If the conditions are cold, change into dry clothes. Put on several layers if necessary. Feed your tired muscles with fluids and a meal packed with both carbohydrates and protein to replenish glycogen energy stores and begin the process of rebuilding tissue. In the days following the event, your body will appreciate the extra effort you have taken to cool down, stretch, relax, and refuel your muscles.

Later in the day, while your swim is still fresh in your mind, record the event in your training log. Include your time, the water and weather conditions, and how you felt about the race, including the start, turns, and finish. Unlike pool events, it is nearly impossible to compare open-water swims, since the water temperature, currents, and the swimmers around you make each race a new adventure. For this reason, consider all the elements that played into your performance.

If you are like most open-water swimmers, the conversation that follows the race is often about when the next event will be. The momentum following your swim is a perfect time to set new goals that may stretch your abilities a bit more or provide a different venue, such as an ocean instead of a lake. Reflect on your training and note in your log how your training affected your swim and where you see potential for improvement. If necessary, work with your coach to adjust your plan as you prepare for your next challenge.

Like all open-water swimmers, you will quickly find that each swim brings different scenery, a new set of conditions, and another chance to improve your open-water swimming skills. With experience, you will feel less like a rookie and more like a veteran, perhaps taking the turns a bit closer to the buoy or making a more assertive start. On the other hand, you might always prefer to hang back outside of the crowd and swim on your own, enjoying the beauty of swimming in nature's pools. Whatever your path, you'll find yourself among the growing number of swimmers riding the fast-moving wave of excitement about open-water swimming.

The excitement about swimming and the benefits of this lifelong sport will only continue to blossom as awareness of fitness grows in the United States. Swimming is a natural sport for adults of all ages looking for a whole-body workout to help them stay fit or to complement other sports. Structured adult swimming programs, such as masters swimming, provide safe and organized venues in which people of all ages and abilities can pursue their swimming goals within the confines of their busy lives. Most swimmers are motivated by the camaraderie of the group and the guidance provided by the coach. A few will pursue the competitive opportunities of pool meets and open-water events. All participants, from former Olympic gold medalists to adults who have just learned to swim, have discovered that masters swimming pays back their efforts with fitness, fun, and friendship. Whether you are just now getting your feet wet or you are a veteran of the sport, settle in, reap the benefits, and enjoy the ride!

Appendix: Sample Workout Sets

The following workout sets can be used with the 16-week training plans found in chapter 13.

Aerobic

Recovery

Repeat 3✕

4 × 100

  1: Kick

  2: Swim freestyle, focus on length in stroke

  3: Alternate freestyle 25 with backstroke 25, focus on shoulder and hip rotation and stroke symmetry

  4: Freestyle swim, build to 75%

Rest 10 to 15 seconds after each 100 and an extra 30 seconds after each set of 4.

Slow interval

Repeat 1✕ or 2✕

6 × 50

3 × 100

1 × 300

Maintain a steady pace at about 65 to 75% effort throughout all distances.

Rest

- 10 seconds after each 50
- 15 seconds after each 100
- 30 seconds after the 300

Aerobic / Anaerobic mix

Fartlek / Speed play

20 × 50

  1: Fast

  2, 3, 4, 5: Easy

  6, 7: Fast

  8, 9, 10: Easy

  11, 12, 13: Fast

  14, 15: Easy

  16, 17, 18, 19: Fast

  20: Easy

3 × 100

  Kick, descend 1 → 3 to best effort

Rest

- Fast 50s on cruise or RI = :05
- Easy 50s on cruise + :15 or RI = :15
- Extra 1:00 after 20
- Kick 100s, RI = :15

IM focus

4 × 25 Fly

4 × 50 25 fly / 25 back

2 × 100

  1: IM

  2: Free

4 × 25 Back

4 × 50 25 back / 25 breast

3 × 100

  1, 2: IM

  3: Free

4 × 25 Breast

4 × 50 25 breast / 25 free

4 × 100

  1, 2, 3: IM

  4: Free

- Focus on DPS through 25s; RI = :10.
- Focus on stroke transition turns in the 50s; RI = :15.
- Descend 100 IM's 1 → 6; RI = :20.
- Always finish each round with a fast 100 free; RI = 1:00.

Anaerobic

Race pace

2 × 500

Break 500s as 50 / 50 / 100 / 100 / 100 / 50 / 50

Rest

- 10 seconds after 50s
- 15 seconds after 100s
- After each 500, swim 4 × 50 easy swim or drill; rest 3 to 5 minutes

100 speed

3 × 100

Early speed: 25 fast / 25 easy / 50 build

3 × 100

Middle speed: 25 easy / 50 fast / 25 easy

3 × 100

Finish speed: 25 build / 50 easy / 25 fast

3 × 100

All fast swim

In all 100s, stay focused on quality, fast turns, streamlines, and breakouts.

Rest

- 20 to 40 seconds after 100s
- Extra 1:00 after each set of 3

Sprint

Variable sprints

Repeat 3× or 4×

4 × 25

1: 12.5 fast / 12.5 easy

2: 12.5 easy / 12.5 fast

3: Start at 75% effort and build to 100% in last 5 yd.

4: All fast, best effort

RI = :15 to :20 after each 25 and an extra :30 after each set of 4.

Montgomery 150s

Repeat 2×

4 × 150

- For each 150, swim 100 at 80 to 90% of race pace, rest 10 seconds, then sprint the final 50 at 100% effort.
- Rest 1:00 after each 150.
- After each set of 4, swim 200 to 300 easy and rest several minutes.
- This set can also be swum as 4 × 75, with 50 at 80 to 90% of race pace, 10 seconds rest, and sprint 25. Jim recommends this option for novice swimmers.

Bibliography

Boyd, Tom. June 26, 2006. Report on USMS Member Segmentation Analysis. www.usms. org/admin/surveys/May2006/segments_report.pdf, page 2.

Chatard, Jean-Claude, and Barry Wilson. 2003. Drafting distance in swimming. *Medicine & Science in Sports & Exercise* 35(7): 1176-1181.

Clothier, P.J. September 2004. Underwater kicking following the freestyle tumble turn. http://digthesis.ballarat.edu.au/adt/uploads/approved/adt-ADT20051026.161431/ public/02whole.pdf.

Costill, D.L., D.S. King, R. Thomas, and M. Hargreaves. 1985. Effects of reduced training on muscular power in swimmers. *Physician and Sports Medicine* 13(2): 94-101.

Gibbons, Meghan. 2005. Into the deep end. *The Washington Post*, May 9. www. washingtonpost.com/wp-dyn/content/article/2005/09/05/AR2005090501054.html.

Keen, Cathy. Florida Museum of Natural History. www.flmnh.ufl.edu/fish/sharks/statistics/ sharksummary_2007.pdf.

Sharp, R.L., and D.L. Costill. 1989. Shaving a little time. *Swimming Technique* 26(3):10-13. http://soloswims.com/shaving.htm.

Skin Cancer Foundation. Year-round sun protection. Skin Cancer Foundation. www. skincancer.org/prevention/year-round-sun-protection.html.

Sokolovas, Genadijus. Energy zones in swimming. USA Swimming. www.usaswimming. org/USASWeb/DesktopDefault.aspx?TabId=297&Alias=Rainbow&Lang=en-US.

Sowers, Virginia. 2006. First masters meet disproved skeptics. *USMS Swimmer Magazine*, March-April. www.usmsswimmer.com/200603/splashback.pdf.

Spawson, Charles. 1992. "Feel" for water—shaving down. www.usms.org/swimgold/esth/ feelwatr.htm.

Stillwell, Belinda. January 2007. Swimming instruction for those fearful of water. *Palaestra*, 36.

United States Masters Swimming. 2008. *USMS Rule Book*. United States Masters Swimming, Inc. Londonderry, NH.

Whitten, Phillip. March 2005. Holding back the years: How much should we decline with age? *Swimming World and Junior Swimmer*, 28.

Index

Note: An *f* or *t* following a page number refers to a figure or table, respectively.

A

adaptation 106
aerobic training 112, 123
anaerobic training 112
ankle stretch 130, 130*f*
aquatic signature 20
arm circles 127, 127*f*
arms. *See under specific strokes, e.g.,*
        breaststroke

B

backstroke 8, 43-50
    arms 45-47, 46*f*, 47*f*
    body position 43-44
    breathing 49
    drills 45, 48
    finish 92
    individual style 49
    kicking 44-45, 44*f*
    mental focus 46
    navigation during 50
    start 76-79, 77*f*, 78*f*
    stroke tempo 47, 49
    turns 84, 85, 86, 91
backstroke flags 50
balance 22-24
Barry, Pat ix, 3
beginning the program 17-18
benchmark sets 6, 117
Boomer, Bill 20
Bottom, Mike 41
breakout 73
breaststroke 8, 61-70
    arms 64-65, 65*f*
    breathing 64-65
    drills 68-69
    finish 92
    integrating kick and arm motions 66-67,
        66*f*
    kick 61-64, 63*f*, 69
    mental focus 70
    turns 85, 87-90, 91
breathing
    backstroke 49
    balance and 23
    breaststroke 64-65
    butterfly 53
    deep breathing exercise 20-21
    freestyle 31-33, 32*f*, 33*f*
    to maximize performance 21-22

open-water swimming 148-149, 152, 187
    timing of 22
breathing patterns 109
build (in set) 108
buoy turns 188-189, 192, 193*f*
butterfly 8, 51-59
    arms 53-55, 54*f*, 55*f*
    body position 52
    breathing 53
    building the stroke 56
    drills 57
    finish 92
    kicking 51, 52-53, 52*f*
    mental focus 59
    rhythm 51, 58
    rule adjustments for 174
    turns 85, 87-90, 91

C

calf stretch 129, 129*f*
caps 97, 146, 175, 195
catch, the 36-37, 37*f*
chafe control 99, 147
championship meets 172, 173
chest stretch 128, 128*f*
circle swimming 16, 17
clapping drill (forward start) 76
clothes, for after swimming 147, 175
coach, finding 13-15
Collins, Mike 196
collisions, avoiding 17
commitment 9
competitions. *See* open-water competitions;
        pool event competitions
competitive swimmers, masters swimming
        programs and 13
computer software 103
concentration 9
conditioning 8-9, 105-106. *See also* dry-land
        training; open-water training;
        workouts
confidence 9
core body strength training 131
Counsilman, Doc ix, 36, 113
crawl. *See* freestyle
cross-training 122, 136-137
crowding, in open-water swimming 188
cruise interval 16, 114, 120-121
currents, in open-water swimming 142-143
cycles 108

D

daily training planning 164-165, 165*t*
deck entries 173
deep breathing 20-21
Derks, Chris 197
descend (in set) 108
detraining 106
diet 167
distance per stroke (DPS) 109, 110-111
distance per workout 122
diving safety rules 72
dolphin diving 150, 150*f*, 190
dolphin kick 51, 52-53, 52*f*
    drills 57, 57*f*
    underwater 57, 77, 85-86
double-leg kick (underwater dolphin) 57, 77, 85-86
DPS (distance per stroke) 109, 110-111
drafting 189-190, 189*f*, 192
drills
    backstroke 45, 48
    balance 23
    breaststroke 68
    breaststroke kick 69
    butterfly 57
    dolphin kick 57, 57*f*
    forward start 76
    freestyle stroke 38, 40
    streamlining 25-26, 25*f*, 26*f*
dry-land training 125-139
    cross-training options 122, 136-137
    goals 125
    injuries and 138-139
    strength training 130-136, 133-135*f*
    stretching 126-130, 127-130*f*

E

earplugs 97, 147
endurance sets 115
energy zones 114
entering a meet 173
entering the water, open-water swimming 144, 149-150, 150*f*, 193
equipment. *See* workout equipment
even-paced sets 109
exercise bands 132
exercise science 6
exhaling 20, 21-22
exiting the water, open-water swimming 144, 151, 193
external rotation stretch 134-135, 135*f*

F

fartlek sets 116
fast-interval sets 116
Fédération Internationale de Natation (FINA) 172, 173

fifth stroke 85-86
FINA. *See* Fédération Internationale de Natation
finishes 91-92
fins 98-99
fitness, monitoring 6, 110-113
fixed-rest sets 118
flags, backstroke 50
flexibility 126-130
flip turns
    backstroke 84, 86
    freestyle 81-84, 82*f*
fluid intake 97, 147
flutter kick 39
foam rollers 132
food intake 147, 176, 190
form resistance 26
forward start 73-76, 75*f*
freestyle 8, 31-42
    arms 33-38, 34*f*, 37*f*
    backstroke as complement to 43, 49
    breathing 31-33, 32*f*, 33*f*
    drills 38, 40
    finish 92
    individual styles 41-42
    kicking 39
    mental focus 35
    straight-arm stroke 41-42
    turns 81-84, 82*f*, 85
frictional resistance 26
front crawl. *See* freestyle
front plank 133, 133*f*
front quadrant, of freestyle stroke 35

G

gastrocnemius stretch 129, 129*f*
goals 4-5, 9, 154
goal sets 6, 117
goggles 96, 146, 175
golf 50s 109
Guthrie, David 70

H

hamstring stretch 129, 129*f*
hand paddles 38, 99-100
heart rate, in fitness monitoring 111-112
heart rate monitors 102, 111
heat assignments 173
heat sheets 173
high-tech swimsuits 177
hip flexor stretch 130, 130*f*
hypothermia 144

I

individualization of training plans 107
individual medley turn 91
injuries 99, 137-139

internal rotation stretch 134-135, 135*f*
interval training 113-114
intraclub meets 172
invitational meets 172

J

jellyfish 145

K

kickboards 40, 98
kicks. *See also under specific strokes, e.g.,*
    breaststroke
    dolphin 51, 52-53, 52*f*, 57
    double-leg 57, 77, 85-86
    flutter 39

L

lactate threshold (LT) 112
La Jolla Roughwater 183
lane base 16, 114, 120-121
lap swimmer training plan 159*t*
lateral movement reduction, in freestyle
    33-34
latissimus dorsi stretch 128, 128*f*
L-lift 134, 134*f*
local invitational meets 172
long-axis strokes. *See* backstroke; freestyle
L-seats 76-77, 77*f*
LT (lactate threshold) 112

M

massage 130, 138
masters program weekly plan 164*t*
masters swimmer training plan 160-161*t*
masters swimming competitions. *See* pool
    event competitions
Masters Swimming program description
    11-12
maximum heart rate (MHR) 111
medicine balls 132
meets. *See* pool event competitions
MHR (maximum heart rate) 111
Montgomery, Jim 35
Moravcova, Martina 59
motivation 6-8
MP3 players 103

N

Nagy, Josef 61
national championship meets 172, 173
navigation
    in backstroke 50
    in open-water swimming 151-152, 151*f*,
        186-187, 192
negative split swim 109
nonflip turn. *See* open turn
nose clips 97
novice swimmer training plan 158*t*

O

Oberstar-Brown, Lia 46
open turn 87-90, 87*f*, 88*f*, 90*f*
open-water competitions 183-199
    after the event 198-199
    event selection 184
    history of 183
    mental focus 197
    open-water workouts 191-194
    pool training 185-191
    race-day planning 194-198
    race tactics 196-198
    training plan 156, 185
    water temperature and 184-185
open-water training 141-152
    breathing and stroke patterns for 148-
        149, 152, 187, 188
    entering the water 144, 149-150, 150*f*, 193
    equipment and clothing 146-147
    exiting the water 144, 151, 193
    gaining confidence in 147-148
    navigation 151-152, 151*f*, 186-187, 192
    for open-water competitions 191-194
    safety 142-146
overdistance sets 115, 190
overload 105
overtraining 154, 166

P

pace clock 100, 110, 118-120
pacing, in open-water swimming 187-188
paddles 38, 99-100
passing 17
pectoralis stretch 128, 128*f*
peek-breathe pattern 151, 151*f*
periodization, in training plans 106, 155
personal care products 98
physical capacity, decrease in with age 107
Pilates 131
plan. *See* training plan
plank 133, 133*f*
pool event competitions 171-181
    after the meet 178, 180
    basic information 171-173
    day of meet 176-178, 179
    entering 173
    mental focus 181
    premeet planning 174-175
    rule adjustments for 174
    training plan for 156
    types of 172
pool rules 15-17
pool workouts. *See* workouts
programs, finding 13-15
pull buoys 100

Q

quadriceps stretch 130, 130*f*

R

race-pace sets 116-117
Ransom, Arthur J. 12
recovery sets 115
red tides 145
regional championship meets 172
relaxation 19-21, 34
relay meets 172, 174
relay start 79-80
reps times distance 108
resistance 24, 26
rest and recovery 154, 155, 157
rest breaks 17
resting heart rate (RHR) 112
rest interval (RI) 108
reversibility of conditioning 106
RHR (resting heart rate) 112
rhythm drill (backstroke) 48
RI (rest interval) 108
rip currents 142, 143
rotary stroke. *See* straight-arm freestyle
    stroke
rounds 108
rowing 135
rules of the pool 15-17
Russian Roll-Over 48

S

safety
    open-water training 142-146
    pool rules 17
    starts 72
Schroeder, Richard 181
send-off interval 108
sets. *See* training sets
shark attacks 146
shaving 177
shin stretch 130, 130*f*
short-axis strokes. *See* breaststroke;
    butterfly
short-term goals 4-5
shoulder-driven freestyle 41-42
shoulder injury, paddles and 99
side lunges 127, 127*f*
side plank 133, 133*f*
sighting, in open-water swimming 151-152,
    186-187, 192
slow-interval sets 115
snorkels 100
snorkel training 101-102
soleus stretch 129, 129*f*
solo swimming 15
somersault 81, 82*f*
specificity of conditioning 106
speed-play sets 116
sprint sets 117-118
stability balls 132
starting the program 17-18

starts 72-80
    backstroke 76-79, 77*f*, 78*f*
    forward 73-76, 75*f*
    protocol for 72-73
    relay 79-80
    rule adjustments for 174
    safety 72
straight-arm freestyle stroke 41-42
straight-interval sets 118-119
straight sets 109
streamlining 24-27, 25*f*, 26*f*
strength training 130-136, 133-135*f*
stretching exercises 126-130, 127-130*f*
stroke count 109, 110-111
stroke length, in freestyle 34-35
stroke pattern, open-water swimming 148-
    149, 188
stroke rate 109
strokes. *See names of specific strokes, e.g.,*
    breaststroke
sun protection 98, 147, 176
swim caps 97, 146, 175, 195
swim fins 51
swim meets. *See* pool event competitions
swimming straight 185-186, 192
swim sets. *See* training sets
swimsuits 96, 175, 177

T

tapering 156
target heart rate (THR) 112
temperature of water 144, 184-185
tempo trainers 100
test sets 117
tethers 100
themed meets 172
THR (target heart rate) 112
tides 142
time, as fitness measurement 110
touch-and-go turn. *See* open turn
training. *See* workouts
training effect 106
training gear. *See* workout equipment
training logs 103, 166-167
training plan 8-10, 153-167. *See also*
    workouts
    daily planning 164-165, 165*t*
    as journey 3, 9-10
    phases of 155-156
    physical training in 8-9
    qualities of 154
    technical aspects of 8
    three Cs of 9
    tips for 166-167
    weekly planning 157, 158-164*t*
training sets 107-109, 115-118
transitional turns, individual medley 91
triathlete training plan 162-163*t*

triceps stretch 128, 128*f*
turns 80-91
    avoiding collisions 17
    backstroke flip 84, 86
    buoy 188-189, 192, 193*f*
    freestyle flip 81-84, 82*f*
    individual medley 91
    open 87-90, 87*f*, 88*f*, 90*f*
    phases of 80

U

underwater dolphin kick 57, 77, 85-86
United States Masters Swimming (USMS)
    11, 13, 172, 173
upper back stretch 128, 128*f*
USMS. *See* United States Masters
    Swimming
USMS Swimmer 11

V

variation in workouts 106
varying-rest sets 119-120
vertical dolphin kick 57, 57*f*
videos 103
visibility, in open-water swimming 145
vision 3-8

W

walking lunges 127, 127*f*
warm-up
    at competitions 178, 179, 195-196
    before workouts 15-16
watches 102, 147
water bottles 97
water conditions, in open-water swimming
    144-145, 184-185
water sense 19-27
    balance and 22-24
    breathing and 21-22

    relaxation and 19-21
    streamlining and 24-27, 25*f*, 26*f*
wave breaststroke 61. *See also* breaststroke
wave resistance 26
weather conditions, in open-water
    swimming 145
weekly training planning 157, 158-164*t*
weight training 131
Weissmuller, Johnny 41
wet suits 146, 148, 184, 190, 195-196
whistle signals, in starting protocol 72
windmill stroke. *See* straight-arm freestyle
    stroke
workout equipment 95-103
    dry-land training 132
    open-water training 146-147, 190
    personal gear 96-98
    pool training 98-100
    rules for 16
    watches and electronic gadgets 102-103
workout programs, structured 13
workouts 105-123. *See also* dry-land
    training; open-water training
    cruise intervals and 120-121
    fitness monitoring and 110-113
    frequency of 122, 157
    frequently asked questions 122-123
    injuries and 137-139
    intensity of 122-123, 157
    interval training and 113-114
    pace clock in 118-120
    planning of. *See* training plan
    terminology 105-109
    training sets 115-118
world championships 172, 173

Y

Y-lift 134, 134*f*
yoga 136

About the Authors

Jim Montgomery has held 10 swimming world records and won 9 world championships, 14 national titles, and 7 NCAA titles. As a member of the 1976 U.S. Olympic team in Montreal, he won three gold medals and one bronze. He was the first person ever to break 50 seconds in the 100-meter freestyle, a feat some have compared to Roger Bannister's breaking the four-minute-mile barrier in track. In 1981 he founded Dallas Aquatic Masters, one of the largest and most successful masters swim programs in the United States, and has been its head coach from day 1. Since 1998, Montgomery has also served as aquatics director at Greenhill School in Dallas. In 1986, he was inducted into the International Swimming Hall of Fame and was the 2002 United States Masters Swimming Coach of the Year. Montgomery has competed and given swim clinics in Japan, Hong Kong, Brazil, England, France, Germany, Italy, Thailand, Mexico, and Finland as well as throughout the United States. He lives in Dallas.

Mo Chambers was a software engineer for a large Silicon Valley company when, at age 30, she decided to take a job teaching a group of eager adult swimmers at a local health club. This side job soon became an all-consuming passion that would bring her national recognition. Within a year she left her engineering job to coach swimming full time. She took the helm of Mountain View Masters Swim Club and in seven years developed the club from 30 to more than 350 members. In 1993-94, she worked with well-known coaches Richard Quick and Bill Boomer on Stanford's women's swim team. In 1996, she was named USMS Coach of the Year. Chambers is a prolific writer for *Swim, USMS Swimmer,* and the ASCA newsletter. Chambers lives in Vancouver, Washington.